D1288300

Plotting Marketing Strategy

A New Orientation

■

Edited by

Lee Adler

Simon and Schuster

New York

An Interpublic Press Book

INDIANA-
PURDUE
LIBRARY
WITHDRAWN
FORT WAYNE

ACKNOWLEDGMENTS:

Acknowledgment is gratefully made for permission to reprint material in copyright:

"Market Stretching" by Theodore Levitt, copyright © 1965 by *Harvard Business Review;* "Investment Philosophy" by Joel Dean, copyright © 1966 by *Journal of Marketing*

HF 5415.1
.A3

All rights reserved
including the right of reproduction
in whole or in part in any form
Copyright © 1967 by Lee Adler
Published by Simon and Schuster
Rockefeller Center, 630 Fifth Avenue
New York, New York 10020

FIRST PRINTING

Library of Congress Catalog Card Number: 67-22941
Designed by Libra Studios, Inc., New York
Manufactured in the United States of America
Printed by The Murray Printing Company, Forge Village, Mass.
Bound by The Book Press, Inc., Brattleboro, Vermont

For

FLORENCE AND DEREK

Contents

■

1

Marketing Vision

■

Lee Adler

■

MARKETING VISION*

LEE ADLER

Since World War II ever-intensifying competition and the need for profits have prompted alert companies to forge a number of new and productive marketing strategies, concepts, and tools. Unfortunately, however, there are signs that a grave illness affects many managements, preventing their effective use of these modern marketing instruments. Among the symptoms are:

1. A tendency to engage in bloody, knock-down-and-drag-out fights with entrenched competitors. Examples abound, especially in the packaged-goods industries.

2. Haphazard or sophomoric application of theoretically sound marketing strategies—market segmentation, selection of companies for merger or acquisition and, above all, product differentiation. Products without truly demonstrable points of difference meaningful to the consumer are legion. Ask any advertising agency copywriter.

3. Devoted marriage to an existing business pattern despite

---

* The conceptual framework for this book derives from an article, "A New Orientation for Plotting Marketing Strategy," by the editor which appeared in the Winter 1964 issue of *Business Horizons*.

evidence that it is in a declining phase. In the beauty aids business, for example, a famous company jealously guarded its department and drugstore trade while sales volume in their product categories relentlessly shifted to supermarkets. To make matters worse, this company persisted in holding onto its older customers, despite ample evidence that women under thirty-five are the heavy users and are also becoming a larger proportion of the entire female population.

4. Emotional attachment to products that have outlived their viability. Take the case of the packaged breakfast food. It had been the foundation item in the original line, and, though tastes in breakfast foods had shifted and new products had been successful competitors for years, its manufacturer, like an indulgent parent, could find no fault with it. Or, when pressed to justify its continued existence, the company rationalized that the brand was a symbol for the company and that its old-time trade was still loyal to it.

5. A passion for the cachet conferred by volume without reckoning the cost of attaining that volume. This bit of irrationality leads to a drive for volume for the sake of volume, rather than volume at a profit. The same thing may be said for the common lust among marketers for larger market shares.

6. Failure to consider alternate routes to profitable volume. Thus, some companies continue to regard the United States as their sole territory while their peers are also vigorously expanding abroad where product potentials are easier to tap. Similarly, some marketers maintain safe advertising-to-sales ratios in fields where advertising makes a powerful contribution to total sales effect. In the meantime, their rivals have learned not to regard advertising as a cost—an inhibiting, negative viewpoint—but rather as an investment that can produce fabulous returns.

MARKETING VISION

What is the nature of this illness that so inhibits creative marketing effort? Levitt called it "marketing myopia."[1] He argued that failure to define a business broadly enough leads to premature

[1] Theodore Levitt, "Marketing Myopia," *Harvard Business Review,* XXXVIII (July–August 1960), pp. 47–48.

senescence. Levitt noted four conditions which tend to foster decay in the midst of apparent bounty: reliance on population growth, confidence in the infallibility of one's current product, reliance on the cost efficiencies of mass production, and "preoccupation with products that lend themselves to carefully controlled scientific experimentation, improvement, and manufacturing cost reduction."

Several other considerations that seem also to interfere with the achievement of marketing breakthroughs can be added to Levitt's discussion. The concern here is not so much with a whole industry as with the growth of individual companies, divisions, and brands.

TRAPPED IN THE SQUARE

The problem is basically lack of vision and self-imposed limitations. There is no better analogy than to the nine-dot square, the familiar puzzle requiring the player to connect all nine dots arranged in the form of a square with no more than four lines, without lifting his pencil from the paper.

Most players don't succeed at first because, even without being told, they think that they have to remain within the square. It's only the bolder and more deeply reasoning who immediately realize that they must go outside the square in order to succeed. (See page 39 for solution.)

Another factor responsible for this nearsightedness is the overdetailing of objectives. It used to be that if a man was asked what his business goal was he would say, "to make money." More likely, he wouldn't even have been asked the question in the first place. A corporate manager today will give some fancy responses, such as:

To implement the marketing concept.

To build my share of market by five percentage points by the end of the current fiscal year.

To assure maximum use of our manpower, financial, and productive resources.

To widen our distribution to 90 per cent of all supermarkets.

To achieve an advertising penetration of 62 per cent by the end of the campaign—

and so on.

It is vital to have goals. A steady parade of marketing experts are calling for businesses to lay down both broad corporate and divisional goals, and specific marketing objectives. For the meticulous enunciation of goals helps the marketer in a number of ways. First, and most basic, goals provide something to shoot at—that is, purpose and focus. Secondly, goals provide an indication of fiscal, manpower, and other needs. Third, goals furnish an instrument to control and channel efforts. And finally, they erect a standard against which to measure performance.

But with all these benefits we should yet be aware of a danger inherent in setting objectives. To be workable a given objective must be concretized and aimed at a single target. While doing so, however, one tends to block broader thinking. Thus, the objective of building Brand X's share of the market from 18 per cent to 23 per cent within two years leaves out such other considerations as "Maybe we should launch another brand in this market," or "Would franchising help broaden our market, lessen our competitive burden?" or "Our technical people say they can make our brand obsolete, and those of our competitors, with a radically new idea. Should we market the idea, or suppress it for the time being?"

Although the process of detailing objectives is necessary, it tends at the same time to scatter objectives. The setting of numerous, detailed targets for an existing business bearing on advertising, sales management, sales channels, expense control, and so on, may not add up to an integrated system of goals leading to market breakthroughs. On the contrary, this process may perpetuate the status quo because it obscures the need for fresh approaches, because its benchmarks and building blocks all emerge from the existing situation, and because it administratively entangles marketers in today to the neglect of tomorrow.

Two other factors abet this tendency to blind business vision. The first is decentralization. Not decentralization itself, to be sure, for when unit managers are given the freedom and responsibility to operate, the spirit of innovation often flourishes. The trouble is with those managements that cannot keep their hands off the divisional steering wheels and insist that profit responsibility belongs to headquarters. When only lip service is paid to decentralization, both practical and psychological obstacles are raised to the free thinking of divisional personnel. This is obviously not intended as an attack on top-management checks and controls, for that would be naive in the extreme. It is an attack on massive control.

The brand-manager system, with all its merits, is an even worse offender in this respect. While acceptable in concept, in practice brand managers are often turned into production schedulers, inventory controllers, budget preparers, sales analysts, and expense-control clerks. They are so busy with the mechanical details of their jobs that they have no time for its vital aspects—market planning, improving the creativity of their advertising, expanding their brands' domains. The growing roles of marketing consultants, package designers, sales promotion creators, and other outside business services testify to the sterility within.

This may be a harsh indictment of many executives, but, I feel, an honest one. We have become manipulators of the tangible, visible thing—the rigid, mechanized substitutes for the Big Idea that sparked the business in its early days. We have become mechanics and bookkeepers.

This problem is a serious one. It leads to such ill-advised actions as discordant mergers, copycat brands, and futile attacks on well-fortified positions. Or it leads to no action at all. The results are failure to grow and to manage change, and increased vulnerability to competition. This is a useless waste when powerful and proven marketing weapons are waiting to be deployed.

BREAKING OUT OF THE SQUARE

To take advantage of opportunities, management needs a vision of the business. This vision, McKay observes, should be spelled out in terms of (a) customers and markets, (b) products and services, (c) technology and production capability, and (d) corporate personality and character—all geared to the satisfaction of customer wants and needs.[2]

Development of this vision enables a company or a division to apply marketing strategies in an orderly, consistent manner. It helps to plan and program marketing innovation. In a more detailed fashion, it guides the selection and use of each marketing weapon geared to the desired direction, pace, and timing of growth.

Put another way, this vision helps marketers break out of their nine-dot squares. It arises from a wholistic view of a business' *raison d'être,* a return to fundamentals. And of all the fundamentals, the most basic is: a company is in business to make money by providing consumer gratifications. Within reason, it does not matter how the company makes money. No law says it must make money with Brand A if Brand A simply no longer has the capacity to make money. Brand B might do a much better job. Or, similarly, if Market C is exhausted, Market D may be wide open.

The vision necessary to grasp this fundamental reality has two dimensions. For breadth, according to Levitt,[3] industries should define their spheres broadly enough to assure continuing growth and to head off competition, or at least to be fully prepared to deal with it. Thus it is not sufficient for an oil company to conceive of itself as being in the oil business; it is far healthier if it regards itself as being in the fuel or energy business, or in the even broader petrochemicals business.

The second dimension is depth. Every company has an essential being, a core, the commercial equivalent of a soul. Deep-thinking managers learn to look for, identify, and capitalize on

---

[2] Edward S. McKay, "The Marketing and Advertising Role in Managing Change." Address before the 54th meeting of the Association of National Advertisers, November 10–13, 1963.

[3] "Marketing Myopia," *op. cit.*, pp. 52–53.

the essence of a company—that which gives it vitality and makes the crucial difference in dealing with rivals and making money.

Consider The Coca-Cola Company. It can be described as a manufacturer of a popular soft drink, or, more correctly, as the manufacturer of syrup used as the base of the soft drink. Or, more recently, as the parent of a whole line of soft drinks—Coca-Cola, Tab, Sprite, Fresca. But a definition of The Coca-Cola Company as a *remarkable distribution network* may be much closer to the truth. The company's great leader, Robert Woodruff, laid down the policy in the 1920s of putting Coca-Cola "within an arm's length of desire." Today, Coca-Cola is distributed in 1,600,000 outlets, more than any other product in the world. Every kind of retail outlet carries the brand. It is put into these outlets by over 1,000 local franchised bottlers in the United States. Because these bottlers, guided by the parent company, have created this extraordinary distribution, it is easier for the company to market new brands. So, with increasing competition on all sides, the heart of this success is the means of achieving widespread availability.

Procter & Gamble Company furnishes another good example. Sure, P&G manufactures soaps and detergents. To define their business in broader terms, as they keep adding products, P&G is in the household cleaner business, the food business, the health and beauty aids business, or in short, in the personal and household products business—a broad enough definition to keep even P&G going for years.

But P&G can also be viewed as a *marketing management philosophy* embodying such vital elements as careful market testing, the assurance of genuinely good products, a high order of merchandising skill and well-supported brand managers. The application of these elements in a determined and unified manner brings marketing success whether the product is a detergent, a dentifrice, or a decaffeinated coffee.

Still another example is the Alberto-Culver Company, a manufacturer of hair preparations that has lately been broadening its line to include a headache remedy, a first-aid item, a dentifrice, and so on. Its president, Leonard Lavin, has said: "If you judge us to be successful (the company went from sales of $400,000 in 1956 to $103,000,000 in 1966), chalk it up to innovator products, excellent packaging, premium pricing, hard-driving promotions, and heavy TV backing of effective creative commercials." [4] Many marketers have innovator products and excellent packaging, and the rest, but not many have the kind of heavy TV backing Lavin refers to. For in my opinion the essence of Alberto-Culver is really a *courageous media investment policy* that results in their profit rate outdistancing their sales rate. The company has said as much:

> We have found an astounding fact: the more we invest in advertising, the less our advertising-to-sales ratio becomes. The sales for our established brands are growing at a greater rate than their substantial advertising budgets. Where a million dollars in advertising used to buy for us $1 to $2 million in gross sales, for our leading brands it now buys added millions of dollars worth of sales, and the ceiling hasn't been reached. Our aggressiveness continues with the added incentive that once we get a brand off the ground, its ability to grow and return profits to the company accelerates at a much greater rate than the increased advertising expenditure.[5]

Now consider an industrial illustration. For many years, since its founding in 1894, The Carborundum Company was content to sell abrasives and offered an extremely broad line of grinding wheels, coated abrasives, and abrasive grain, with a reputed 200,000 different product possibilities by varying type, grade, and formulation. But the focus was on the product. In the mid-1950s, Carborundum perceived that the market for abrasives could be broadened considerably if, looking at abrasives through its customers' eyes, it would see the product as fitting into *metal polishing, cleaning, or removal systems.* Now Carborundum is concerned with all aspects of abrading—the machine, the contact wheel, the workpiece, the labor cost, the overhead rate, the abrasive, and, above all, the customer's objective. "That objective," says Carborundum's President, W. H. Wendel, "is never the abrasive *per se*, but rather the creation of a certain dimension, a type of finish or a required shape, always related to a minimum cost. Since there are many variables to consider, just one can be misleading. To render maximum service, Carborundum must offer

---

[4] Address before the New York Marketing Executives Association, April 1962.
[5] John S. Lynch, "Turmoil in Toiletries—The Rise of Alberto-Culver," *Food Business* (November 1962), p. 19.

a complete system." To offer that system required a considerable overhauling of the company.

First, the firm needed to enhance its knowledge of the total system. As Mr. Wendel explains, "We felt we had excellent knowledge of coated abrasives products, but that we didn't have the application and machine know-how in depth. To be really successful in the business, we had to know as much about the machine tools as we did the abrasives." To fill this need, Carborundum made three acquisitions—The Tysaman Machine Company, which builds heavy-duty snagging, billet grinding and abrasive cut-off machines (and has, since the acquisition, tripled its business); Curtis Machine Company, a maker of belt sanders; and Pangborn Corporation, which supplied systems capability in abrasive blast cleaning and finishing.

The company's abrasives divisions were reorganized and management realigned to accommodate the new philosophy and its application. The company found that *centering responsibility for the full system in one profit center* proved to be the most effective method of coordinating approaches in application engineering, choice of distribution channels, brand identification, field sales operations, etc., and was particularly valuable in order to integrate the acquisitions into the new program.

An Abrasives Systems Center was established to handle development work and to solve customer problems.

Technical conferences and seminars were held to educate customers on the new developments.

Salesmen were trained in machine and applications knowledge.

As a consequence of these developments, the company has opened up vast new markets. To quote Carborundum's president again, "Customers don't want a grinding wheel, they want metal removed. . . . The United States and Canadian market for abrasives amounts to $700,000,000 a year. But what companies spend on stock removal to bore, grind, cut, shape and finish metal amounts to $30,000,000,000 a year."

But even this achievement is only part of the Carborundum story. The firm also recognized that the real key to its success is not just a unique capability to devise and market economical materials-engineering systems but rather this capability married to *ceramics technology.* This blend of talents links together Carborundum's diverse operations. ("Very few of our divisions don't have kilns," notes Mr. Wendel.) It has also provided the focal point for further logical expansion of markets—including consumer goods (Spode china), ceramic fibers, and refractories—via internal development, acquisitions, and joint ventures.

CORPORATE MARKETING CONCEPTS

At the heart of the matter, it is a company's uncluttered isolation and articulation of its essential being, coupled with its energetic determination to exploit this being, that is at the root of marketing success. Then mental constipation vanishes and a company is able to harness available marketing tools to maximum effect. These tools become more psychologically accessible; they can be used with more insight than before.

Let's relate this notion to the marketing concept since ream upon ream has been written on this topic. To avoid semantic pitfalls, let's define the marketing concept in terms of two key elements: consumer rather than factory orientation, and an integrated use of all of the tools of marketing—advertising, sales promotion, marketing research, pricing strategy, etc. The marketing concept is urged upon companies as almost the ultimate salvation. In my opinion, the pendulum has swung too far! We now pay only grudging attention to, if we don't altogether ignore, the realities of a firm's complex of resources and, consequently, its ability to apply the marketing concept. A business' human, financial, and physical resources, its experience, products, channels of distribution, sales force, technological capabilities, skills, preferences, and psyches of its managers will all determine the degree to which it can orient itself to its market. Put another way, there is a need for more dialogue between the needs of the company and the needs of the market. The two must jibe. In other words, there is a need not for *the* marketing concept, but rather for each company to shape its own *unique, exclusive corporate marketing concept.*

Where does this concept come from? Usually it is the product of deep soul-searching, sometimes enduring for years. Drucker cites the case of a manufacturer of packaged goods who decided after five years of hard work that what his customers—retail grocers—bought was not goods which he could get from many other sources, but managerial help.[6] This included advice on buying, inventory-keeping, bookkeeping, and display. The manufacturer then shifted to a *sales service concept*. Its retail salesmen became retail counselors first, product salesmen second. If the grocer was helped, the order followed.

International Minerals and Chemicals Corporation evolved a similar marketing vision in a far different field, that of fertilizers. There are many fertilizer manufacturers in the United States. Most of them are small and few make their own raw materials, preferring to buy them in bulk from one of a handful of large chemical companies, such as International Mineral. Raw-material prices tend to be similar, as do the range and quality of their technical services to fertilizer companies.

Some years ago International Mineral began to wonder how it could successfully obtain and keep a larger slice of the fertilizer-company business. It came to the conclusion that it would have to offer prospective customers some solid reasons for dealing with it—and these reasons would have to be ones that its competitors could not duplicate easily.[7]

Just what these reasons were was found out by commissioning a nationwide study of the problems facing fertilizer companies. The research firm was instructed to study everything about the fertilizer business and not just confine themselves to packaging or production problems. After several months of work answers began to appear. The biggest single problem facing the fertilizer companies seemed to be the difficulty of estimating potential sales in their marketing territories on a county-by-county basis.

In addition, the fertilizer companies found difficulty in determining just how good a credit risk a customer was; how to get customers to pay their bills on time; the hiring, training, motivation, and compensation of salesmen; the training and motivation of retailers who sold their products; figuring efficient shipping routes and freight costs; in-transit breakage and insurance; advertising and sales promotion, etc.

---

[6] Peter Drucker, *The Practice of Management* (New York: Harper & Bros., 1954), p. 54.

[7] Bud Reese, "IMC Offers Customer Service to the Nth Degree," *Industrial Marketing* (November 1961), pp. 97–101. See also Robert A. Kelly, "Excitement: Neglected Sales Tool?," *Sales Management* (April 17, 1959), pp. 33–34, 108.

As a result of these findings, International Mineral set up, within its own company, a management consulting organization which was made available free to its customers to help them in these areas of their business. In addition, a simple manual was developed from which its customers could get solutions to some of their problems. A further step was the careful training of International Mineral's salesmen, so they were able both to explain and promote the new service.

Results soon justified the steps taken. Fertilizer companies had been provided with a solid reason for preferring to do business with International rather than any other chemical company in the same field. Its sales rose rapidly, and it raised commodities like potash out of the commodity class.

In redefining their businesses in these unique and exciting ways, the most successful concerns have perceived that the core of a business is often a concept, a philosophy, a policy, a talent, an orientation toward a market, a capacity to fill a certain customer need. It is less often identified with a particular product, a process, a set of procedures, or a supply of raw materials.

These nimble marketers have also made sure that their "inner light," to use an appropriate Quaker concept, contains a competitive edge. They answer the question: Why should people buy from us rather than from our competitors? They also do one other thing: in arriving at their own marketing visions, they take the future into account as much as possible. Sweeping changes impend in our population, culture, technology, and business society. Growing discretionary income, consumer education, and leisure time are drastically affecting purchasing and consumption habits and desires. So too are the rapidly evolving role of women, the vast increase in young people with their strange subculture and in senior citizens with their special needs.

Technological change is dramatic: Radio Corporation of America Chairman David Sarnoff foresees a common electronic communications network in one language serving the entire world; large-scale underwater exploration is opening new avenues of development; water desalination; socially acceptable drugs that modify personality; automatic shopping from the housewife's kitchen; computer-operated stores and houses; no-plumbing houses; controlled thermonuclear power; synthetic protein foods;

control of hereditary defects . . . one can go on at great length ticking off changes. Not all of them will affect every company. But some of them will affect every company.

None of this is to be interpreted dogmatically. As in everything else, there are exceptions to prove the rule. Some firms have won fame and fortune by their ability to perceive and satisfy previously unsatisfied customer needs. This is the essence of the marketing-oriented vision of a business. Others have been equally responsive to their marriage to a supply of raw materials or to their technological capabilities.[8] Actually, there are few pure case histories of either. What happens in practice is a combination of both—which is to say a dialogue between the laboratory and the market.

The marketing-oriented firm knows that consumers are always trying to tell it things, and learns to listen carefully. For example, during the past 30 to 40 years a segment of the dry cereal market was expressing dissatisfaction. How do we know? Well, every morning some people would add bananas, strawberries, or blueberries to their corn flakes. It's only in the past year or two that the manufacturers have added freeze-dried fruit to the cereal in the package. One might argue that this innovation could not have happened earlier because the technological advance had not been made. However, we might ask whether if the cereal makers had fed this consumer need into their product planning ten years ago, they might not have developed the freeze-dry process sooner.

Now take the quite different case of Dorr-Oliver. The company began as a manufacturer of processing equipment for the hydrometallurgical industries. The company soon recognized that their unique strength was far-reaching separations technology rather than only metallurgical skills. As a result, they have broadened their business tremendously by developing separation equipment for water treatment, sugar refining, food processing, pharmaceutical and chemical production. They have even devised a unique waste-disposal system, the components of which borrow heavily from technology developed in areas outside the sanitary field.

As I note elsewhere, it is not uncommon for technology-based companies to find themselves in many industries as the result of

---

[8] Robert J. Williams, "Two Roads to New Products," *Madison Avenue Magazine* (May 1963), p. 38.

shrewd extensions of their technical capability. Thus too we have The Pall Corporation situation. Pall began with special filter media for aircraft fuel systems. Having developed unique skills at filtration, the company redefined its mission as "fluid clarification"—a definition that has taken Pall into water and sewage purification for industry, municipalities, homes, boats, and trailers.

Or consider United Shoe Machinery Corporation. The essence of United Shoe Machinery, in my judgment, is a native Yankee ingenuity at designing and manufacturing machines with the digital dexterity of the human hand. This is a far different definition from saying "We make shoe machinery" (although the company's name hasn't yet caught up with this vision of itself). And USM applies this skill to making machinery and equipment for many industries quite remote from shoes, including the apparel, automotive, electronic, building, packaging, and other fields—as well as a broad line of specialty fasteners, adhesives, and custom-fabricated products.

The railroad's aversion to change is a classic case of marketing myopia. Norfolk & Western, however, has not just redefined itself as being in the transportation business, rather than a coal hauler. It's gone way beyond that. Norfolk & Western conceives of itself as a "total distribution system geared to the logistics of business." [9]

Westinghouse used to define its mission as "designing, producing and marketing materials, products, equipment, systems and services to create, distribute, apply and utilize controlled power." Now the company describes itself in terms of "opportunity-orientation," a willingness to invest in any area of suitable profit and growth potential in which Westinghouse has or can acquire capabilities. This vision has spearheaded the firm's entry into real estate in Coral Ridge, Florida, and even more interesting, into the soft-drink business. Westinghouse Broadcasting now owns two 7-Up bottling plants. Reasoning: Our expertise is advertising, not just the mechanical operation of electronic media; advertising is a potent force in soft-drink marketing; therefore, we can make a contribution to a soft-drink enterprise.

Xerox has broadened its vision from a facility for electrostatic

---

[9] Norfolk & Western, "New Way to Market a Big Railroad," *Industrial Marketing* (March 1966), p. 66.

reproduction to the visual handling and communication of information. Applications include Magnavox Telecopier, a device for sending pictures from a transmitting to a receiving device via telephone wires, and Xerox' entry with American Education Publications and Basic Systems, Inc., into the burgeoning education industry via a marriage of "hardware" and "software."

The problem of identifying a company's "inner light" is particularly acute—and necessary—in the case of multiproduct, multidivision enterprises. These hydra-headed colossi, many in the industrial field, may baffle all efforts at seeing them whole. Yet it is possible:

> Keuffel & Esser, for example, makes about 10,000 different products for engineers and draftsmen, and in the audiovisual and specialized optical fields. Keuffel & Esser has defined its vision as helping technical people to design and measure better. The company's slogan "Creative products for creative engineers" is one way of expressing this concept for marketing-communications purposes.[10]
>
> International Telephone and Telegraph has proliferated so much via the conglomerate merger route that it now has over 100 divisions and subsidiaries around the world. The company operates in such major business areas as manufacturing communications equipment, running communications systems, consumer electronics goods, appliances, broadcasting, finance, car rentals. The common denominator for most of these businesses is "engineering precision and quality." [11]

Coming at this from the direction of creating effective advertising, Lewis M. Williams wrote a decade ago:

> There are countless products whose principal sales features are institutional: such features as engineering know-how, fine workmanship, excellent research facilities used with imagination, and above all a passionate "family pride" in true craftsmanship that permeates the whole organization. Those features are supremely advertisable.
>
> Essential facts about a product—in what respects it is superior, what benefits it delivers to its users—are the news that prospects are eager to know; and it is ridiculous not to proclaim them.
>
> But is it not equally absurd to ignore what may be called the "spir-

---

[10] "Corporate Campaigns Solidify Image," *Printers' Ink* (February 1966), p. 45.
[11] "How Does ITT's Ad Formula Work?," *Printers' Ink* (February 1966), p. 35.

itual" values built in by the manufacturer—values so vital to achieving a quicker, more economical sale?

That it will also be a more durable sale seems certain, because the actual buying grows not alone from a recognition of the product's merits, but from a belief in the integrity of the maker.[12]

It is these "spiritual values" we seek. We can sometimes get a glimpse of these from company slogans. Standard Oil Division, American Oil Company, has challenged its own organization as well as reaching out compellingly to its customers with the line "You *expect* more from Standard and you *get* it." Borg-Warner captures the idea of its technical capabilities with the theme "The Great Engineers at Borg-Warner." Westinghouse conveys confidence with "You can be sure if it's Westinghouse," while General Electric has a great phrase (and rather ducks the issue) with "Progress is our most important product". FMC Corporation "puts ideas to work." Bendix says, "A thousand products, a million ideas." Monsanto is "where creative chemistry works wonders for you." Alcoa used to talk about "imagineering." Du Pont wraps it up with "better things for better living . . . through chemistry." Esso "research works wonders with oil." And United States Steel simply states, "Only steel can do so many jobs so well."

JUGGLING THE PARAMETERS

How does a manager set about searching for the vision of his own business? What are needed are search principles to serve as analytical tools and as checklists to help systematize and order this kind of intimate self-assessment. Recognition of these visions often springs from several sources:

1. Identification of unique skills or talents within the company. This might be creative skill in advertising, a capacity to communicate persuasively with a certain market segment, translating American experience into profitable marketing overseas, effecting sound mergers, or a flair for product design, whether the product is re-entry vehicles or chocolate pudding.
2. Competitive pressures.
3. Recognizing what the leader of a business enjoys doing most

[12] Lewis M. Williams, "Institutional Advertising—Can It Do a Sales Job For You?," *Printers' Ink* (April 20, 1956), p. 27.

(often highly correlated with what he's good at). Ferranti, in Great Britain, speaks of the goal of its business as "maximizing joy value."

4. A boldness of spirit. The bravest, and wisest, companies let their customers define their businesses for them; in the long run, customers do anyway. Courage is also manifested in being willing to invest heavily today for the promise of greater return tomorrow.

5. A more incisive definition of what the customer is really buying.

These lead to juggling the parameters of one's world, to enlarging the set of alternatives perceived as possibilities for action. Which is, of course, what we mean when we describe someone, whatever his field, as being a "man of vision." Put in terms of gestalt psychology, we must break habitual frames of reference. We've already studied some examples of these factors at work. Now ponder these further illustrations:

Gerber Products Company made baby foods for years. In 1965 the company began to implement its unique vision, neatly captured in the slogan "Babies are our business . . . our only business," by bringing out lines of baby clothes, tissues, wash cloths, and medicated disposable diaper liners.

Ford Motor Company entered the rent-a-car business in 1964. By doing this, Ford redefined itself as a transportation provider, rather than as an auto manufacturer—a gigantic conceptual leap. (Actually, to the extent that auto makers have catered to their customers' after-sale needs, they might have been defined more broadly prior to Ford's move.)

While Ford was launching itself into the rent-a-car field, the industry leader, Hertz, was remolding itself on the basis of rental skills without any constraining reference to the particular items rented. Now you can rent practically anything from Hertz, including perambulators, dance floors, coat racks, and hospital equipment.

The transportation and travel industry supplies other illustrations as well. Beset by competition from increasingly inexpensive jet airplane flights, especially on the North Atlantic, the steamship companies are evolving new visions of their business. They are becoming less the transoceanic transporters they once were. Instead they are entering, on an ever-expanding scale, the *floating resort and recreational center business.* This fascinating example of marketing vision is underscored by the growing diversion of ships from regular service to cruising.

By contrast, most airlines have chosen to restructure their universe more narrowly. They see their business as furnishing air carriage from one runway to another, as every air traveler knows only too well as he struggles with all the steps that precede and follow the period aloft. This excludes local helicopter operators who are making hay out of the airlines' abdication of marketing responsibility.

Charles Pfizer & Company has identified its essential being as a combination of technical skills and superb production facilities. It has brought these to bear in cosmetics, toiletries, and proprietary drugs—all products which can profit from the requirements of ethical drug manufacturing. Pfizer has acquired Leeming/Pacquin, Coty, Desitin, Barbasol, and still other consumer-goods companies to put its new self-conception to work as quickly as possible.

This reorganization of the boundaries of the system in which a business operates may be visible or tangible in the sense of geographic markets or naming the competition within a SIC category. What this restructuring will then do is redefine who the enemy is in a constructive fashion. This is the case with the steamship lines; their rivals are now less the transatlantic airlines than they are stationary resorts and hotels in Florida and the Caribbean.

But the fresh perception of one's universe may also be less tangible. For example, I once spent several days traveling with sales representatives of The Coca-Cola Company's Fountain Division in order to become more familiar with problems at the point of sale. After numerous calls on luncheonettes, drugstores, concessionaires, restaurants, and other users of Coca-Cola syrup, I noticed that the salesmen never referred to the product. Their concern was with selling the dealer a new dispenser with the current slogan embossed on it, or getting him to use more Coca-Cola window display material, menus, back-bar signs, offering promotion ideas to help tie in sales with frankfurters, popcorn, hamburgers; suggesting ideas on physical layout, etc. In short, the salesmen were really advertising and merchandising counselors. And if they did a good job, then syrup continued to flow automatically. Shortly after that experience I came across a statement by Neil McElroy, chairman of Procter & Gamble, to the effect that "We are as much in the advertising business as we are in the manufacturing business" [13]—which makes the same point even more cogently.

MULTIPLE VISIONS

This further reference to Procter & Gamble brings up the question of whether a company may have more than one marketing self-concept. The answer is "yes," although these visions may be interlocked. For example, we have spoken of P&G as a marketing-management philosophy. One of the tools of marketing which P&G uses to a considerable extent is advertising. In 1966 the firm invested $245,000,000 in advertising in measured media, making it the world's largest advertiser. Hence the justification for McElroy's statement. Moreover, the essence of P&G has also been defined by a former executive as the *superb management of information*—the willingness to buy and objectively analyze more marketing-research data than any of its competitors. This policy and practice, too, fitted into the overall scheme of a marketing-management philosophy (and, I suspect, may also characterize the most agile competitor in any field).

In other cases, however, a company may have separate visions of the business, each pertinent to different sectors. No fewer than four concepts may be identified in the instance of American Home Products Corporation:

An astute, rigorous accounting policy applied to marketing which has expressed itself in:

a determination to maximize short-term profitability; brands must show a stipulated rate of profit or be dropped without ceremony.

a refusal to engage in unrewarding competitive slugfests.

a willingness to milk brands in the declining phase of their life cycle.

extremely tight budget control; it is said that expenditures of over $50 must be approved by the President.

---

[13] *Printers' Ink* (September 28, 1962), p. 43.

holding down on marketing costs; American Home Products is described as priding itself on being the only company to make money in test markets.

A concomitant of the above policy planks is a tendency to develop specialty products with low-purchase frequency and little competition; this is evidenced in the proprietary drug and household specialties products areas, examples being Denalen dental cleanser, Freezone corn remover, Neet depilatory, Quick Dip Silver Polish, Wizard Nursery Spray, Compound "W" wart remover.

An uncanny skill in finding and acquiring profitable-looking ventures; e.g., Anacin, Woolite, Three-In-One-Oil, Brach's Candy, Ecko household products. The other side of this coin is American Home Products' ability to get rid of poor performers; e.g., Clapp's Baby Foods.

A strong mass-merchandising capability involving low-cost, fast-moving, nondurable consumer packaged goods moving through food and drug outlets and readily responsive to promotional pressures. Lines such as Chef Boy-ar-Dee foods, Dristan cough and cold remedies, and Aerowax protective coatings illustrate this principle at work.

A bold creative impulse and freedom in utilizing it: the company has reportedly launched new product development on the strength of an advertising idea for a previously nonexistent product.[14]

Yet the above four factors do not even cover all of American Home Products' businesses. These policies and philosophies apply to the packaged-goods divisions—Boyle-Midway, Whitehall, and American Home Foods. The company's other major divisions, Wyeth Laboratories and Ayerst Laboratories, reflecting their interests in ethical drugs, march to a different tune.

Other firms have collapsed multiple values into a department-store outlook. Several of Westinghouse's divisions can be seen as comprising a department store for electronics products and capabilities. Lehman Brothers may be viewed as a department store of finance. And many banks might ameliorate their images, and humanize themselves in the process, if they saw themselves as retailers of money.

[14] "The Invisible Marketer," *Television Age*, XII, No. 7 (October 26, 1964), pp. 24 ff.

HAZARDS

The introspective search for an exclusive self-perception is not without hazards. A marketing vision of a business is necessarily a rather grand and sweeping statement, since it must find the common denominator for all, or at any rate, many of the divisions, products, functions, specialized skills, and other elements which collectively impart to each business its unique personality. Three particular hazards are common:

First, a tendency to compose so general a definition as to be either inoperable and/or fail to distinguish the company from the pack. Few firms can carry off a very general definition. Two that can are American Telephone and Telegraph and Sears, Roebuck.

Theodore N. Vail worked out the answer for AT&T as far back as 1905.[15] He said: "Our business is service." Not "telephone service" or even "communications service," but simply "service." This led the company to (a) an ever-improving technology, to create customer satisfactions; (b) "indoctrination in dedication to service for all employees"; (c) a public-relations program which stressed service; and (d) "a financial policy which assumed that the company had to give service wherever there was a demand and that it was management's job to find the needed capital and to earn a return on it."

That AT&T has succeeded is amply evidenced by the remarkable array of services it offers business and private customers today—Telstar, WATS lines, automatic dialing, data transmission via computers chattering to each other across long-distance lines.

Sears, Roebuck's marketing vision has been stated by the company as "an organized system for efficient and economical distribution, dedicated to serving the public with a broad range of goods and services, and to meeting any change in demand." As Charles H. Granger notes:

> Probably 90 out of 100 large organizations have some stated objectives of this general type. But the difference is that Sears not only states its objectives; it lives by them. In the last ten years the number of mail-order plants has remained steady at 11, and the number of retail stores

---

[15] Peter Drucker, *op. cit.*, pp. 49–50.

has increased slightly from 694 to 748 (although many have been modernized and expanded). But the company is now upgrading itself into a style house, as its recent advertising demonstrates. Here are examples of the variety of Sears, Roebuck activities—

It runs a fleet of 5,000 service and installation trucks.

Through Allstate it is the largest stock company insurer of automobiles in the country, and fourth largest in the fire and casualty field.

It is in the life insurance business.

The Allstate Motor Club and Allstate Tours operate in the travel field.

It has entered the savings and loan business.

Homart Development Company recently opened its first shopping center, with a half-dozen others in various stages of planning.

Sears, Roebuck Acceptance Corp. has about $500-million of installment contracts.[16]

A concomitant of this danger is the tendency to try to reduce the "inner light" to a catchy phrase people can grasp. When the product spread runs from abrasives to zymoscopes, telescoping profound values into a slogan may result in a fearfully broad and frequently innocuous description. The same thing can happen when a raw material enters into a myriad of end-use products. After many years and a couple of hundred tries, the closest Owens-Corning has come to describing itself is "Fiberglas . . . makes good things better . . . makes new things possible." If a slogan won't work, better not to have one; if it takes a paragraph—or a page—of sonorous language to express the marketing spirit of a firm, so be it.

A second pitfall stems from the attempt to project a unique vision into an inhospitable sphere where its potency is vitiated. Some years ago, a radio station executive who fully understood the use of radio advertising in the development of rural and small-town markets developed a detergent product. His advertising format and content were tailored to the market, e.g., the use of folksy humor, country music—"corn," as urbanites would call it. So too were his arrangements with radio stations; in the early days he purchased time on a commission basis. The business throve and the single product soon blossomed into a full line. After the company had become a big factor in the rural and small-

[16] Charles H. Granger, "The Hierarchy of Objectives," *Harvard Business Review* (May–June 1964), p. 72.

town Midwest, it sought to expand to both coasts. But the bucolic approach failed, as did attempts to use conventional marketing approaches. In the fullness of time, the company reverted to its original methods.

A third danger in the hunt for a common denominator is a product-oriented rather than a market-oriented vision.

An appliance manufacturer, after much soul-searching, described itself with seeming cleverness as being in the business of making everything with an electric plug at the end of it. This definition led the firm into such new businesses as electric toys and electrical gardening equipment. In none of these new businesses did the company have the marketing expertise or channels of distribution; as a result it has since abandoned these new enterprises.

A maker of household protective coatings identified itself in terms of its principal raw material—wax. This prompted the company to investigate opportunities in wax candles. This concern, fortunately, recognized that candles move through different channels, and to different consumers from its current customers and that it would be too costly to market them.

As noted above, this is not to condemn all definitions of a business' mission with respect to its raw material. The manufacture of sewer pipe, for instance, requires seven or eight different clays. These clays are found in a limited number of locations and the company controlling the sources of supply has a powerful competitive edge. In this case, self-definition in terms of the raw material makes a lot of sense. In the same way, it would be foolish for Gorton's of Gloucester not to include a reference to fish in its self-definition, or for Swift to ignore cattle and hogs.

On the other side of the coin, articulation of a corporate marketing concept oriented to serving a market may also misfire. Already well entrenched in the retail jewelry trade, a manufacturer of cigarette lighters sought to market another line of goods handled largely by jewelry stores. But the manufacturer lacked the product-development skills needed for the new line and, even though he easily achieved broad-scale sales coverage, the venture succumbed.

I feel constrained at this juncture to note that there are cases where the concept of marketing vision does not apply at all. There are some companies seemingly without such a unifying marketing self-perception—Textron, Avco, W. R. Grace may be good examples. In such instances another spirit pervades and unifies instead of a marketing vision; it may be a managerial vision. This vision may be actuated in terms of a common accounting system, standards for judging profit return on sales or investment, superior skills in evaluating executive performance, or similar nonmarketing functions.

These illustrations reinforce the point made earlier that it is not right to urge the "marketing concept" on manufacturers willy-nilly. The concept evolved must be equally responsive to the needs of the market and of the firm. If the dialogue is one-sided, if the needs of either are slighted, disaster may be the outcome.

These illustrations also point up the creativity and judgment involved in enunciating a marketing vision. There are no blacks and whites, only shades of gray. One company's meat is another's poison. We are dealing with an art, not a science.

WHAT BUSINESS ARE WE REALLY IN?

We may now focus more directly on an important aspect of this subject. A correct identification of the heart of a business may prompt hitherto unforeseen avenues of market development. Put another way, such identification may change the nature of a business dramatically.

A long-time manufacturer of patent medicines perceived, as in the case of American Home Products, that the core of his business was a talent for marketing packaged goods, not just home remedies. Casting about for additional outlets for this expertise, he noted that other manufacturers of packaged goods needed this kind of skill. This led to his acquisition of several toiletries companies and a dog food company.

Most of the major American tobacco companies have, for a variety of reasons, pursued the same course. Witness their entry into pet foods, confectionery products, fruit drinks, shaving materials, personal-grooming items during the late 1950s and, with increased zeal, in the 1960s.

Drucker also cites the case of a manufacturer of machine tool parts who gave up manufacturing and became a welding consultant. This move put him in a class by himself, instead of being one of hundreds in his manufacturing business.

"As long as he kept on manufacturing," says Drucker, "he used his really productive resource, his welding expertise, at a very low rate of productivity and return."

McGraw-Hill is not a publisher of trade magazines and books, but "serves man's need for knowledge." The breadth dimension of its vision lies in all kinds of communications vehicles and content, while the depth dimension is rooted in skill in communicating *ideas.*

Pinpointing a marketing vision in terms of innovation is a common way of changing the dimensions of a business. As Paul E. Funk has noted, this phenomenon is common in technical fields. Westinghouse's Underseas Division, for example, has concentrated on a *systems approach* to underseas exploration which would utilize the corporation's main capabilities. Thus, rather than bog down in the mass production of submersibles, Westinghouse will furnish all the engineering equipment for underwater development—precision navigation systems, manipulation systems, computers to run centralized engine rooms. This puts Westinghouse in many businesses—military underwater applications (rescue operations, mine warfare countermeasures, machinery noise radiation measurements, and salvage operations), petroleum discovery and recovery, fishing. ". . . we're in any business we want to be in," says the company.[17]

But extensions of a business, thanks to innovation, are also mushrooming in consumer areas, as exemplified by aerosol packaging, disposable goods of all sorts, credit cards, insurance coverages.

Because corporations, like individuals (or, more correctly, because they are the reflections of the individuals who lead them), have distinctive personalities, aspirations and frames of reference, the same foundation of experience, at least as it appears to the outsider, may yield quite different visions of their businesses. Near the close of World War II, two companies, both manufacturers of similar packaged foods made of grain, set about the task of identifying their major strengths and weaknesses in order to formulate effective platforms for growth and expansion. They arrived at very different conclusions. Company A saw its major strength to be the development and marketing of products resulting from the milling of grain. This led to expansion into cake mixes, dry

[17] Steve Blickstein, "Innovation Is the Name of the Game," *Sales Management,* (November 11, 1965), pp. 41, 86.

breakfast cereals, and similar lines. Company B, by contrast, concluded that a merchandising personality it had developed was one of its major assets. Company B, therefore, linked its fortunes to the further exploitation of that name by designing a broad line of consumer goods using many different raw materials. Both firms have been eminently successful, even though their paths diverged radically from the same origin.

THE VALUES OF VISION

The quest for true marketing identity, painful as it may be, offers substantial benefits:

It helps management to see, or to crystallize, its special flair as the first step in further exploiting it. Many companies are smarter than even they may realize. Recognition of their unique talents can help to sharpen or extend their use of them. Revlon, for example, sells beauty, not skin or hair care. As Charles Revson, the company's President, puts it, "In the factory we make cosmetics, in the drugstore we sell hope." The company transformed cosmetics from packaged goods to fashion goods and introduced the factor of seasonality and style obsolescence. And, having come this far, Revlon has since projected its fashion expertise into other businesses, including women's dresses, raincoats, and decorative accessories. It is Revlon's capacity to communicate persuasively and memorably to beauty-hungry American middle class women that is at the heart of its success, rather than the chemical fact of its being a cosmetics manufacturer.

These women yearn to be sirens, luring men to seduction. But they are restrained by inhibitions imposed by their surroundings, their culture and upbringing. So they live outwardly as suburban homemakers and inwardly as Mata Haris. Revlon understands this conflict and appeals to both sides of it. Hence, the demure, wholesome women depicted in its ads, with only a veiled hint of sexiness. Hence the particular promise articulated for Revlon products—beauty, social ease, but not an unleashed libido. Hence, too, the almost diabolically clever choices of product and color names, each suggesting innocence on the one hand and joyous sin on the other—Fire and Ice, Demure Adventuress, Bare Beige, Jungle Peach, Hot Coral, Lilac Champagne, Blasé Apricot, Dark Apple, Stormy Pink, Naked Pink, and Paint the Town Pink.

It provides a focus for unified corporate identification, particularly valuable and needed by today's multiproduct corporate behemoths. While marketing vision probes more deeply than the requirements of corporation image formation or institutional advertising, the process can be of considerable aid in deciding what the corporate personality ought to be, and in furnishing a cohesive message for achieving it.

It helps to stimulate and capitalize on innovation, and prompts new marketing-action programs.

It enables a company to use available marketing strategies in more sophisticated and effective ways.

It is this last point that leads to the core of this book. A factor analysis of the marketing operations of hundreds of American companies in many product fields yielded two central observations. One we have already discussed—successful marketers define their businesses in unique, exciting ways that open new horizons. The second is that a limited number of basic marketing strategies recur continuously in the operations of successful marketers. In the case of less alert marketers, it was found that these strategies were either not used or used haphazardly, incorrectly, or without real understanding of their power. These strategies are not new. What is new is fitting them into a conceptual whole, making them more accessible as a systematic approach for marketing planners, and, above all, illuminating the vital two-way street between marketing vision and marketing strategy. For the two nourish each other. Sometimes articulation of the vision prompts the use of a certain strategy. A case in point is the recognition of packaged-goods marketing expertise as the heart of a business leading to the use of merger and acquisition as a marketing strategy. Alternatively, a company's use for years of a given strategy may in time lead to recognition of its broader potential; Revlon is a good example.

The balance of this book is, therefore, devoted to a detailed discussion of these strategies in order to provide marketers with a systematic approach to the evolution of breakthroughs for their businesses. Some of these are action strategies. Others might be called *strategies of thought* in that they seek to encourage a fresh point of view, a restructuring of one's frame of reference, a breaking out of the nine-dot square. Hence the discussion blends theory and practice.

These strategies may be summed up as follows:

1. *The End-Run:* To hurdle marketing roadblocks, create your own battlefront, rather than accept the arena established by your competition.

2. *Concentration:* To dominate, consolidate, and apply marketing pressures against specific targets rather than dissipate effort over a broad front.

3. *Market Segmentation:* Direct marketing effort against consumer-need groups defined along psychological, physiological, social, or cultural dimensions.

4. *Market Stretching:* Extend markets over time, customer groupings, trade channels, geography, by utilizing the concept of the product life cycle to plan life-giving infusions of marketing effort before a product is launched.

5. *Multibrand Entries:* Capitalize on the fact that two brands in a category will usually generate more sales than one.

6. *Brand Extension:* Use an established brand name to extend a product line.

7. *Product Innovation:* Modify, improve, revivify products, search ceaselessly for new products to sustain marketing vitality and assure growth.

8. *International Expansion:* Exploit expanding global opportunities.

9. *Investment Philosophy:* For a rational profit-oriented approach to marketing, treat promotional outlays as capital investments.

10. *Distribution Breakthroughs:* Hack your own fresh path through the distribution jungle rather than merely staying wedded to traditional channels.

11. *Merger and Acquisition:* View the corporate marriage as a marvelous instrument for marketing goods.

12. *Iconoclasm:* Seek unorthodox solutions to orthodox problems. Depart ye from the ways of thy father if thou wouldst survive and grow.

A leading expert, drawn from either the academic or business world, has contributed a chapter on each of the above strategies, tailored to the overall theme of this book.

Although the individual strategies have been dissected separately for the sake of analytical clarity, they are, of course, intertwined in practice. Segmenting a market helps one to concentrate. Product change is often an essential for effective segmentation. Brand extension can lead to new distribution channels. New distribution channels can lead to multibrand entries. Success with a number of brands of the same product is merely testimony to cunning segmentation of a market along psychological, physiological, or other not-so-apparent dimensions. And so on. In the final analysis, all the strategies are end-runs, and the action components of a fresh image of the business boldly stamped on the past to provide insurance against decay and a foundation for growth.

Because these strategies are interlocked, it is inevitable and desirable that some authors have touched on subjects covered also by others. What may therefore appear here and there as duplication is deliberate. Equally deliberate is the inclusion of occasional divergent viewpoints, as, for example, on the role of the product-life-cycle concept. The contributors have been encouraged to "be themselves" in terms of style, length, examples, tailoring form to suit content and point of view, rather than conform to arbitrarily imposed editorial standards.

Nothing in this volume constitutes rules to be blindly heeded. It's worth repeating that in marketing all is art. No two situations are alike. What works well for one business will not work for another; what works well under some competitive circumstances will not work under other circumstances; what works at one point in time will not work at another. What we offer therefore is a systematic approach, but not a system; guidelines, but not gospel.

Solution to Problem on Page 13.

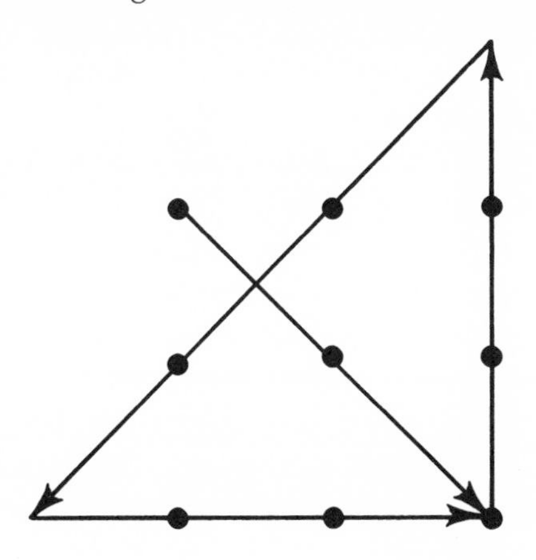

2

The End-Run

■

John Phillips

■

During a period when the premium on innovation grows ever greater there appears to be a concomitant growth of forces in the business world least likely to stimulate change. Managers seem to be sharpening their skills steadily insofar as the operation of the current business is concerned. But while they tend the machinery very well indeed, most fail to provide the creativity needed to sustain and revitalize their businesses to meet the challenges all around them. Underlining this problem is the growing belief that the world of the future needs experts, not leaders. The need to manage creativity—to rekindle the light in the founder's eye in the eyes of his successors—has thus become crucial.

This chapter is particularly important because the strategy it sets forth really underlies every other marketing strategy. In a sense, the "end-run" is as much a strategy of thought or a philosophy as it is an action approach. For one executes an end-run by utilizing one or more of the strategies covered in later chapters.

John Phillips comes to this discussion as a most practical marketing philosopher, since he has himself succeeded in applying this strategy at higher and higher levels of responsibility throughout his business career.

Mr. Phillips was raised on a farm in Wisconsin. Early in his career he was a partner in a business, Miss Wisconsin Cheese, based on the first method of marketing and advertising natural aged cheeses under a brand name in packages. This business was sold to Armour & Company in 1955. He then worked with Armour as Marketing Director of Special Products, helping reorganize their business away from commodity operations and into modern packaged-goods marketing procedures.

Mr. Phillips joined American Home Products Corporation in 1960 as Vice President, dealing primarily with future activities, acquisitions, and new products. He became President of R. J. Reynolds Foods, Inc. in 1966.

Mr. Phillips' experience in forging a packaged-goods business into being against a strongly entrenched competitor, then going from that to working on the complex problems of a massive company that had encountered great problems, followed by experience with a highly successful packaged-goods company, developed strong interests in the forces that help or hinder the future of a company.

His chapter covers these forces and suggests procedures for their management.

■

THE END-RUN

JOHN PHILLIPS

The use of football terminology is oddly apt in arguing for creativity in marketing. For whatever definition of "creativity" we use, the hallmark of that mental process is a breaking away from norms and well-worn ways of doing things, and its product is *significant* innovation—in effect, an "end-run" around the status quo.

In the broadest sense, these end-runs can occur on two levels. The first affects the very foundation and survival of a business. The second level concerns the *utilization* of the strategies and tools of marketing to outmaneuver competition and gain competitive advantage in day-to-day struggles in an established market.

THE CYCLE OF BUSINESS LIFE

Just as nearly every product passes through a life cycle, so, too, do entire businesses go through certain stages. Every business is in one of three phases:

1. The development of a new idea into a business.
2. The expanding phase of the idea or ideas that brought the business into being.
3. The declining phase as new ideas begin to supersede the concepts on which the business was founded.

Pause to reflect on several businesses and you will find you can usually set them into one of these three categories.

What does this have to do with "marketing vision"? The fact is that all business is dependent on what it markets. Thus the longer it can keep itself in the first phase, or developing timely marketing ideas, the longer it can postpone the inevitable third phase. The word "inevitable" is used deliberately. Carried one step further, it can be said with certainty that every business will ultimately fail. The proof is they always have—it appears to be just a matter of when.

The premise of every business failing is stated for a positive and constructive purpose, although some readers may doubt it at this point. The constructive purpose is that if the ultimate end is recognized, it becomes clearer that a principal responsibility of leaders of a business is to postpone for years, and hopefully centuries, this eventual consequence. Marketing vision can be put to no better purpose.

Stated another way, successful businesses rarely fall into serious difficulties because of accounting problems or production problems or sales force problems or delivery problems or personnel problems. When they ultimately get into serious trouble it is usually because the advantages offered in what they sold or how they sold or the basis for their being in business are no longer present.

What is it that keeps efforts to perpetuate a business from being continually made, just as time and thought are regularly devoted to the accounting, production, sales force, delivery, and personnel areas of the business?

One of the factors is that accounting, production, sales force, and similar activities are tangible and visible. We live with them every day in a real way. Most managers have progressed in business by doing these tangible things well. Most managers, by circumstance, do not usually come into a business when it is in the first, or idea stage, so it is very natural to assume that the successful prolonging of the business will come from careful management of the tangible factors in the business.

Careful management of the tangible factors is an absolute necessity. The point is, though, that this alone is not sufficient to perpetuate the success of the business.

THE MANAGEMENT OF CREATIVITY

The problem lies in the management of ideas and creativity. Leaders of a business have always found difficulty in regularly reviewing the changing business situation around them and then making sure creative action is directed against emerging problems.

To illustrate this problem from the end effect, consider these examples:

Why did virtually no buggy or wagon manufacturers attempt to enter the automobile business?

Why were no automobile-engine manufacturers successful in entering the airplane-engine field?

Why were so few aircraft companies successful in entering the electronics field related to space and missiles?

Why did virtually no steam-locomotive companies enter the field of diesel locomotives?

Why did no railroad companies attempt to establish airlines?

Why were virtually no butter manufacturers successful in entering the oleomargarine field?

Why did very few vegetable canners enter the field of convenience prepared foods?

Why did virtually no theatrical companies enter the movie field?

Why did virtually no phonograph companies enter the radio field?

As a more current illustration of this problem, there are companies with which you may be familiar that logically should have made early entries into the following new growth fields, but did not do so:

Catering services to offices, factories and airlines
High-quality motels at airports
Lawn-care products
Dietetic soft drinks

Birth-control pills
Sidewalk surfers
Toothpaste that would really reduce cavities
High-quality frozen desserts
Aerosol packaging equipment
Outdoor-living equipment
Medical electronic equipment
High-quality rubber and plastic kitchen equipment
Automobile seat belts that roll up
Lower-cost contact lenses
Hair-coloring products
Pure meat chunk dog food
Disposable hospital supplies
Dandruff shampoo that works
A replacement for leather that looks and acts like leather
Long-acting cold tablets
Metal skis
Paperback books

Some companies may answer that while one of the preceding examples may have fitted with their business, it seemed like too much of a change to inspire research on the idea before it was exploited by others. But when you reflect on it, isn't this part of the answer to why every business fails? The field any business is in will inevitably fade in importance, so the only choice is to keep branching out into new fields. This doesn't mean that the food field, for example, will fade in importance, but that advantages in products or services offered by a food company will eventually be superseded by other approaches in the food field.

The changes affecting a business take place at a faster rate than is generally recognized. *Forbes* magazine has published a list showing the top 100 companies in the United States in terms of assets in 1945 and where they stood 20 years later in 1965.

Companies such as Curtiss-Wright (26th), Armour (28th), International Nickel (35th), Liggett & Myers (36th), Pullman (39th), Bendix (42nd), United Fruit (46th), M-G-M (56th), American Smelting (57th), Warner Brothers (60th), Phelps Dodge (62nd), and Schenley (67th) are no longer in the top 100 in assets. This does not mean their assets have necessarily declined, but illustrates the problem of keeping equivalent business growth at a high rate in the midst of change.

Some companies still in the top 100 list with declines in their relative standings are Montgomery Ward, from 25th to 56th; Swift, from 27th to 83rd; Woolworth, from 34th to 57th; United States Rubber, from 48th to 64th; and A&P, from 50th to 65th—again illustrating the problem.

Every large, successful business got its start by someone's breaking away from an established way of doing things by evolving a new idea and developing it.

The problem, in contrast, is that most people spend their time in business in managing the marketing or managing the production or managing the office or managing the accounting or managing the financing or managing the delivery that relate to the ideas on which the business was built in the first place. This preoccupation with tangibles is so intensive as to suggest, to their practitioners, that these management areas are the keys to the future. But they are only part of the answer.

Greatly improved systems of management are now in existence. Out of these have emerged phrases such as "professional managers," "marketing orientation," "complete marketing," and "consumer viewpoint." So we now think management has become much more of a science; but unfortunately this applies almost entirely to what is in existence and tangible, such as production lines, shipping procedures, sales coverage, and office procedures.

What all this progress too rarely provides is what will prolong the first stage of every successful business—the development of new ideas—and so extend the life of the business.

Thus the problem boils down to how to continue to identify new areas of opportunity and then give them the same dedicated support that originally built the business. The crux of the problem is that very few businesses have worked out a way to manage creativity. And worse, as we have worked out and emphasized management techniques for daily business problems, we have made more difficult the inspiring of creativity and a continued search for new directions.

The very phrase "managing creativity" is contradictory. The trouble is that creativity is an area of business that is never in physical existence and so is elusive and intangible. However, many of the management techniques now used on tangible aspects of business and taken for granted are revolutionary when compared with techniques of forty years ago. So I firmly believe techniques for managing the future of a business will come into existence. Companies that discover them will have a great advantage. This is undoubtedly the greatest opportunity for the future.

SHORTER-TERM END-RUNS

The foregoing has been concerned with the encouragement of new marketing visions of a business for their long-term effects in carving out new opportunity areas. But there are also nearer-term considerations where the same strategy of thought applies. Not only does the management of tangibles seem to preclude broader thinking about the future of a business, it also discourages the creativity needed in the day-to-day competitive struggle. Managers can become so immersed in the physical and visible elements of a business that they trap themselves in their own nine-dot squares.[1]

Just as the goal of marketing creativity for the long term is to outmaneuver change, so the goal of shorter-term end-runs is to outmaneuver competition in today's marketplace. More specifically, the purpose of the end-run is to avoid unnecessary, costly, time-consuming, or otherwise undesirable battles with entrenched competitors or other nearly insuperable obstacles. The objective is to create the arena rather than uncritically accept one made by the competitor.

During the late 1940s and early 1950s, Lever Brothers Company made a number of unsuccessful assaults on P&G's solid position in the heavy-duty detergent field.[2]

Finally, in 1957, Lever acquired "all" from Monsanto for the automatic washing machine market. In this way Lever succeeded in outflanking P&G in a high-volume segment of the laundry market.

---

[1] See p. 39 for explanation of nine-dot square.

[2] Spencer Klaw, "The Soap Wars: A Strategic Analysis," *Fortune*, LXVII (June 1963), 123 ff.

Not to be outdone, P&G counterattacked "all" frontally with Dash. This tactic worked for a time, but by 1961 "all" had regained its lost ground. Then P&G launched its own end-run —Salvo low-sudsing tablets. What P&G could not accomplish directly it accomplished indirectly. Between Dash and Salvo P&G won half the low-sudsing business in several years. By 1963 P&G was well ahead of Lever with a 16.1 per cent share of the heavy-duty soap and detergent market with two brands, as against only 12.7 per cent for Lever's "all" and Vim low-sudser combined.[3]

Another illustration would be a tobacco company broadening its viewpoint to consider itself an expert in mass distribution and advertising rather than a cigarette manufacturer. Thus, acceptance of the boundaries of a marketing battlefront, or of the weapons to be used, does not nurture the development of demonstrable differences from competition. But a penetrating vision of one's business strips away these restrictive definitions and leads to refreshing new horizons.

The parallels drawn between football and marketing have a common ancestor in military strategy. For example, in his account of World War II, General Douglas MacArthur castigated other United States commanders for their head-on attacks against the Japanese, while expressing pride in his own leapfrogging strategy in New Guinea and the Philippines.[4] MacArthur noted that casualties and losses of materials in the two battles for Okinawa and Iwo Jima alone—both frontal assaults—were greater than those he experienced in all of his campaigns in the Southwest Pacific.

We see many examples of this end-run strategy practiced by shrewd marketers. Some are grand and sweeping designs. Others are more modest in scope. It is essential to note that these end-runs may be developed at any point in the marketing spectrum.

The following examples relating end-runs to the various facets of marketing are illustrative:

Relative to Revised Visions of a Business: "We're not in the railroad business," Chicago, Burlington & Quincy Railroad advertisements have announced, "we're in the distribution business." This revamped attitude forced the Burlington line to think of themselves as an extension of the shipper's total distribution system and

[3] The Gallagher Report, Vol. XII, No. 19 (May 13, 1964).

[4] Douglas MacArthur, *Reminiscences* (New York: McGraw-Hill Book Co., 1964).

to use the latest tools available to execute this vision and thereby outflank other carriers.

The railroad leases an IBM 360 computer to move freight cars more efficiently. A private microwave system was installed to speed computer data between key cities on the line. Burlington bought a plane to fly prospective customers to inspect industrial sites along its right of way. The line's police have quit chasing hobos and now worry about reducing freight damage.

Consolidated Foods, Inc. describes its corporate mission as the management of money, not simply as being in the food business.

Relative to Marketing Communications: Obviously, the sensible thing to do if you're advertising a high-priced line of men's toiletries is to select "class" media such as *The New Yorker, Holiday,* and the like. At least, convention in the toiletries business urges this communications channel. Yet when Swank introduced Jade East—its line of men's colognes and after-shave lotion—it took an opposite course. While also appearing in the conventional media, they used spot TV to break out of the common mold. And break out they did. Jade East soon became one of the leading lines, despite entrenched competition.

A fresh creative stance in advertising can supply even more leverage than creative media selection. Once again the detergent field provides a good example. Colgate's all-purpose cleanser, Ajax, overtook P&G's Mr. Clean by stressing a new copy point: the benefits of its ammonia content. At first Mr. Clean counterattacked by challenging the ammonia story. But this strategy didn't work and so P&G was compelled to bring out a new product, Top Job, to be able to neutralize effectively Colgate's fresh and imaginative approach with its own creative implementation of the ammonia-copy platform. It is significant to note here that ammonia was not a new ingredient in these products; what was new was its use in advertising to furnish a distinctive difference. And yet what prevented long-time ammonia marketers, such as Parsons and Bo-Peep, from capitalizing on this opportunity?

Relative to Product Innovation: "Product fragmentation" is proving to be a most potent marketing weapon. To elucidate the values of introducing variations of an existing product, A. C. Nielsen cited the case of one product category in which four new variants, based on new flavors and physical properties, expanded the total market 78 per cent during a five-year period.[5] In another product classification, specialty brands seized 18 per cent of the total market, and in still another category one specialty grabbed 34 per cent of the market in four years while the regular, long-established entries were barely able to maintain stable volume levels.

It is reported that new fuel systems for cars may revolutionize the gasoline business. If the petroleum companies do not have the courage to effect change themselves rather than remain wedded to the established pattern, change may be forced on them.

Relative to "Market Stretching": For many years United Shoe Machinery had included in their industrial line a tool to "blind-fasten" metal parts together, that is, attach pieces of metal together securely from one side only. Several other companies made a similar product. About five years ago United Shoe Machinery had the bright idea of making this tool about one-third the size, about as big as a pair of pliers, and selling it to the "do-it-yourself" market. The product is now being sold in hardware stores and discount houses all over the country with great success.

Relative to Distribution: For chemical processors, ethylene has several advantages as a raw material. But until recently many companies were forced to use one or more of 13 substitutes because ethylene normally is sold as a gas and distributed via pipeline. This requires the consuming plant to be very near the ethylene plant and connected by pipeline. Enjay Chemical Company, a major ethylene producer, hurdled this barrier to the expansion of its ethylene business by developing the idea of producing ethylene in liquid form, which could be distributed by special cryogenic tank trucks.

THE RIGHT MENTAL CLIMATE

These, then, are a potpourri of examples of the end-run. The capacity to conceive of end-runs, both those useful in the daily competitive maelstrom and those that help to forge altogether new businesses, and the courage to execute them are crucial to

---

[5] A. C. Nielsen, Jr., "The Challenge of the Marketing Explosion." Speech presented before the American Association of Advertising Agencies, November 17, 1965.

survival and growth. As Peter Drucker wrote, ". . . to reach objectives, detours may have to be made around obstacles. Indeed, the ability to go around obstacles rather than charge them head on is a major requirement for managing by objectives." [6]

Obviously, the right mental set is needed on the part of both the leader of a business and his executives. The right organizational setup and administrative freedom are also essential so that creativity is not frustrated. Top management must understand, lead, and bless programs of advanced development which will enunciate and implement new marketing visions to keep the business always in the pioneer phase.

ELEMENTS IN SUCCESSFUL FORWARD PLANNING

At this point it is not prudent to attempt to give complete answers to the steps that can improve the management of creativity as it applies to improved products and services, new products and services, new areas of business, and new ways of marketing them. The opportunity probably lies in pursuing these steps:

1. Forward planning cannot be delegated by the President of a business to a manager of forward planning. The President can turn to staff people for assistance, but this responsibility must also remain a daily part of his activity—as important as any aspect of the business.

2. Select staff people for the forward planning activity who have had successful line experience and also demonstrate an instinctive understanding of the forces at work that control the destiny of a business.

3. Guard against selecting people who gravitate to forward planning staff work because it does not demand tangible near-term results and thus is interesting, gives great opportunity for loose theoretical thought, and is safe as far as demanding results for several years is concerned—or, in some unfortunate circumstances, for many years.

4. Find ways to keep experienced line operators with theoretical thought ability, as described in Item 2 above, psychically rewarded and satisfied in the staff work required for forward plan-

[6] Peter Drucker, *The Practice of Management* (New York: Harper & Bros., 1954), p. 61.

ning. Perhaps this is the heart of the problem. Business and social environment honors, respects and rewards, in daily ways, the so-called doers. Yet all our examples show that the creators and innovators, who are not clearly perceived as doers, are the key to perpetuating success. The paradox is that the people who easily gravitate to the forward planning area in a business rarely possess the total business judgment required to secure the needed respect from line operators to get their ideas readily accepted and put into action—especially if they require major risk, as the crucial ones must.

5. So, to repeat, forward planning cannot be delegated by the chief executive. He needs help and the help must come from people with business insight and experience who are then willing to forgo a sense of near-term accomplishment for the hope of affecting a favorable direction to the long-term course of business. The compensation for the loss of a sense of near-term satisfaction must come from the attitude of the chief executive. He can probably best balance this by continuing to make clear to all his associates that his job has two parts—daily operation and long-term future. By example and statement he can create an attitude of recognition for the people who labor in both activities. But this can occur only if he retains the day-to-day responsibility for the future to himself, even though he turns to other people for help—just as he usually does on the tangible activities of the business.

■

Summary

"End-runs," the action product of creativity in marketing, are vital on two levels—for the long-run preservation of the business as well as for providing competitive advantage in the everyday battles of the marketplace.

Preoccupations with the tangible and visible factors in a business cannot replace, and should not stultify, the crucial need to manage ideas and to prepare for and initiate change.

The objective of shorter-term end-runs is to outflank competition by the execution of a modified vision of the business. These end-runs may utilize any tool of marketing, including product innovation, distribution breakthroughs, market stretching, and so on.

The right corporate climate and organization are needed to execute end-runs; this includes the right mental set on the part of the individual executive and, above all, on the part of top management.

The core requirement is to identify new areas of opportunity and then give them the same dedicated support that built the business in the first place. To accomplish this, staff people can help, but forward planning cannot ultimately be delegated; it must lodge with the President. Staff people must have had successful line experience as well as a high order of conceptual ability. They should be sufficiently rewarded psychically to be satisfied with staff work.

3

Concentration

■

Harper W. Boyd, Jr

■

"To dominate, concentrate" might well be the war cry of many marketers. The principle is easy enough to state: Consolidate enough resources—effort, funds, manpower, creativity—in one area to "own" it rather than to spread oneself thin over a wider sector.

A realistic self-perception lies at the root of concentration. The very fact of self-definition and determination to exploit a firm's unique self-vision almost automatically leads to concentration on that vision rather than dissipating scarce resources over a broad front, which in turn expresses itself in any number of diverse marketing actions. There may be concentration on a sales strategy, an advertising message, a distribution channel, a product line, a market segment, a medium of communication, a price range—the list is almost endless. Thus the principle of concentration not only underlies the successful development of a marketing vision but also certain basic strategies covered in this book, notably market segmentation and multibrand entries.

It is this principle that accounts for all the justifiable preoccupation with heavy-user groups. That's why beauty-aids companies zero in on young women, beer marketers direct their attention to young men, laxative and tonic producers to older, lower-income people, soft drink bottlers to teenagers, floor-wax makers to suburban housewives, cigarette manufacturers to men, and so on through all the heavy users in each field.

To develop the concept and implications of concentration as it applies to marketing, we have called on Harper W. Boyd, Jr., who has been Professor of Marketing in the Graduate School of Business of Stanford University since 1964 and previously taught at Northwestern University for 14 years, rising to Director of the Graduate Division of the School of Business. Dr. Boyd has also accumulated ample experience in the business world as Director of the Bureau of Commercial Research, London, England; as Research Director of Market Research Corporation of America; and as a consultant to many companies, advertising agencies, trade associations, research houses, United States government agencies, and foreign governments, including Egypt and Australia.

Dr. Boyd's list of writings is so extensive as to defy enumeration here. Especially worthy of note, in addition to many articles, monographs and papers, are his co-authorship of *Marketing Management and Administrative Action* (McGraw-Hill Book Co., Inc., 1963) and *Advertising Management* (Richard D. Irwin, Inc., 1967). He has also co-authored a number of textbooks in marketing and marketing research.

CONCENTRATION

HARPER W. BOYD, JR.

In recent years we have witnessed the wholesale adoption of certain military terms by many writers in marketing; e.g., strategy, tactic, and logistics. While these terms have been used with considerably less precision than intended by the military scientist they have, nevertheless, been useful in conveying the need to think of marketing as a dynamic and fluid area of management. Perhaps of even greater importance has been that these terms have lent emphasis to the concept that there is a hierarchy of actions which lead to a plan of action.

Even the serious reader of marketing literature might easily be led to believe that many students of marketing are also students of the science of warfare. But if this were true one would be hard pressed to explain why certain principles of war have never been "translated into" the field of marketing. Of all these principles the one dealing with the concept of *concentration* would seem to be the most applicable. According to one noted military writer, "The principles of war, not merely one principle, can be condensed into a single word—'concentration.' But for truth this needs to be amplified as the 'concentration of strength against weakness.' "[1] It is the purpose of this chapter to explore in some depth the application of this principle to marketing management.

CONCENTRATION AS THE GRAND STRATEGY

In a very real sense the principle of concentration can be thought of as a grand or master strategy. This would position it as an overriding company policy and as such "superior" to strategy. "As tactics is an application of strategy on a lower plane, so strategy is an application on a lower plane of 'grand strategy' . . . the term 'grand strategy' serves to bring out the sense of 'policy in execution.' For the role of grand strategy—higher strategy—is to coordinate and direct all the resources of a nation."[2]

If the word "company" is substituted for "nation" in the above quotation it is clear that we are talking about the concentration of sufficient resources relative to the needs of the market and the resources of competition to dominate one or more market segment. Actually we are concerned about the effect—*domination*—brought about by the grand strategy of *concentration.* It should be clear that we are dealing mainly with concepts which cannot easily be quantified—and no attempt to do so will be made in this chapter.[3] Thus what constitutes *effective dominance* will vary depending upon the market segment under attack and the objectives of the firm. One can easily imagine situations where a company would have to have a very large share of a market in order to benefit from domination (e.g., a small-volume local market) versus those where a market share of even 15 to 20 per cent would represent effective

[1] B. H. Liddell-Hart, *Strategy: The Indirect Approach* (London: Faber & Faber Ltd., 1951), p. 347. Clausewitz, in speaking about the principles of war, said much the same, as witness his statement: "In a word, the first principle is *to concentrate as much as possible*" (quoted in Major-General J. F. C. Fuller, *The Conduct of War* [London: Eyre & Spottiswoode, 1961], p. 69).

[2] See Liddell-Hart, *ibid.*, pp. 335–336.

[3] This statement should not be construed as suggesting investments in any market past the point where they will generate greater profits elsewhere. We are arguing that the master strategy of concentration provides greater aggregate returns because of the efficiency of the marginal dollars invested.

dominance (e.g., a very large national market). And in a similar fashion the concept of *effective concentration* is a relative one.

In our discussion we will not be content to discuss merely concentration as grand strategy without pointing out what it implies in terms of implementation. Therefore the concept of concentration will be applied: (1) to any single strategy, such as channels of distribution, personal selling, or advertising; (2) to any combination of strategies; (3) to any tactic, such as advertising media or copy claim; and to any combination of tactics.

SETTING OBJECTIVES

An overriding objective is useful only to the extent that it serves as a guide to action (the development of strategies) *and* unifies and challenges the talents of the organization. More and more it is coming to be recognized that the marketplace is the prime source of the firm's overriding objective.[4] It is not sufficient, however, for a firm merely to locate its objectives in some aspect of consumer demand. To have meaning the objectives must be specific in terms of *what* wants and *what* needs of *what* parts of the market the firm wishes to satisfy.

Still, a broad—even generic—affirmation of intentions is of considerable value in helping a company move toward concentrating its resources. It makes a great deal of difference whether a company realizes that it is not selling products but the functions which these products perform in satisfying a customer's need. Phrased in these terms companies sell such "things" as energy, nutrition, comfort, intellectual development, and measurement rather than oil, bread, pillows, textbooks, and slide rules. The concept has merit in flexibility, since energy can be obtained by products other than oil, and bread serves other functions than nutrition. This means that objectives can be phrased and interpreted differently by companies in the same industry.

Objectives have consequences and the "need" (or problem-solving) approach will often help a company redefine its purpose in life along imaginative lines—again making more inevitable the concentration approach.

[4] See J. B. McKitterick, "What Is the Marketing Management Concept?," in Frank M. Bass, ed., *The Frontiers of Marketing Thought and Science* (Chicago: American Marketing Assn., 1957), pp. 71–82.

For example, a cosmetic company sees itself as helping to solve a subtle psychological *need* pertaining to a youthful, wholesome appearance along with a certain amount of sophistication. This leads the company to realize that its product has certain style or fashion overtones. And this realization, in turn, leads to a concentration on certain merchandising and creative approaches, fashion containers, and the relation of the seasons to the product mix.

Usually the mission of servicing a need can be made sufficiently challenging to occupy the talents of an organization. Such a challenge as ". . . good, cheap, fast, worldwide telephone service for everybody,"[5] total fabric care, and instruments to measure time, can with proper interpretation provide demanding and exciting goals which force management to concentrate on finding ways and means to attain them. Such goals should minimize the temptation for the organization to set up a multiplicity of goals which ultimately tend to dissipate prime resources. This, of course, is not to say that diversification is bad *per se*. Rather it strongly suggests that one does not move toward diversification *until* one has achieved dominance in some area—and even here it is usually better to move toward the production of goods that serve related needs than dissimilar ones. We noted earlier that one advantage of the concept of generic use was that it lends itself to a variety of relatively unique interpretations—all of which were related to the basic need.

It is critical for management to understand fully the significance of the strategy of concentration. To be effective, this grand strategy demands that it be applied throughout the total firm. It is perhaps most obvious at the objectives level where the resources available must be "fitted" in such a way as to achieve some measure of dominance. Often this requires that objectives be collapsed. Too often management fails to realize that more may be accomplished by sequencing objectives through time in contrast to tackling a number of objectives simultaneously; doing only a few things well at a time versus spreading resources. Objectives setting is not unlike a line of dominoes. Once the lead domino is toppled the others fall "in line." A single product versus a line of products, a given market area, a small number of high-volume

[5] Charles H. Granger, "The Hierarchy of Objectives," *Harvard Business Review* (May–June 1964), p. 70.

accounts, dealing only with certain types of wholesalers—all are examples of ways to set limited objectives.

A large commercial printing company doing a variety of work for a variety of customers found it had no strong position with any single type of customer because it had no unique set of skills. In its attempt to be all things to all people it had not generated a strong position with any important set of customers. By targeting on repetitious commercial contract work, which required color and binding (e.g., retailer mail-order catalogs), the company was able over time to develop a combination of skills which enabled it ultimately to go after—and get—publication contracts. To get to this point the company had to reorganize and retrain its personnel, partially re-equip its plant, and develop an understanding of the publishing business. When it was operating as a job shop its personnel had to run so hard to keep the plant busy that no unique skills emerged—except at the market-coverage level. The company, with its large overhead, which resulted from handling a variety of jobs, couldn't compete against the specialists who had relatively less overhead and lower prices. A critical point in the conversion process was the decision to purchase high-capacity specialized machinery to replace general-purpose equipment, which was inefficient because it had to be flexible over a range of jobs.

MARKET SEGMENTATION

Market segmentation may be defined as the act or process by which a market is divided into two or more parts. The rationale for "dividing up" a market—any market—is that it is not homogeneous with respect to customer responses to company changes in product, price, channels of distribution, and promotional strategies. Thus segmentation is an attempt to group buying units in such a way that their reactions to marketing efforts will be similar. Another way of saying this is that elasticities will vary between segments but will be minimized within segments.

It is obvious that segmentation is but a part of the objectives-setting process, since one has to start with a clear definition of *the* market (the need as it relates to people or firms) before one "breaks" it apart. Most firms practice market segmentation in one way or another—consciously or unconsciously. In dealing with our concepts of concentration and domination the notion of segmentation looms large in importance, among other things, since it enables the firm to:

target its product through the development of attributes that appeal highly to the needs of a reasonably homogeneous group, as contrasted to designing one which is a compromise.

determine the appeals that are best for the segment and concentrate on this, as opposed to trying to say a variety of things about the product or service because of the variety of audiences.

concentrate on the media which are most effective, rather than use a "shotgun" approach.

focus on those channels that cater to the needs of the segment concerned, versus using more "broadcast" channels.

In a very real sense we are talking about the advantages of *specialization* brought about through the definition of a market goal which groups people according to a similarity of need and an orientation to a common "solution."

The United States Time Company (Timex) has been uniquely successful in *concentrating* on the low-price segment of the watch market through the manufacture and sale of watches priced at retail from $6.95 to $39.95. This market had been essentially left uncovered by the more traditional watch companies. Timex reportedly now sells more watches than any other watch company in the world—including 40 per cent of the watches in this country. To date the company has shown little interest in attempting to sell other segments of the watch market, let alone get into any other business. Given such a market target, the company found that its ability to specialize in its production of a limited line produced significant economies which, in turn, were fed into the process through which the company sought and achieved domination. An important by-product stemming from their concentration on the low-price market was that the company found it possible to sell the bulk of its output through a variety of unconventional outlets (especially drugstores) that, once stocked with the fast-selling Timex, were understandably reluctant to carry the other brands of low-priced watches which followed Timex into the market.[6]

[6] See *Business Week,* November 16, 1963.

Another kind of segmentation is illustrated by Breck in the shampoo market. By segmenting the market through the development of a line of individualized shampoos for dry hair, oily hair, and normal hair, the company apparently matched the way women thought of their hair. Thus they did not believe that any *one* shampoo (e.g., all-purpose Halo) could meet their individual needs.[7] Dominance, in this case, was achieved by concentrating meeting of the needs of several subsegments once the overriding objective had targeted on the segment of women's hair care.

Catering to the specific physical parts of a person, as illustrated above, is a relatively common objective, as witness the preoccupation of companies with teeth, eyes, hair, beard, feet, lips, skin, legs, and so on. It should be pointed out that such an objective has considerable danger unless the company recognizes that the physical part of a person involved is merely part of a person's total gestalt. Cultural norms and life style can and do affect the use of such products and this, in turn, often requires different treatments in the form of different products if the firm is to be successful. Still, the "parts" objective has appeal, since by concentrating on a specialized "part" a firm can make good use of its resources and often build a relatively dominant position in the market.

ALTERNATIVE WAYS OF SEGMENTATION

It is probably impossible to devise and apply a scale to "potential" buyers that will measure precisely their elasticity in a direct and precise manner vis-à-vis a firm's marketing expenditures. This problem is compounded when it is recognized that the firm has to group its individual strategy expenditures into a total marketing-mix expenditure and that the parts interact with one another. What we seek is a reasonably simple set of characteristics by which to segment the market and from which we can infer behavior relative to our efforts. In point of fact, we first infer behavior and then devise our efforts—including the extent of our efforts. Thus the concept of concentration leading to dominance

[7] Daniel Yankelovich, "New Criteria for Market Segmentation," *Harvard Business Review* (March–April 1964), p. 88.

is, to a considerable extent, based on our ability to segment the market in a meaningful way.

We can classify (segment) using a scheme which, hopefully, enables us to *ascribe* behavior. This is frequently done with household goods using demographic characteristics (age, education, occupation, sex, presence of children, etc.), social class, personality attributes, or some combination of these (e.g., life cycle). Social class has been used by a number of companies as a way to segment the market.[8]

The Kroehler Manufacturing Company, the largest furniture manufacturer in the United States, concentrates its efforts primarily at the upper-lower- and lower-middle-class American families. Its success can be attributed primarily to its ability to design a product line with these groups in mind; the high styles or extreme types of construction are avoided. The company also stayed out of the low end or "borax" field. Construction tends to feature such attributes as ruggedness, durability, and comfort at a reasonable price. Combinations—such as an upholstered chair and sofa set—are emphasized.

Given such a product line the company was able to generate considerable pressure on the market by spending substantial sums (several millions of dollars each year) on advertising, using such mass media as *Life*, the *Saturday Evening Post, Better Homes and Gardens*, etc. About 12,000 dealers are used, and collectively they place locally about one million column inches of advertising each year.

A more common way of segmenting is on the basis of past behavior relative to the product group in question, or inferred behavior based on past behavior relative to a substitute product. Some companies segment on the basis of heavy versus light buyers —or in the relative profitability of buyers.

Cummins-Chicago Corporation increased their sales dramatically (95 per cent) primarily by concentrating on those 20 per cent of the establishments that bought 80 per cent of the type of

[8] For a discussion of social classes and how they differ with respect to their buying behavior see Pierre Martineau, "Social Classes and Spending Behavior," *Journal of Marketing* (October 1958), pp. 121–130. Also see Lee Rainwater, Richard P. Coleman, and Gerald Handel, *Workingman's Wife* (New York: Oceana Publications, Inc., 1959).

product the company sells—invoice canceling and perforating equipment. By reducing substantially the number of accounts to call on, the company was able to encourage concentration of sales calls, isolate key buying influences within each prospective client's establishment, target their advertising, including direct mail, and help their distributors concentrate their efforts.[9]

More, much more, could be said about segmentation; in fact, we have but touched the subject. But the main purpose of the discussion was simply to point out its relevancy to the concept of concentration.

MAJOR STRATEGIES

With regard to product and product line it is difficult to separate out the critical effect of the firm's objective—including the target segment or segments. Still, there are many ways in which a company can visualize itself servicing a given market; e.g., producing a long or a short line. A case in point would be the success of the specialty meat producers such as the Oscar Mayers versus the Swifts and the Armours.

Zenith, for many years, was almost uniquely successful by going against the industry trend of line proliferation and sticking to a relatively small line of household products, primarily radios and TV sets. By increasing its share of a fairly static market, Zenith, during the period from 1955–1960, was able to double its sales and increase its after-tax earnings to about 20 per cent of net worth. By further concentrating on style and quality the company was able to take advantage of a situation which saw, because of declining prices, most competitors sacrifice these product attributes. The above strategy enabled the company to obtain greater dealer loyalty since most were able to sell Zenith sets at higher than average margins. Also, because its sets were easier to service, Zenith won the respect of repairmen who, by word of mouth, further built a quality reputation for the company.

---

[9] "Sighting the 20% That Buy 80%," *Sales Management*, April 15, 1960. For a reasonably technical discussion regarding the value of concentration on profitable accounts see Charles H. Devin, *Marketing Productivity Analysis* (New York: McGraw-Hill Book Co., 1965), pp. 72–87.

The discussion thus far should not be interpreted as saying that a firm should not shift its emphasis from an established product to a new one. Times and opportunities change, and a company must adjust. A position of dominance is often of considerable help in making such a move.

Emery Air Freight initially concentrated its resources on the "emergency" segment of the air freight market. By developing a unique product line consisting of door-to-door delivery service via Emery's own trucks, a world-wide procurement service, and a time of delivery service by which customers were kept informed of the progress of their shipment and the time of its arrival, the company quickly achieved domination.

Emery's management believed, however, that its growth lay in selling the planned usage of air freight on a more regular basis versus the sale of a product for the emergency market. Without question, the firm's dominant position in the industry made it possible for it to shift its emphasis in the direction of the planned-usage segment of the market. Its outstanding reputation made it easier to contact and sell top management on the new service.

The product-life-cycle concept would seem to lend itself well to our discussion of concentration as a master strategy.[10] Briefly stated, the product-life-cycle concept is a relatively simple one. The cycle consists of three phases: (1) the introductory one, in which the critical ingredients are engineering skill and ability to launch the new product; (2) the growth phase, in which unit profits climb sharply for all concerned; and (3) the maturity phase, in which, despite increased volume, profits decline.[11] The firm that concentrates its resources to achieve dominance during phases one and two should reap substantial rewards, since its efforts and returns are spread over time in contrast to the follower who "comes in" after a particular phase has already gotten under way.

The Dow Chemical Company followed the development of polystyrene plastic, moved quickly to develop an extensive market development program for Styron—the company's brand name. A detailed marketing plan was developed which included the use of a product-evaluation committee to evaluate end products to

[10] See also Chapter 5.

[11] See Arch Patton, "Top Management's Stake in the Product Life Cycle," *The Management Review* (June 1959), pp. 9–14, 67–71, 76–79.

determine whether any plastic was appropriate; whether styrene should be used and if so, what formulation; whether the product was adequately designed from a functional point of view; and whether workmanship was sufficient.

Dow published a quarterly publication which was sent to retail buyers of toys and housewares. Each article approved by the product-evaluation committee was pictured and the name and address of the manufacturer was given. All approved articles were allowed to use the Dow Styron label and Dow advertised its product extensively to the consumer.

The company also undertook for its customers extensive research which resulted in, for example, a heavier polystyrene formula for use in the production of plastic toys and factory-colored Styron for the wall-tile market.

As a result of these and other activities the company was able not only to accelerate the demand for polystyrene but also to seize and hold a commanding position in the industry, which was comprised of such other large companies as Monsanto Chemical Company, Bakelite Company, and Koppers Company.

Packaging is a variable which lends itself to the domination concept—especially for those products which are sold through supermarkets. Many producers of such products have learned the importance of having a package which will literally "reach out" to the housewife. Ernest Dichter reports that his research shows that the Cheer detergent box was uniquely successful in obtaining this "reaching out" quality via its dynamic action design (clean wash flapping in the breeze) coupled with its bold color scheme of blue, red, white, and yellow.[12]

CHANNELS-OF-DISTRIBUTION STRATEGY

Channels of distribution offer most firms a considerable opportunity to apply the concept of concentration, if only because there are typically so many different ways by which a channels strategy can be implemented.

---

[12] Ernest Dichter, "The Man in the Package" in Stewart H. Britt and Harper W. Boyd, Jr., eds., *Marketing Management and Administrative Action* (New York: McGraw-Hill Book Co., 1963), pp. 310–321.

The direct-to-user channel lends itself to domination, since the seller has the option of concentrating his fire on a limited number of high-potential accounts or of dispersing his fire among a large number of accounts; or a firm may adopt the policy of dominating a less conventional channel—one which is spurned by its competitors.

Electrolux has apparently been successful in its sale of vacuum cleaners over the years by concentrating on the use of house-to-house selling as well as by concentrating on a single appliance. Clearly the company has dominated this channel for this product over the years, and its other strategies, such as pricing, advertising, and product line, have been geared to maintaining dominance through its house-to-house selling.

The earlier discussion of Dow would fit here, since this company saw the advantages which could be obtained by dominating, through proper and imaginative servicing, the important accounts by direct selling. Cryovac in the sale of its packaging system early recognized the need to dominate on a direct basis and proceeded to discard its distributor organization.

SELECTION OF RETAILERS

Companies often find it desirable to dominate a growth segment of the retail trade—in terms of either a type of retailer or a given number of retailers of the same type. Large companies are often vulnerable to this kind of attack by a smaller competitor, since they are geared to mass marketing, which results in less attention being paid to any one type of retailer.

In the early 1950s Pepsi-Cola in its fight against Coca-Cola made a critical marketing decision.

> It could try to attack Coca-Cola on all fronts at once and scatter its shots, or it could concentrate its firepower. The market for soft drinks breaks into two large categories. The first is on-premise sales—i.e., fountain sales, vending-machine sales, and the sale of already refrigerated bottles for on-the-spot consumption. The second is the "take home" market—the sales of unrefrigerated bottles for consumption in the home. It was this second sector that Steele singled out for his major attack. This was where Pepsi was already at its strongest; and it would be easier to get outlets in places like grocery stores and supermarkets

where many brands are displayed than in snack bars or soda fountains where, as a rule, only a single brand of cola is sold.[13]

The above-described channel strategy sparked an advertising campaign targeted at the housewife who was the key to the take-home market. The theme was "the light refreshment." Coke bottlers demanded that Coke retaliate by challenging the implication that Coke had more calories than Pepsi. But Coke refused.[14]

Coke had reasons for this policy. First, while Pepsi might have the option of attacking Coke at a single point, Coke had to defend its entire line, its fountain and vending sales as well as its home market. Its ads had to be more general.[15]

An illustration of selecting a limited number of retailers all of the same type is afforded by the Drexel Furniture Company, which franchises only about 3,000 outlets to carry its products. By concentrating on this relatively small number of stores the company has been able to achieve considerable within-store domination and excellent support, including displays, maintenance of a basic stock, and good local advertising.

A large electric clock manufacturer serves as an illustration of the disadvantages which can occur when efforts are dispersed over too many retailers. This company attempted to sell literally every store that carried low-price electric alarm clocks—department stores, hardware stores, mail-order houses, appliance stores, jewelry stores, drugstores, etc. Sales were made through a sales force to wholesalers who in turn sold to over 100,000 outlets. The company employed a group of retail missionary men to open new retail accounts. Once "opened," such accounts were turned over to the appropriate wholesalers to service. Despite these and other efforts this company constantly found itself with serious distribution problems. It dominated no single group of stores. Yet its competitors (with fewer resources) achieved strong trade support through concentrating on specific types of stores. Thus one competitor dominated the appliance stores, another the jewelry stores, and so on.

---

[13] Alvin Toffler, "The Competition That Refreshes," *Fortune* (May 1961).
[14] *Ibid.*
[15] *Ibid.*

SELECTION OF MIDDLEMEN

Working with either a small number of middlemen via an exclusive franchise or a given type of middleman to the exclusion of others is a relatively common way to achieve some degree of channels dominance. Too often, though, firms submit to proliferating their use of middlemen as a way of picking up increased sales at a relatively low cost. If the product is being "pulled" through the channels, this may work. But if not, the seller runs the risk of dividing up the profits available to the middlemen to such an extent that few will provide aggressive support of the product.

An example of a company that successfully entered an established market late by concentrating on middlemen is Jones and Laughlin Steel Company with its stainless steel. In wooing the independent warehouseman the company went counter to the policies of its large competitors (e.g., Republic Steel Corporation and Armco Steel) who were selling as much stainless direct as possible. J&L was able to convince the best warehouses that it was committed to selling *through* them and not around them. The result was that J&L signed up about 140 good warehousemen and has been able to become a factor in the market.[16]

ADVERTISING STRATEGY

We are not concerned here with the frequent claim that if you can't look "big" in a given medium, don't enter it. Rather, we are concerned more with overall communication strategy which has to do with both copy (message) and media. We too often forget that we must always make a basic choice between *reach* and *frequency* in the construction of our message. This is really the same as saying that we must decide on how much redundancy we want in our message. We can center on a single message and repeat it over and over again if we think that our audience, for whatever reason, may have a hard time either receiving the message or understanding it. In other words, we always have the choice of transmitting more information in a message or transmitting less and repeating it more.

[16] "Cracking a 'Tiffany' Market," *Business Week,* July 8, 1961.

The above is a hard problem, since too slow a rate bores and too fast a rate confuses, and different people respond differently to different rates, thus making it difficult to set an optimum rate. But if the audience has some degree of homogeneity then our problem of rate is made less difficult. Thus by specialization we can do a better job of getting across our message.

Many students of advertising are quick to point out how difficult it is to get a message across, if only because of the large number of messages being beamed at consumers daily. While it is dangerous to generalize, this would seem—all other things being equal—to indicate that redundancy has merit—at least up to a point—versus a policy of dispersion.

Effective communication occurs when the source (the sender) encodes in such a way that the intended receiver (destination) can relate it to those parts of his experience which are similar to those of the source. It is clear that the more the source and the destination have in common the more apt the message is to be encoded efficiently. This "commonness" is more apt to occur when a firm specializes—or at least organizes so that specialization can occur. It should also be noted that we are talking about the heart of the marketing concept—i.e., the importance of knowing thoroughly the needs and wants of a firm's prospective customers. Given such an understanding, the firm should be better able to undertake a communication program evolving a concentration of copy claims of sufficient magnitude to appropriate that claim for its product. Certainly this statement contains elements closely related to the concept of concentration.

A message is more likely to be successful if it builds on what already exists; i.e., the knowledge, attitudes, and values of the receiver. The notion of segmentation discussed earlier is thus important, since it provides this desired homogeneity and facilitates concentration, and ultimately perhaps dominance.

The Kroehler Furniture Company's objective of selling essentially to lower-middle- and upper-lower-class households made possible a copy platform which concentrated on providing a message which took advantage of such existing attitudes as concern with durability and conservatism, values relating to a child-oriented household, and insecurities which pertained to the way in which different styles of furniture are grouped within a home.

What has already been said about copy applies in principle to the selection of media. Again the reach-versus-frequency problem is faced. In discussing the strategy of market aggregation with reference to the buying efficiency of promotional funds Alan Roberts says:

> Within certain dollar ranges, at least, the efficiency of promotional budgets may respond elastically to changes in size. That is, each dollar added to the promotional investment in a single product may result in a proportionally larger increase in promotional efficiency. The explanation of this lies in the basic per-thousand costs of advertising media. Media costs tend to follow this law: The larger and more general the medium, the smaller the cost per thousand; the more limited or specialized the medium, either geographically or by editorial or audience appeal, the greater the cost per thousand. The more that markets may be aggregated, the lower the cost per thousand in buying advertising to reach that mass market, at least within the range of certain promotional budgets.
>
> For the major consumer advertisers, however, promotional budgets frequently pass the range of efficiency discussed above. The size and diversity of the mass-consumer markets require supplemental advertising investment in local and/or specialized audience media. The latter then become an important part of the company's total national advertising program. At this point, one rationale for the strategy of aggregation tends to disappear; indeed, national advertisers move toward segmentation strategy in proportion to their targeting of selective local and/or specialized markets.[17]

Too often the advertiser disperses his funds in an apparent attempt to obtain reach and in so doing scatters his resources to such an extent that he obtains literally no impact. Given the intense intramedia competition, the advertiser must realize that many small space buys are often inefficient compared to fewer big space buys. It is simply too easy to get lost in the crowd.

PERSONAL SELLING STRATEGY

To a considerable extent what has been said about concentration with respect to the advertising strategy applies to the personal selling strategy. Especially is this true with the reach-versus-frequency problem.

---

[17] Alan A. Roberts, "Applying the Strategy of Market Segmentation," *Business Horizons* (Fall 1961), pp. 65–66.

As accounts become larger and the number of accounts of any significant size fewer, the sales force—both qualitatively and quantitatively—has changed. Dominance can be achieved only by concentrating the sales function in a limited number of persons. More and more it appears that sellers are using the account-executive idea whereby a generalist handles all contacts with a large buyer. He, this generalist, is often supported by a diversified staff of specialists ranging from technical to merchandising specialists. He represents the customer to his management and because of his responsibility more often than not takes the customer's point of view even against that of his own management.

Dominance in a sales force vis-à-vis other competing forces can usually be obtained only by adapting the strategy of concentrating on a limited number of accounts. Although this type of concentration has been discussed earlier, a last example can do no harm.

A few years back Bostitch made the decision to capitalize on sales specialization. Highly talented salesmen were selected to work with high potential accounts. A pilot sales specialist program in the automotive field gained the company a 300 per cent increase in sales in one year.[18]

CONCLUSION

Concentration leading to domination can be a powerful master strategy in marketing. In this chapter the concept has been explored under a variety of conditions ranging from objectives to such strategies as product and product line, channels, advertising, and personal selling. No attempt has been made to set up precise criteria for determining the amount of resources required to achieve dominance or the determination of the point at which domination is reached, following which inputs can be reduced. Rather we have sought merely to explore the concept and its implications.

An important conclusion regarding the concept has to be that domination can rarely be achieved with any success unless management targets its objectives on a specific audience (segmentation) and literally gets to know more about this group than the group knows about itself. A second and allied conclusion is that

[18] "Bostitch Learns How to 'Use' People," *Sales Management*, March 18, 1960.

once the segment is agreed upon, concentration and domination with respect to the best strategies often follow automatically.

Yet another conclusion—and an obvious one—is that concentration in any one strategy has an obvious effect on the other strategies comprising the marketing mix. Frequently it will be found that the marketing mix can be made more efficient by spending the additional funds required to achieve some degree of domination with respect to one strategy because it reduces the required inputs required for the other strategies, or because it makes them substantially more efficient at their present—or even expanded—expenditure level. An example here would be product dominance.

It should also be noted that one might well undertake to forgo dominance in one strategy in order to achieve it elsewhere in the marketing mix. Often a firm is required to add to—even proliferate—its product line to gain a dominant position within its channels.

And, finally, we should note that concentration is closely akin to the notion of specialization, although the employment of either does not guarantee dominance. Rather, it merely increases the possibility of achieving dominance. In a world of complexity to which many businesses respond by elaborate diversification the concept of dominance through concentration or specialization must indeed sound strange and out of place. But the principle should appeal to marketers as a means of simplifying the job of determining and solving the needs of a group of customers, marketers who in studying its possibilities will again see and understand some of the much-documented advantages of specialization.

■

Summary

"Advantage is gained in war and also in foreign policy and other things by selecting from many attractive or unpleasant alternatives the dominating point." *

---

* Winston S. Churchill, *The Second World War* (New York: Houghton-Mifflin Co., 1948), I, 225.

Concentration can rarely be achieved with any success unless management targets its objectives on a specific audience (segmentation) and literally gets to know more about them than the group knows about itself.

Concentration on any one strategy has an obvious effect on the other strategies comprising the marketing mix. Frequently the whole mix can be made more efficient by spending the additional funds required to achieve some degree of concentration with respect to one strategy because it reduces the input required for the other strategies, or because it makes them substantially more efficient at their present—or even expanded—expenditure level.

Concentration is closely akin to the notion of specialization, although the employment of either does not guarantee dominance.

The principle is intimately related to strategies of product lining, distribution channels, marketing communications, and personal selling.

4

Market Segmentation

■

Maurice E. Bale

■

As total markets have grown, it has become increasingly difficult for the traditional handful of brands in each market to satisfy all members of each consuming group. This fractionalization of markets has been further stimulated by intensifying specialization and differentiation of customer wants brought on by growing customer disposable income, refinement of tastes, sophistication, and psychic disposition to cater to individual desires.

As a result, market segmentation has become one of the most fundamental of all marketing strategies. Its purpose is, of course, to identify and concentrate on fractions of a total market capable of yielding a disproportionate volume and profit in return for the gratification of the special needs of that segment. The key point to focus on is the skill with which factors that truly divide markets are identified, vital target groups defined, segments harmonizing with a company's own talents and offerings selected, and marketing programs tailored accordingly.

Insight into the core of one's own business facilitates the use of the principle of market segmentation in ways that are uniquely right for the individual marketer. In the cosmetics field, for instance, taking into account the variety of consumer characteristics, desires, usage situations, and psychological states, consider what manufacturers of make-ups and skin-care preparations have achieved. Once upon a time there was a single product called cold cream. Now cold cream, although it still exists, has also been "spun off" into foundation, cleansing, vanishing, nourishing, conditioning, hormone, astringent, lanolin, marrow, and wrinkle cream.

Our author is particularly qualified to discuss this topic, having demonstrated his grasp of market segmentation from his first assignment in the United States—to establish Brylcreem in the American market. This he did so well that, in due course, it became the best-selling hair dressing in this country.

Maurice E. Bale is a Canadian, who started his career in the department store field as a trainee with Hudson Bay Company in Winnipeg. In 1937 he joined Harold F. Ritchie & Company Ltd. as a salesman in the Grocery Division. He moved up in this company, through various positions, to national sales manager of the Grocery Division, handling such products as Dole's canned fruit and juices, Sunmaid raisins, Ralston Purina, and Ovaltine.

In the fall of 1952 he was promoted to Executive Vice President and General Manager of Eno-Scott & Bowne, Beecham's United States subsidiary, and elected president of this company in November 1964. (The company name was changed in 1960 to Beecham Products, Inc., in order to associate it more closely with the parent.)

In 1963 Mr. Bale assumed the added responsibility of becoming chief executive officer for all of Beecham's interests in the Western Hemisphere and Australasia. In June 1966 he was elected a director of Beecham Group Ltd., the parent company.

■

MARKET SEGMENTATION

MAURICE E. BALE

The segmentation, or splitting up, of practically every United States mass market in the twenty years or so since World War II has provided unique opportunities for alert and imaginative businessmen, as well as a fascinating field for students of economics and sociology.

To understand what has happened, as well as the strategies needed to deal with the new phenomenon of segmentation, it will be helpful to take a brief backward look at the pre-war American economy. In those days, in nearly every consumer-goods field, the emphasis was on mass production, mass marketing, and the maintenance of a limited number of giant national brands.

In the cigarette industry, for example, Camels, Luckies, Chesterfields, and Philip Morris, all of them regular size and nonfilter, accounted for 73 per cent of total United States volume. In the soap field, Ivory, Lux, and Palmolive completely dominated the business; all other brands were relatively unimportant. In the automotive industry, Chevrolet, Ford, Buick, and Plymouth were so far ahead of competitors that market shares gained by other makes were almost negligible.

My own personal experience during those years was in the food brokerage business, and there we were dealing constantly, and almost exclusively, with big-volume, mass-market leaders. Branded items like Dole pineapple, Sunmaid raisins, and Ralston cereal were so dominant in their fields that we considered them staples. Even the products which we dealt with as specialities were almost invariably the unchallenged leaders in their own fields. A product like Saniflush, for example, had practically a monopoly in its own market, as did Ovaltine and Welch's grape juice in their respective categories. No matter where you looked, the story was the same: a few big, well-known national brands reaching and owning American mass markets.

Furthermore, at that time it seemed to many businessmen and others that this was the natural and inevitable trend of the economy—that the big brands were going to get bigger and bigger and more and more standardized and that consumers would conform more and more to mass-marketing patterns. As a matter of fact, in many intellectual quarters, as you may remember, there was a good deal of worrying about this. Every American, according to certain writers and professors, would soon become indistinguishable from every other American—each wearing an Arrow shirt, eating Kellogg's corn flakes, chewing Wrigley's gum, drinking Coca-Cola, lounging in his B.V.D.s, gargling with Listerine. The individual buyer with individual tastes was going to be obliterated by the twin juggernauts of mass production and mass brands.

Well, unfortunately for the theorists, it didn't happen that way. What did happen, following World War II, was a sudden, dramatic, and quite unpredicted marketing revolution, a revolution with startling social as well as business implications. In the great postwar revival practically every industry in America went surging ahead. But—and this was the unexpected outcome—in practically no industry did the old, established brands retain their commanding position. Furthermore, in practically no field have we ever seen a return to the prewar patterns of market domination by a few big brands.

Instead, with the tremendous flow of new products, nearly every American mass market—in foods, drugs, toiletries, almost any field you want to name—has shown signs of splitting up into a number of smaller markets, markets based on varying consumer tastes, preferences and buying habits. This splitting up, or segmentation process, is probably the most challenging single aspect of modern American marketing and it is proceeding today at an accelerated pace.

Let us look at just a few examples. In the cigarette field, for instance, once dominated by the Big Four—Camels, Luckies, Chesterfields, and Philip Morris—there are today no less than 17 brands with a significant share of the industry total. And these brands include regular and king size, filter and nonfilter, mentholated and nonmentholated, and several shadings of differences in each of these categories. Prewar, the American smoker seemed satisfied with one basic size and type of cigarette. Today he shops around among many different varieties.

Or take the automotive industry. Though there are fewer American manufacturers in the field than there were before World War II, their market has segmentized in truly astonishing fashion. Where once you had three basic price ranges in the automobile business—high, medium, and low—you now have as many as ten different price fields, ranging from very high and medium-high down to low, economy, and compact. Furthermore, manufacturers are producing many more types and makes of cars. Ford Motor Company, for instance, concentrated prewar on Lincoln, Mercury, and Ford. Today it produces Continental, Thunderbird, Mercury, Comet, Ford, Mustang, Falcon, and Cougar, and has plans for other new lines.

The food industry, in nearly every one of its product categories, has seen striking and continuous market segmentation and fragmentation. The fruit juice field, for example, once almost the exclusive property of Welch's, has expanded to support an astonishing variety of fresh, frozen, canned, and bottled juice items. The ready-to-eat cereal market today has more than 60 different brands and types of products, fighting for a share of business. The baked-goods field no longer centers around the standard white loaf but supports dozens of fresh and frozen varieties.

And in the segmentation process, many of the old selling beliefs and shibboleths have all but disappeared. Twenty-five years ago, for instance, it seemed unlikely that there would ever be a market for instant coffee. I remember that we tried our best to push Nescafé in those days, but with very little success. But then suddenly, postwar, a huge new instant-coffee market opened up. By 1963 it accounted for 29 per cent of total coffee volume. It is a major factor in the American coffee business today.

Now, why have such things happened? Why are they continuing to happen at a faster and faster pace, and on a broader and broader scale? More important, what lessons can be drawn from all these profound changes by alert and progressive marketers?

In my opinion, the basic reasons for market segmentation contain, in themselves, clues for the strategies which must be followed in dealing with it. At the risk of seeming to oversimplify, let me suggest the following:

1. *Consumers are different.* They differ widely in tastes, interests, personal desires and preferences, and in their physical, emotional, and psychological needs. No matter how convenient and comforting it may be for a manufacturer to think of his market as a vast sea of average, standardized buyers, there are really no such people.

2. *Consumers like to express their differences.* Contrary to what was once believed, they don't necessarily want to use the same brand of toothpaste or toilet water or travel facilities as everyone else. They want products and services which most closely fulfill their own personal desires. They are interested primarily in themselves, not in conforming to any mass pattern.

3. *Consumers will express their differences whenever they have (a) sufficient income, and (b) sufficiently attractive product*

choices. Beyond question, a primary factor in the segmentation of American mass markets has been the sharp rise in incomes in all classes of United States society. Coupled with this has been the dramatic increase in the variety and profusion of new products offered in the marketplace. Taken together, the two influences have made segmentation almost inevitable.

You will notice that in this abbreviated explanation I have concentrated entirely on the consumer's role. This, of course, is fundamental to all sound marketing thinking. But it becomes doubly important in dealing with segmentation.

Beyond question, the companies which have been most successful in segmentation have been those with the most sensitive understanding of the consumer mind. On the other hand, corporations which through habit, inertia, or production-oriented thinking have clung to outworn customer and product concepts have, without exception, suffered through the segmentation process.

Essentially, the challenge facing any marketer today comes down to this:

(a) To discover, define, understand, and isolate significant consumer segments of a total mass market.

(b) To develop quality products which can be produced at a profit in serving these market segments.

(c) To mount carefully planned, fully conducted programs for exploiting these opportunities.

Curiously enough, non-United States companies have sometimes been quickest to grasp these fundamentals and to cash in on American market segmentation. Schweppes, the British bottled mixer, is an outstanding example. Its United States success is all the more remarkable in that it crashed a bottled-beverage industry dominated by American giants—Canada Dry, Coca-Cola, Pepsi-Cola and others—all of whom were perfectly capable of producing products roughly comparable to Schweppes—if they had only happened to think of the idea. Actually what Schweppes did was to move in, open up, exploit, and take over a highly specialized segment of the bottled beverage market—the gin-and-tonic field. Before Schweppes, most Americans drank gin only in martinis and Tom Collinses. Since Schweppes, gin and tonic has become a standard American drink and Schweppes has cashed in heavily on its own marketing skill and foresight.

Or consider Volkswagen. This shrewd German marketer caught the American automotive industry, and most of its European contemporaries, almost sound asleep. It invaded the United States with such a solid product and marketing program that before the others got around to producing compacts and miniatures to compete, VW had carved out for itself a substantial market segment, which it still enjoys. In this connection, it is worth noting that it has been the *overall* excellence of the Volkswagen marketing operation—not simply fine advertising but also dealerships, service arrangements, sales policies, parts, supplies, and many other factors—which have made it by far the most successful foreign invader of the United States automotive field.

An almost equally impressive case is that of Sony, the Japanese electronics firm. Sony, in the midst of a brutally competitive American television-set industry, has coolly, calmly, and shrewdly staked out a segment of the business for itself. It has done so by concentrating on a section of the market which the giants didn't seem to think worth troubling about—the miniature TV-set business—the nine-inch and even five-inch screens, which everyone thought had died out in the early 1950s. Sony, since 1958, has built up a $37-million export business, half of it in the United States.

Significantly, the success of all three of these companies, Schweppes, Volkswagen, and Sony, followed precisely the same pattern. Each went after not the total, but part of a market. Each demonstrated superior understanding of its own segmented part. Each provided superior products to fill the needs and desires of its own carefully selected audience. And each employed a professionally structured marketing mix to attain its goals.

Actually these are the same three steps which must be followed by any company which hopes to compete in the segmentation era. So let us turn now to a more detailed examination of each one of them.

DEFINING A MARKET SEGMENT

The oldest, most traditional, and in some ways most primitive method of defining the various elements of a total market is what is most times called *producer segmentation.* This is simply dividing a market according to product types and according to the ingredients or production techniques used in their manufacture.

Nearly every industry employs some form of such producer segmentation. The liquor industry, for example, breaks down its volume by gins, rums, bourbons, scotches, and vodka; the gasoline industry by regular and high-test gasolines and straight and premium motor oils; the aviation industry by first-class and tourist, or economy, accommodations; the radio-set industry by AM and FM or console and portable.

There is nothing particularly wrong with such producer segmentation, providing that the designated market segments are not looked at as ends in themselves, or made the whole focus of marketing strategy.

The key to product success lies in the needs and wants of consumers, not in the performance of a product within the limits of some manufacturer-dictated segment. Furthermore, too much preoccupation with producer segmentation can sometimes blind a company to the shifting realities of the marketplace.

One well-known food manufacturer, for example, based his share of market and volume objectives, and his marketing planning, on the manufacturing processes and ingredients used in his product. By this measurement he had a successful product and an 80 per cent share of an apparently stable business. However, many other new products, made with different ingredients and by different processes, had poured into the market and were being used by consumers for the same purpose. The volume of these new products was about ten times as great as our marketer's own narrowly defined production-process segment. Thus he actually was enjoying a steadily declining market share (it had dropped to 8 per cent of total) instead of the deceptively optimistic picture which he read in his marketing plans.

Perhaps the best thing to be said about producer segmentation is this: It represents a first rough step in breaking a market into its component parts, and it has a certain, though limited, usefulness in basic strategies and planning. Its weakness is that it is manufacturer- rather than consumer-oriented, and it seldom provides clues to latent or shifting consumer needs and desires. In any case, you can take it as axiomatic that marketers who have been most successful in dealing with segmentation have been those who have carried their thinking beyond the producer or manufacturer stage.

DEMOGRAPHIC SEGREGATION

A second, and highly popular method of defining markets is through *demographic segmentation.* This involves dividing the consumers in a total market according to age, income, sex, geographical location, race, and other groups, and focusing marketing and advertising activities on one or more of the groups isolated in this fashion. Demographic segmentation represents a considerable advance over producer segmentation, since it is based on a study of customers, not manufacturing processes or ingredients, and you may easily find that breaking your market down in this way will disclose unexpected opportunities.

For example, if your studies show that 65 per cent of the purchases in your product group are made by unmarried males below the age of 35, you may well decide to concentrate your marketing effort toward this particular group, and to disregard all others. If analysis indicates mothers with young children account for 50 per cent or more of the market for a particular class of product, you may wish, in the interests of efficiency, to select this as your target audience.

If a total market shows signs of greater strength in small-town and small-city areas than in big metropolitan counties, your best strategy may be to focus on this. Similarly, if you find that sales bulk is disproportionately higher among lower-income, lower-educated consumers, you may do well to revise your entire product and marketing plans to fit and serve these groups.

Demographic segmentation can often be of tremendous help in defining markets. It does, however, have certain drawbacks and weaknesses which you should bear in mind:

1. To a certain extent the breakdown of customers into neat little demographic bundles—by age, income, education, etc.—is an artificial division. In many cases consumer buying habits don't follow strict demographic patterns.

2. Frequently attempts to segment a market demographically

lead to the mistaken conclusion that there is an "ideal" or "typical" buyer who will react like a jack-in-the-box, or trained seal, to demographic stimulation.

3. Too often a preoccupation with demographic segmentation leads a marketer to concentrate only on the "big numbers," the larger segmented units, and to disregard the smaller segments in which, because of a competitive situation, superior product quality, or lack of direct exploitation, his greater opportunities may lie.

An illustration of the first two of these points is the case of a laundry-product manufacturer who defined his "target audience" as a young housewife with a large family, living in an urban area, with an income of over $5,000 a year. This was a happy, precise, businesslike little portrait. The only trouble was that a subsequent analysis of sales showed that large numbers of older women with smaller incomes and no children were purchasing and repurchasing the product.

The explanation, of course, was that they liked the particular qualities which the product gave them. The manufacturer, after his initial confusion, had to conclude that people weren't buying his product *because* they were young, urban, over-$5,000-a-year mothers, but for entirely nondemographic reasons. Furthermore, he was forced to realize that appeals to his market based on its demographic unity weren't half as effective as appeals based on product quality and performance.

This is not to say, however, that the use of demographic data cannot be enormously helpful in plotting certain phases of marketing strategy, especially in the selection and use of advertising media. It is merely a caution about the too-enthusiastic application of such material.

The second point is a subtler one, and will be dealt with in more detail later on. It is simply the fact that, in studying demographic data, there is a perfectly normal and entirely human tendency to look only at the larger shares, the bigger numbers. You may easily assume that if the majority of your consumers fall into a particular group—say married males, age 25–34—then your life or death depends on how well you reach this segment. It may. But then again, it may well not.

SPECIAL-INTEREST SEGMENTATION

A third method of market segmentation, and often a very practical one, is by *special interests.* As the country has grown larger and wealthier, huge consumer groups with high spending power have evolved around special interests and activities.

For example, the boating market has an estimated 40 million people and annual retail expenditures or rating of $2½-billion.

Teenagers, who are more of a special-interest group than simply an age class, spend an estimated $12- to $20-billion a year for a wide variety of products, many of them with a definite or exclusive teenage appeal.

The photography market for all types of cameras and equipment has an annual volume of more than $1½-billion.

The estimated 140 million Americans who hunt and fish spend better than $4-billion a year in pursuing their hobbies.

Often a careful study of these or other special-interest segments will disclose new product and profit opportunities for wide-awake marketers.

PHYSIOLOGICAL- AND PSYCHOLOGICAL-NEED SEGMENTATION

By far the most challenging type of market segmentation, however, is that which is based on *physiological or psychological consumer needs.* In such segmentation, markets are broken down not by product, or demographic categories, but by groups which reflect varying consumer desires. Furthermore, this type of segmentation thinking often results in the emergence of new, highly specialized and precisely defined markets.

Perhaps one of the most spectacular recent examples of this technique has been the extraordinarily successful Mustang, introduced by Ford Motor Company. Mustang's history is especially interesting because of the sharp contrast it provides with older, more traditional, methods of new-car introduction.

In the old days, when the automotive industry classified its cars by product segments—high-priced, medium-priced, and low-priced—it was generally assumed that price was the prime factor in car purchasing. Furthermore, the industry tended to think of car buyers in terms of vertical movement. They assumed that a Chevrolet owner was on his way to becoming a Buick owner, and then a Cadillac owner, right up the price ladder.

Providing logical rungs for the ladder became a major concern of car manufacturers, and this thinking was what led Ford to introduce the Edsel. It decided it needed another entry on the road from Ford to Lincoln—a medium-priced entry. Basically the Edsel may have failed for a number of reasons, particularly styling. But the whole logic of the Edsel introduction was based on producer orientation and thinking, not on consumer needs and wants. Such orientation is always hazardous.

By contrast, Mustang was a classic example of defining, building for, and selling to a new, highly specialized market segment. Essentially that segment was the unexpectedly large group of motorists who wanted to combine low-cost, dependable transportation with sports-car fun and styling. Ford, in introducing Mustang, appealed shrewdly to this group with a combination of basic low price and a host of optional extras that could be added to express the owners' own personality and imagination.

Mustang has proved far more than just another new line of car. It is the spectacular pace-setter for a brand-new market segment. This lesson, that markets break down most meaningfully in terms of specialized consumer needs and wants, is basic in dealing with segmentation.

In searching your own market for segmentation opportunities, you will not want, of course, to overlook traditional product categories of your industry. You will do well to study demographic breakdowns of consumers for clues that can develop new marketing strategies. And you will certainly want to examine the potentials in special-interest groups. But for the majority of marketers, the real breakthroughs are most apt to come from a more intensive study of consumer needs and desires.

STUDYING MARKET SEGMENTS

If the definition and selection of sizable consumer groups within a total market is the first step in the process of dealing with segmentation, then the intensive and continuing study of these groups is a necessary preamble to such selection.

For these studies there are no magical formulas or infallible techniques. Methods will vary as widely as the kinds of markets and types of consumers or consumer attitudes you are examining. Among the more widely used techniques are:

(a) Straight consumer research involving questionnaires, personal interviews, group interviews, and a variety of psychologically structured tests aimed at uncovering new customer insights.

(b) Product tests, involving new products, old products, competitive products. These are often as valuable for the consumer information they develop as for their product data and preferences.

(c) Advertising tests on appeals, copy themes, and product concepts. Reader-viewer responses to various advertising headlines, layouts, or story boards frequently turn up clues for further market exploration.

In all such studies, however conducted, it is well to bear in mind that you are aiming for two kinds of information: (a) a deeper understanding of particular consumer needs or desires; (b) some quantitative idea of the size of the market segments which have these needs or desires.

A leading food manufacturer, for example, studied the customers for several of his products, in terms of these five variables:

(a) *Weight concern*—the spectrum of buyers from compulsive eaters to those unconcerned about weight.

(b) *Home preparation*—housewives who have a need to prepare complete recipes to those who sometimes or always seek the convenience of prepared products.

(c) *Time of day*—eating needs of different homes at breakfast, lunch, dinner, and various snack times.

(d) *Food value*—need for nutrition versus indulgence.

(e) *Value-price*—people willing to pay a premium for quality down through those interested only in lowest price.

By analyzing such data both qualitatively (in terms of varying consumer desires) and quantitatively (in terms of the size of each market segment) he was able to come up with several concepts for new products, and to reposition certain of his old products for greater market penetration.

A brewer, in a series of tests, found that beer drinkers can be divided into groups according to their outlook on life, and, furthermore, that these groups or market segments are quite different and are reached by different brands. In one series of interviews beer drinkers were given a picture-adjective test in which they were asked which brand different types of people would drink. Later they were given a number of projective psychological tests to explore further this subject of brand-user personalities. Here were the results for three brands:

Brand	*Picture Adjectives Associated with the Brand*	*Brand-User Personalities*
A	Outdoorsman Worker Lively Sportsman Muscular	Optimistic, more physical than mental, informal
B	Weak character Poor Young Single Oddball	Pessimistic, tentative, uses restraint in pleasure-seeking
C	Farmer Middle Class Well-to-do Professor Married	Conformist, lead uneventful lives, conservative

In-depth probing along these lines provided substantiating evidence that differing brands with differing images were both appealing to and reaching different personality types. This in turn pointed to opportunities to position new brands to appeal to the different market segments.

Such examples are typical of some of the research techniques used in developing information on consumer segmentation. There are, of course, dozens of others. My personal opinion is that you will find your research studies most productive when they are based on an awareness of these principles:

(a) Market segmentation is a dynamic and constantly changing phenomenon, not a static one.

(b) Any market which seems to have reached a static position in regard to its products or product concepts provides an especial challenge for new, segmented marketing.

Our own experience at Beecham with our hair-dressing product Brylcreem illustrates both of these points very well. Brylcreem was first marketed in Britain in 1928 and was introduced in the United States in 1936. For 15 years it made very slow—in fact pitifully slow—progress here in America. By 1951 it had 1.3 per cent of the men's hair-dressing market, in which the three leading products together held 65 per cent.

Brylcreem's rise began only when we revised our entire marketing strategy, our complete marketing mix, and our whole advertising approach—when we in fact set out to capture a segment of the total market. At that time every one of Brylcreem's major competitors was a liquid and packed in bottles. We decided to concentrate on our product advantage—Brylcreem was packed in a handy, unbreakable tube—and to develop advertising themes which appealed specifically to those buyers who appreciated a cream rather than a liquid dressing. You may remember our "Little dab'll do you" slogan.

This segmentation strategy was coupled with a new, stronger marketing mix, involving an orderly plan of market-by-market penetration and heavy use of spot TV, and Brylcreem was on its way. Its progress was substantial. In four years, by 1955, it had captured a 10 per cent share of the market. In eight years, by 1959, it had climbed to first place among all United States hair dressings, ahead of the famous brands sold in bottles.

Seemingly, when Brylcreem started its climb, the market had frozen around a single type of product. Actually the segmentation potential was always there in terms of buyers' wants, though neither we nor anyone else guessed the size of the segment. Furthermore, and to illustrate the changing nature of the process, in 1951 Brylcreem was the only hair dressing in a tube. Today there are seven, all bearing the names of top toiletry companies. The conditions of segmentation have altered entirely from what they were 15 years ago, though I am happy to report that Brylcreem remains the leading white cream on the American market, as it is world-wide.

This fact, that markets and consumer tastes are in a constant process of flux and change, and that segmentation itself produces profound changes and opens up entirely new directions, emphasizes and reinforces the importance of continuing research and study. Human nature being what it is, people seldom reach the point of complete satisfaction with anything. When one aspiration is met, a whole new set of aspirations are developed. So it is with consumer needs as regards products. When a need is fulfilled by a product, the consumer begins to develop—perhaps only subconsciously—a whole new set of needs.

The floor-wax industry is an amusing case in point. At one time there were women, thousands of them, who were willing to take a can of wax, rub it on a floor, and buff it to a shine. The advent of self-polishing waxes added new segments of women who wanted their floors to look nice but were unwilling to scrub and rub. As the old problems were solved, new problems arose. And today women are buying a floor wax whose principal benefit is that it is easy to remove. At first the problem was putting it on—now the problem, and hence the opportunity, is in taking it off.

Only the most careful, intimate, detailed, continuous study can spot and anticipate in profitable marketing terms the swings and variations of consumer desires.

PRODUCTS FOR SEGMENTED MARKETS

We noted earlier that defining and understanding a market segment were the first requisites of sound strategy. We come now to an even more important, but in certain ways far less understood and appreciated aspect of segmentation, the development of products to fit carefully defined market groups. Actually the high percentage of new-product failures in practically every consumer field is discouraging testimony to the product ineptness and bad planning of many modern marketers. In this connection, the following passage from a speech by Dr. Blaine Cooke, Vice President, Marketing, for United Airlines, is particularly interesting:

> In the era of the marketing concept, it is necessary to consider with some care what we really mean by a product.

If I understand the marketing concept correctly, it suggests that a product, any product, is only incidentally a physical artifact, resulting from a production process.

Except in cases ordinarily having pathological significance, no consumer buys a product for its own sake. He does not in fact buy products at all; he buys expectation of satisfaction of his needs or desires.

Such needs and desires differ, of course, and the differences create the phenomenon of market segmentation.

It may be argued persuasively that a product concept and a market segment are essentially two ways of describing the same reality. In this sense, a marketer must view a product which fails in much the same light that a Christian Scientist views a cold in the head—that is, as a thing which exhibits physical manifestation but has no ultimate reality.

It is not a metaphysical excursion but a very practical marketing observation that a product which failed is not in a marketing sense a product at all; it is merely an interesting but meaningless spinoff of the process of production.[1]

The key point in this stimulating and provocative argument is Dr. Cooke's contention that a product *concept* and a market segment are "two ways of describing the same reality." In saying this he puts his finger on the reason for the vast majority of product failures. They are products without product concepts. They are conceived and developed in a vacuum, not in terms of the market segments they must reach and serve.

From the standpoint of the manufacturer, there are a number of explanations for this. Too often the marketer is in too much of a hurry. He neglects the long, tedious, necessary steps of product testing. Too often he allows production enthusiasm or production feasibility to overshadow the need for in-depth consumer research. Too often his pride blinds him to the fact that he has simply a "me-too" product with no demonstrable superiority over others in the field. And finally, too often, he makes mistakes in the timing of his product introductions out of his inability to gauge and assess the shifting conditions of the marketplace.

These lessons are hard to come by, and most of us who market to consumers have made most, if not all, of these errors at some

[1] From a speech before the American Marketing Association, as reported in *Advertising Age,* July 18, 1966.

time in our business careers. At Beecham, for instance, we had a resounding failure a few years ago with Silvikrin shampoo. Silvikrin is a highly successful product overseas, and I suspect that this fact alone tended to warp our judgment. Somehow we let ourselves dream that Silvikrin would, inevitably, bring a touch of British magic to the American scene. This, of course, was absurd. Any product, domestic or imported, must stand or fall on its special appeal and suitability to the particular conditions, competition, and tastes of a United States market segment. Nothing else matters.

In the case of Silvikrin we probably didn't do enough research, enough testing. Perhaps the difference in the condition of American women's hair had a lot to do with it. And certainly the sudden appearance of a new major competitor in the field had a dampening effect on both our timing and our impact. We did manage, with our initial advertising, to motivate a lot of people to try Silvikrin. But repeat sales didn't materialize in volume. We failed, and that's all there was to it.

Looking back, I am convinced that our failure was due, basically, to the cause which Dr. Cooke has pointed out. Silvikrin in this market was a product without a genuine product concept. It was not planned, developed, and produced for a particular market segment.

In general, the products which achieve real breakthroughs in segmented marketing all seem to have two things in common: (a) specialized ability to fill segmented needs; (b) high and consistently maintained quality.

The matter of high quality probably deserves special emphasis, because any segmentation success quickly attracts imitators, and only through the maintenance of the highest-quality standards can you hope to defend a new franchise.

French's mashed potatoes are a good case in point. French's opened up the instant-potato market and soon was challenged both by well-known name manufacturers, such as Pillsbury and Borden, and by price and private-label brands. The fact that French's has retained a vigorous leadership position in the field has been due primarily to its scrupulous insistence on maintaining its quality standards.

SEGMENTATION AND THE MARKETING MIX

Assuming that the consumer needs of a particular market segment have been thoroughly studied and grasped and that a quality product for meeting these needs has been developed, the next step is the determination of the overall plan or marketing mix. Here the continuing challenges are for completeness and coordination. The fact that a marketer is targeting on a segment, not a total market, makes it all the more important that he does not neglect any essential element in his plan and that all elements work together toward his pinpointed objective. Frequently, in tackling a new segmentation program, it will be necessary to rethink and restructure some of the policies and procedures followed in the past.

Among the elements which should be thoroughly integrated into the marketing mix are:

1. Packaging
2. Pricing
3. Distribution program and procedures
4. Merchandising
5. Test marketing
6. Market-by-market timetable
7. Data analysis procedures and progress checkpoints
8. Advertising themes and testing
9. Advertising media program
10. Advertising production and timetable
11. Continuing marketing and advertising research
12. Alternative plans and procedures for meeting special conditions

Obviously, the exact nature of each of these elements will differ by products, by companies, and by the market segment sought. There are no hard-and-fast rules which can apply in all cases. However, it will be found that any company, as it engages in segmentation marketing, begins to build up its own invaluable backlog of specialized experience and learns to draw on the past in its future planning. It will also be found, I believe, that the more that is known about segmentation procedures, the more scrupulous a marketer is going to become in planning and perfecting each element in his marketing mix.

LESSONS IN THE MACLEANS CASE HISTORY

Certainly we have found the above to be true at Beecham, and the point is well illustrated by the history of Macleans toothpaste. Five years ago, when we began planning to introduce Macleans to the American market, we were confronted with what many friends and industry specialists assured us was a hopelessly discouraging outlook. At that time over 70 per cent of the United States toothpaste market was controlled by the two giants, Colgate and P&G (through its entries Crest and Gleem). In addition to these three brands, many other well-known products, including Stripe, Ipana, and Pepsodent, were battling for the rest of the business.

United States toothpaste advertising, at that time, amounted to $40-million a year, an almost staggering total for any new brand to compete against. Furthermore, nearly all United States toothpastes were concentrating on a single advertising theme—"decay prevention." You remember the TV commercials, "Look, Mom, no cavities," and all the excitement that accompanied the first endorsement of a fluoride toothpaste by the American Dental Association. It certainly didn't seem like a very easy market to crack, and our first product tests comparing Macleans with its notable competitors did little to allay our fears. They showed that substantially more people in blind tests preferred the taste of Colgate, Crest, or Gleem. In some tests the ratio was almost two to one.

I suspect that, in many ways, we were just plain lucky that we didn't become so discouraged by these first results that we threw up our hands and admitted defeat. But we didn't, and because we didn't we learned an extraordinarily valuable lesson about research studies: you must dig deep to find real meanings.

Further analysis of our research showed one highly interesting point. The people who *did* like Macleans liked it very much. They were, in fact, crazy about it. Admittedly, they were fewer in numbers than the Crest-Gleem-Colgate adherents. But they were extremely and vocally enthusiastic. And the more carefully we weighed the fact, the closer we got to a second important lesson about market segmentation—pay attention to strong minority groups. It's so easy in analyzing a set of figures to look only at the biggest numbers. But your opportunity may well lie with the smaller ones.

Furthermore, in the case of Macleans we got additional and highly valuable information from our study of advertising themes. We found, as you might expect, that the strongest themes seemed to be the best known and most widely used—the decay-prevention claims, particularly in reference to children's teeth, which Crest, Gleem, and Colgate were featuring. But we also found that a very substantial segment of the American public was not so much interested in the child and decay-prevention story as they were in a product benefit, which, in other markets, Macleans had stressed for years—the benefit of whiter teeth. Whiter teeth, with all the implications of attractiveness to the opposite sex, was a far more important benefit to a sizable segment of the toothpaste market than "Look, Mom, no cavities." And Macleans, as a product, had the properties to back up such a claim.

When we finally (and it was a slow process) grasped the implications of these findings, we made them the basis of our Macleans introduction strategy. Then, armed with these and many carefully worked out pricing, packaging, merchandising, and marketing policies, we set to work.

Our timetable called for opening on the West Coast in April 1962 and moving across the country in four successive waves. As each wave progressed, we incorporated findings into our marketing and advertising operations for the next area. Our nationwide program was completed in October 1965, and by that time we had moved up to fourth place among all United States toothpastes, a rather considerable accomplishment. In the process we picked up 7½ share points of the American market, and I am pleased to be able to report that Macleans continues its healthy trend. In many areas we are now pushing hard for third place among all toothpaste brands.

Such results, of course, are bound to be gratifying to any marketer, and I am sure that we at Beecham can be forgiven if we point to them with pride. But, in a larger sense, it is what we have learned from the Macleans experience, rather than any immediate success, which counts most. In terms of long-range benefits affecting our future operations, I would list these lessons as follows:

1. The importance of in-depth product and market research.
2. The importance of digging for research meanings.
3. The importance of isolating significant market segments regardless of size and without regard to the practices or philosophies of even major competitors.
4. The importance of gearing advertising themes to basic product-concept, market-segment thinking.
5. The importance of a total marketing mix covering all phases of a program.
6. The importance of continually developing new strategies, treatments and advertising-marketing tools to provide momentum and growth for your efforts.

■

Summary

Markets become segmented because (a) consumers are different in tastes, interests, physiological and psychological needs; (b) consumers like to express their differences; and (c) they will express their differences whenever they have sufficient income and sufficiently attractive product choices. In other words, segmentation begins with the consumer and his needs. Intensive, detailed knowledge of the consumer is therefore vital in the use of this strategy.

The challenge facing today's marketer is (a) to discover, define and understand significant consumer segments; (b) to develop quality products which can be produced at a profit to serve these segments; and (c) to mount carefully planned programs to exploit these opportunities.

Producer, demographic and special-interest segmentation have varying degrees of utility as criteria for dividing markets. But the first may be dangerously misleading and the second, by itself, can be unrewarding.

Segmentation in terms of consumers' physiological and psychological needs is the most potent way to use this strategy.

The fragmentation of markets is a dynamic and constantly changing phenomenon, not a static one. When a market does appear static, it offers particularly good opportunities for further segmentation. Markets therefore require continuous study.

Marketers should not be misled by big numbers. Often the best potential lies in neglected minority segments.

5

Market Stretching

■

Theodore Levitt

■

Markets can be created, expanded, or resuscitated in many different fashions. Which of these approaches a business uses depends on its resources, its competitive situation, its perception about the future, its goals, and the marketing vision it evolves for itself.

For example, it is becoming more common for industrial chemical producers to "go consumer." This can come about only from a redefinition of a business. Dow Chemical Company, for example, has broadened its horizon with plastic food wraps, oven cleaners, even Christmas tree decorative materials, among a long list of consumer products. A number of makers of hair-care products have gone consumer another way; specialists serving the beauty salon trade, Helene Curtis, Rayette, Ozon, Breck, Clairol, and VO-5, have all made their mark by selling direct to the consumer.

Paradoxically, market segmentation can lead to the broadening of markets. Zealous specialization evokes a countervailing force: a strong desire is born for all-purpose products sold to and used by practically everyone. The detergent industry is ripe for one; now there are specialized products for heavy-duty laundering, fine laundering, manual dishwashing, automatic dishwashing, cleaning floors, kitchens, bathrooms, and so on. As a result, uses for even the most general cleansers are narrowing. The floor wax business is also setting the stage for an all-purpose product with its profusion of pastes, waxes, and polishes—including a product that removes the other products. In this context, the recent burgeoning of one-step cleaning and waxing in floor waxes and one-step dusting, waxing, and polishing in furniture waxes may be the industry's way of broadening user segments. Thus the sharp strategist recognizes when the time has come to throw the gears into reverse and use the tool of product or product line simplification.

We have thus, in the above brief examples, three ways of stretching markets: (1) "go consumer"; (2) "go retail"; (3) "go all-purpose." Each of these, however, calls for new product development or product modification. But fundamental to all of these is a concept for extending the life cycle of products, whether new or old. This involves stretching markets *over time* as well as across other trade channels or customer segments. And it is this concept that Theodore Levitt explores in depth in this chapter.

Dr. Levitt, Professor of Business Administration at the Harvard Business School, is the author of numerous articles on management and marketing subjects, including the prize-winning article, "Marketing Myopia," in the *Harvard Business Review,* which holds the all-time record in reprint sales of nearly 200,000.

He is on the board of directors of several corporations and a consultant to numerous companies in a wide variety of manufacturing, service, and retailing companies.

Professor Levitt is the author of the best-selling business book, *Innovation in Marketing* (McGraw-Hill Book Co., Inc., 1962), winner of one of the McKinsey Foundation Book Awards for the best business books of the year in 1962, and of *Industrial Purchasing Behavior: A Study in Communications Effects* (Boston, Harvard Business School, Division of Research, 1965).

■

MARKET STRETCHING

THEODORE LEVITT[1]

Most alert and thoughtful senior marketing executives are by now familiar with the concept of the product life cycle. Even a handful of uniquely cosmopolitan and up-to-date corporate presidents have familiarized themselves with this tantalizing concept. Yet a recent survey I took of such executives found none who used the concept in any strategic way whatever, and pitifully few who used it in any kind of tactical way. It has remained—as have so many fascinating theories in economics, physics, and sex—a remarkably durable but almost totally unemployed and seemingly unemployable piece of professional baggage whose presence in the rhetoric of professional discussions adds a much coveted but apparently unattainable legitimacy to the idea that marketing management is somehow a profession. There is, furthermore, a persistent feeling that the life-cycle concept adds luster and believability to the insistent claim in certain circles that marketing is close to being some sort of science.[2]

The concept of the product life cycle is today at about the stage that the Copernican view of the universe was 300 years ago: a lot of people knew about it, but hardly anybody seemed to use it in any effective or productive way.

Now that so many people know and in some fashion understand the product life cycle, it seems time to put it to work. The object of this chapter is to suggest some ways of using the concept effectively and of turning the knowledge of its existence into a managerial instrument of competitive power. The essence of what will

[1] This chapter was pre-published as an article, "Exploit the Product Life Cycle," in the *Harvard Business Review* (November–December 1965).

[2] For discussions of the scientific claims or potentials of marketing, see George Schwartz, *Development of Marketing Theory* (Cincinnati: South-Western Publishing Co., 1963); and Reavis Cox, Wroe Alderson, and Stanley J. Shapiro, eds., *Theory in Marketing* (Homewood, Ill.: Richard D. Irwin, Inc., 2nd Ser., 1964).

be proposed in this chapter is the idea that a product's productive life can, with proper care and attention, be prolonged or stretched. In Lee Adler's felicitous phrase, "market stretching" is a promising strategy for the life extension of many products.

Since the concept has been presented somewhat differently by different authors and for different audiences, it is useful to review it briefly here so that every reader has the same background for the discussion which follows later in this chapter.

HISTORICAL PATTERN

The life story of most successful products is a history of their passing through certain recognizable stages. These are shown in Exhibit I and occur in the following order:

Stage 1. Market Development: This is when a new product is first brought to market, before there is a proved demand for it, and often before it has been fully proved out technically in all respects. Sales are low and creep along slowly.

Stage 2. Market Growth: Demand begins to accelerate and the size of the total market expands rapidly. It might also be called the "takeoff stage."

Stage 3. Market Maturity: Demand levels off. It grows, for the most part, only at the replacement and new family-formation rate.

Stage 4. Market Decline: The product begins to lose consumer appeal and sales drift downward, as when buggy whips lost out with the advent of automobiles and when silk lost out to nylon.

Three operating questions will quickly occur to the alert executive:

Given a proposed new product or service, how and to what extent can the shape and duration of each stage be predicted?

Given an existing product, how can one determine what stage it is in?

Given all this knowledge, how can it be effectively used?

A brief further elaboration of each stage will be useful before dealing with these questions in detail.

DEVELOPMENT STAGE

Bringing a new product to market is fraught with unknowns, uncertainties, and frequently unknowable risks. Generally demand

EXHIBIT I. PRODUCT LIFE CYCLE—ENTIRE INDUSTRY

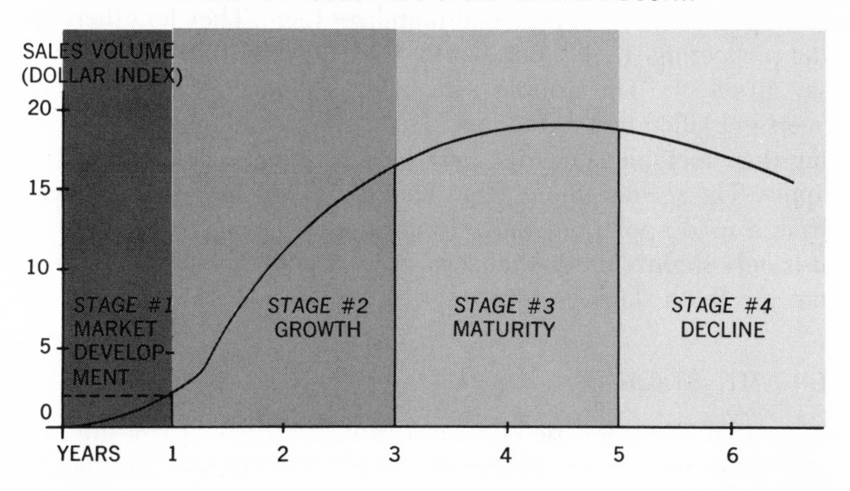

has to be "created" during the product's initial market-development stage. How long this takes depends on the product's complexity, its degree of newness, its fit into consumer needs, and the presence of competitive substitutes of one form or another. A proved cancer cure would require virtually no market development; it would get immediate massive support. An alleged superior substitute for the lost-wax process of sculpture casting would take lots longer.

While it has been demonstrated time after time that properly customer-oriented new product development is one of the primary conditions of sales and profit growth, what have been demonstrated even more conclusively are the ravaging costs and frequent fatalities associated with launching new products. Nothing seems to take more time, cost more money, involve more pitfalls, cause more anguish, or break more careers than do sincere and well-conceived new-product programs. The fact is, most new products don't have any sort of classical life-cycle curve at all. They have instead from the very outset an infinitely descending curve. The product not only doesn't get off the ground, it goes quickly underground—six feet under.

It is little wonder, therefore, that some disillusioned and badly burned companies have recently adopted a more conservative policy—what I call the "used-apple policy." Instead of aspiring to be the first company to see and seize an opportunity, they systematically avoid being first. They let others take the first bite of the supposedly juicy apple that tantalizes them. They let others do the pioneering. If the idea works, they quickly follow suit. They say, in effect, "The trouble with being a pioneer is that the pioneers get killed by the Indians." Hence they say (thoroughly mixing their metaphors), "We don't have to get the first bite of the apple. The second one is good enough." They are willing to eat from a used apple, but they try to be alert enough to make sure it is only slightly used—that they at least get the second big bite, not the tenth skimpy one.

GROWTH STAGE

The usual characteristic of a successful new product is a gradual rise in its sales curve during the market-development stage. At some point in this rise a marked increase in consumer demand occurs and sales take off. The boom is on. This is the beginning of Stage 2—the *market-growth stage.* At this point potential competitors who have been watching developments during Stage 1 jump into the fray. The first ones to get in are generally those with an exceptionally effective "used-apple policy." Some enter the market with carbon copies of the originator's product. Others make functional and design improvements. And at this point product and brand differentiation begin to develop.

The ensuing fight for the consumer's patronage poses to the originating producer an entirely new set of problems. Instead of seeking ways of getting consumers to *try the product,* the originator now faces the more compelling problem of getting them to *prefer his brand.* This generally requires important changes in marketing strategies and methods. But the policies and tactics now adopted will be neither freely the sole choice of the originating producer nor as experimental as they might have been during Stage 1. The presence of competitors both dictates and limits what can easily be tried—such as, for example, testing what is the best price level or the best channel of distribution.

As the rate of consumer acceptance accelerates, it generally becomes increasingly easy to open new distribution channels and retail outlets. The consequent filling of distribution pipe lines generally causes the entire industry's factory sales to rise more rapidly than store sales. This creates an exaggerated impression of profit opportunity, which, in turn, attracts more competitors. Some of these will begin to charge lower prices because of later advances in technology, production short cuts, the need to take lower margins in order to get distribution, and the like. All this in time inescapably moves the industry to the threshold of a new stage of competition.

MATURITY STAGE

This new stage is the *market-maturity stage.* The first sign of its advent is evidence of market saturation. This means that most consumer companies or households that are sales prospects will be owning or using the product. Sales now grow about on a par with population. No more distribution pipe lines need be filled. Price competition now becomes intense. Competitive attempts to achieve and hold brand preference now involve making finer and finer differentiations in the product, in customer services, and in the promotional practices and claims made for the product.

Typically, the market-maturity stage forces the producer to concentrate on holding his distribution outlets, retaining his shelf space, and, in the end, trying to secure even more intensive distribution. Whereas during the market-development stage the originator depended heavily on the positive efforts of his retailers and distributors to help sell his product, retailers and distributors will now frequently have been reduced largely to being merchandise-displayers and order-takers. In the case of branded products in particular, the originator must now, more than ever, communicate directly with the consumer.

The market-maturity stage typically calls for a new kind of emphasis on competing more effectively. The originator is increasingly forced to appeal to the consumer on the basis of price, marginal product differences, or both. Depending on the product, services and deals offered in connection with it are often the clearest and most effective forms of differentiation. Beyond these, there will be attempts to create and promote fine product distinctions through packaging and advertising and to appeal to special market segments. The market-maturity stage can be passed through rapidly, as in the case of most women's fashion fads, or it can persist for generations with per capita consumption neither rising nor falling, as in the case of such staples as men's shoes and industrial fasteners. Or maturity can persist, but in a state of gradual but steady per capita decline, as in the case (until the recent advent of swarms of college-age young people) of beer and steel.

DECLINE STAGE

When market maturity tapers off and consequently comes to an end, the product enters Stage 4—*market decline.* In all cases of maturity and decline the industry is transformed. Few companies are able to weather the competitive storm. As demand declines, the overcapacity that was already apparent during the period of maturity now becomes endemic. Some producers see the handwriting implacably on the wall but feel that with proper management and cunning they will be one of the survivors after the industry-wide deluge they so clearly foresee. To hasten their competitors' eclipse directly, or to frighten them into early voluntary withdrawal from the industry, they initiate a variety of aggressively depressive tactics, propose mergers or buy-outs, and generally engage in activities that make life thanklessly burdensome for all firms and make death the inevitable consequence for most of them. A few companies do indeed weather the storm, sustaining life through the constant descent that now clearly characterizes the industry. Production gets concentrated into fewer hands. Prices and margins get depressed. Consumers get bored. The only cases where there is any relief from this boredom and gradual euthanasia are where styling and fashion play some constantly revivifying role.

PREPLANNING IMPORTANCE

Knowing that the lives of successful products and services are generally characterized by something like the pattern illustrated in Exhibit I can become the basis for important life-giving policies and practices. One of the greatest values of the life-cycle concept is for managers about to launch a new product. The first step for them is to try to foresee the profile of the proposed product's cycle.

As with so many things in business, and perhaps uniquely in

marketing, it is almost impossible to make universally useful suggestions as to how to manage one's affairs. It is certainly particularly difficult to provide widely useful advice on how to foresee or predict the shape and duration of a product's life. Indeed, it is precisely because so little specific day-to-day guidance is possible in anything, and because no checklist has ever by itself been very useful to anybody for very long, that business management will probably never be a science—always an art—and will pay exceptional rewards to managers with rare talent, enormous energy, iron nerve, and great capacity for assuming responsibility and bearing accountability.

But this does not mean that useful efforts cannot or should not be made to try to foresee the shape and duration of a new product's life. Time spent in attempting this kind of foresight not only helps assure that a more rational approach is brought to product planning and merchandising; also, as will be shown later, it can help create valuable lead time for important strategic and tactical moves after the product is brought to market. Specifically, it can be a great help in developing an orderly series of competitive moves, in expanding or stretching out the life of a product, in maintaining a clean product line, and in purposely phasing out dying and costly old products.[3]

FAILURE POSSIBILITIES . . .

As pointed out above, the length and slope of the market-development stage depend on the product's complexity, its degree of newness, its fit into customer needs, and the presence of competitive substitutes.

The more unique or distinctive the newness of the product, the longer it generally takes to get it successfully off the ground. The world does not automatically beat a path to the door of the man with the better mousetrap.[4] The world has to be told, coddled, enticed, romanced, and even bribed (as with, for example, cou-

---

[3] See Philip Kotler, "Phasing Out Weak Products," *Harvard Business Review* (March–April 1965), p. 107.

[4] For perhaps the ultimate example of how the world does *not* beat such a path, see the example of the man who actually, and to his painful regret, made a "better" mousetrap, in John B. Matthews, Jr., R. D. Buzzell, Theodore Levitt, and Ronald E. Frank, *Marketing: An Introductory Analysis* (New York: McGraw-Hill Book Co., 1964), p. 4.

pons, samples, free application aids, and the like). When the product's newness is distinctive and the job it is designed to do is unique, the public will generally be less quick to perceive it as something it clearly needs or wants.

This makes life particularly difficult for the innovator. He will have more than the usual difficulties of identifying those characteristics of his product and those supporting communications themes or devices which imply value to the consumer. As a consequence, the more distinctive the newness, the greater is the risk of failure resulting either from insufficient working capital to sustain a long and frustrating period of creating enough solvent customers to make the proposition pay, or from the inability to convince investors and bankers that they should put up more money.

In any particular situation the more people who will be involved in making a single purchasing decision for a new product, the more drawn out Stage 1 will be. Thus in the highly fragmented construction-materials industry, for example, success takes an exceptionally long time to catch hold; and having once caught hold, it tends to hold tenaciously for a long time—often too long. On the other hand, fashion items clearly catch on fastest and last the shortest time. But because fashion is so powerful, recently some companies in what often seem the least fashion-influenced of industries (machine tools, for example) have shortened the market-development stage by introducing elements of design and packaging fashion to their products.

What factors tend to prolong the market-development stage and therefore raise the risk of failure? The more complex the product, the more distinctive its newness, the less influenced by fashion, the greater the number of persons influencing a single buying decision, the more costly, and the greater the required shift in the customer's usual way of doing things, the more these conditions are likely to slow things up and create problems.

. . . VERSUS SUCCESS CHANCES

But problems also create opportunities to control the forces arrayed against new-product success. For example, the newer the product, the more important it becomes for the customers to have a favorable first experience with it. Newness creates a certain special visibility for the product, with a certain number of people standing on the sidelines to see how the first customers get on with it. If their first experience is unfavorable in some crucial way, this may have repercussions far out of proportion to the actual extent of the underfulfillment of the customers' expectations. But a favorable first experience or application will, for the same reason, get a lot of disproportionately favorable publicity.

The possibility of exaggerated disillusionment with a poor first experience can raise vital questions regarding the appropriate channels of distribution for a new product. On the one hand, getting the product successfully launched may require having—as in the case of, say, the early days of home washing machines—many retailers who can give consumers considerable help in the product's correct utilization and thus help assure a favorable first experience for those buyers. On the other hand, channels that provide this kind of help (such as small neighborhood appliance stores, in the case of washing machines) during the market-development stage may not be the ones best able to merchandise the product most successfully later when help in creating and personally reassuring customers is less important than wide product distribution. To the extent that channel decisions during this first stage sacrifice some of the requirements of the market-development stage to some of the requirements of later stages, the rate of the product's acceptance by consumers at the outset may be delayed.

In entering the market-development stage, pricing decisions are often particularly hard for the producer to make. Should he set an initially high price to recoup his investment quickly—i.e., "skim the cream"—or should he set a low price to discourage potential competition—i.e., "exclusion"? The answer depends on the innovator's estimate of the probable length of the product's life cycle, the degree of patent protection the product is likely to enjoy, the amount of capital needed to get the product off the ground, the elasticity of demand during the early life of the product, and many other factors. The decision that is finally made may affect not just the rate at which the product catches on at the beginning but even the duration of its total life. Thus some products that are priced too low at the outset (particularly fashion goods, such as the chemise, or sack, a few years ago) may catch on so quickly that they become short-lived fads. A slower rate of consumer acceptance might often extend their life cycles and raise the total profits they yield.

The actual slope, or rate of the growth stage, depends on some of the same things as do success or failure in Stage 1. But the extent to which patent exclusiveness can play a critical role is sometimes inexplicably forgotten. More frequently than one might offhand expect, holders of strong patent positions fail to recognize either the market-development virtue of making their patents available to competitors or the market-destroying possibilities of failing to control more effectively their competitors' use of such products.

Generally speaking, the more producers there are of a new product, the more effort goes into developing a market for it. The net result is very likely to be more rapid and steeper growth of the total market. The originator's market share may fall, but his total sales and profits may rise more rapidly. Certainly this has been the case in recent years of color television; RCA's eagerness to make its tubes available to competitors reflects its recognition of the power of numbers over the power of monopoly.

On the other hand, the failure to set and enforce appropriate quality standards in the early days of polystyrene and polyethylene drinking glasses and cups produced such sloppy, inferior goods that it took years to recover the consumer's confidence and revive the growth pattern.

But for a firm to try to foresee what a product's growth pattern might be is not very useful if it fails to distinguish between the industry pattern and the pattern of the single firm—for its particular brand. The industry's cycle will almost certainly be different from the cycle of individual firms. Moreover, the life cycle of a given product may be different for different companies in the same industry at the same point in time, and it certainly affects different companies in the same industry differently.

ORIGINATOR'S BURDENS

The company with most at stake is the original producer—the company that launches an entirely new product. This company generally bears most of the costs, the tribulations, and certainly the risks of developing both the product and the market.

EXHIBIT II.
PRODUCT LIFE CYCLE
—ORIGINATING COMPANY

SALES VOLUME
(DOLLAR INDEX)
15
10
5
0
YEARS
1
2
3
4

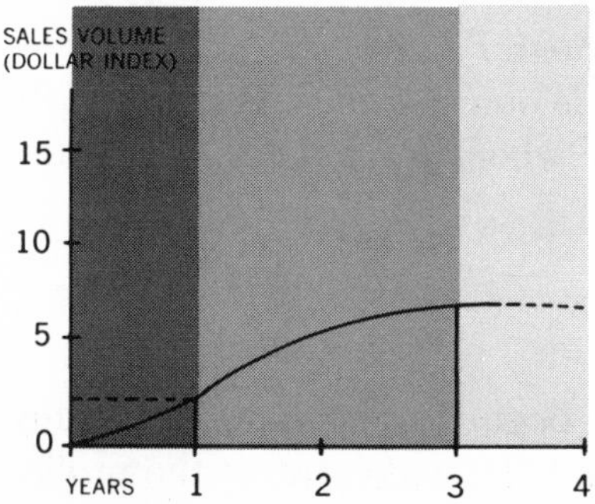

EXHIBIT III.
UNIT PROFIT CONTRIBUTION LIFE
CYCLE— ORIGINATING COMPANY

UNIT CONTRIBUTION
(DOLLARS)
$4
3
2
1
0
−1
−2
−3
YEARS
1
2
3
4

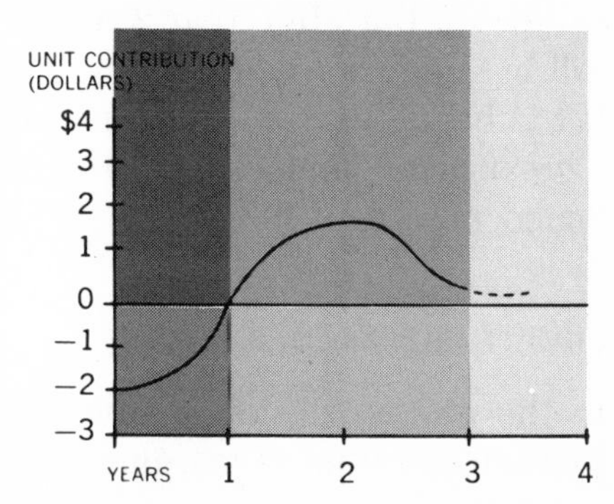

COMPETITIVE PRESSURE

Once the innovator demonstrates during the market-development stage that a solid demand exists, armies of imitators rush in to capitalize on and help create the boom that becomes the market growth, or takeoff, stage. As a result, while exceedingly rapid growth will now characterize the product's total demand, for the originating company its growth stage paradoxically now becomes truncated. It has to share the boom with new competitors. Hence the potential rate of acceleration of its own takeoff is diminished and, indeed, may actually fail to last as long as the industry's. This occurs not only because there are so many competitors but, as we noted earlier, also because competitors often come in with product improvements and lower prices. While these developments generally help keep the market expanding, they greatly restrict the originating company's rate of growth and the length of its takeoff stage.

All this can be illustrated by comparing the curve in Exhibit II with that in Exhibit I, which shows the life cycle for a product. During Stage 1 in Exhibit I there is generally only one company—the originator—even though the whole exhibit represents the entire industry. In Stage 1 the originator is the entire industry. But by Stage 2 he shares the industry with many competitors. Hence, while Exhibit I is an industry curve, its Stage 1 represents only a single company's sales.

Exhibit II shows the life cycle of the originator's brand—his own sales curve, not that of the industry. It can be seen that between Year 1 and Year 2 his sales are rising about as rapidly as the industry's. But after Year 2, while industry sales in Exhibit I are still in vigorous expansion, the originator's sales curve in Exhibit II has begun to slow its ascent. He is now sharing the boom with a great many competitors, some of whom are much better positioned now than he is.

PROFIT SQUEEZE

In the process the originator may begin to encounter a serious squeeze on his profit margins. Exhibit III, which traces the profits per unit of the originator's sales, illustrates this point. During the market-development stage his per-unit profits are negative. Sales volume is too low at existing prices. However, during the market-growth stage unit profits boom as output rises and unit production costs fall. Total profits rise enormously. It is the presence of such lush profits that both attracts and ultimately destroys competitors.

Consequently, while (1) industry sales may still be rising nicely (as at the Year 3 point in Exhibit I), and (2) while the originating company's sales may at the same point of time have begun to slow down noticeably (as in Exhibit II), and (3) while at this point the originator's total profits may still be rising because his volume of sales is huge and on a slight upward trend, his profits per unit will often have taken a drastic downward course. Indeed, they will often have done so long before the sales curve flattened. They will have topped out and begun to decline perhaps around the Year 2 point (as in Exhibit III). By the time the originator's sales begin to flatten out (as at the Year 3 point in Exhibit II), unit profits may actually be approaching zero (as in Exhibit III).

At this point more competitors are in the industry, the rate of industry demand growth has slowed somewhat, and competitors are cutting prices. Some of them do this in order to get business, and others do it because their costs are lower owing to the fact that their equipment is more modern and productive.

The industry's Stage 3—maturity—generally lasts as long as there are no important competitive substitutes (such as, for example, aluminum for steel in "tin" cans), no drastic shifts in influential value systems (such as the end of female modesty in the 1920s and the consequent destruction of the market for veils), no major changes in dominant fashions (such as the hour-glass female form and the end of waist cinchers), no changes in the demand for primary products which use the product in question (such as the effect of the decline of new railroad expansion on the demand for railroad ties), and no changes either in the rate of obsolescence of the product or in the character or introductory rate of product modifications.

Maturity can last for a long time, or it can actually never be attained. Fashion goods and fad items sometimes surge to sudden heights, hesitate momentarily at an uneasy peak, and then quickly drop off into total obscurity.

STAGE RECOGNITION

The various characteristics of the stages described above will help one to recognize the stage a particular product occupies at any given time. But hindsight will always be more accurate than current sight. Perhaps the best way of seeing one's current stage is to try to foresee the next stage and work backward. This approach has several virtues. It forces one to look ahead, constantly to try to reforesee his future and competitive environment. This will have its own rewards. As Charles F. Kettering, perhaps the last of Detroit's primitive inventors and probably the greatest of all its inventors, was fond of saying, "We should all be concerned about the future because that's where we'll have to spend the rest of our lives." By looking at the future one can better assess the state of the present.

Looking ahead gives more perspective to the present than looking at the present alone. Most people know more about the present than is good for them. It is neither healthy nor helpful to know the present too well, for our perception of the present is too often too heavily distorted by the urgent pressures of day-to-day events. To know where the present is in the continuum of competitive time and events, it often makes more sense to try to know what the future will bring, and when it will bring it, than to try to know what the present itself actually contains.

Finally, the value of knowing what stage a product occupies at any given time resides only in the way that fact is used. But its use is always in the future. Hence a prediction of the future environment in which the information will be used is often more functional for the effective capitalization on knowledge about the present than knowledge about the present itself.

SEQUENTIAL ACTIONS

The life-cycle concept can be effectively employed in the strategy of both existing and new products. For purposes of continuity and clarity, the remainder of this chapter will describe some of the uses of the concept from the early stages of new-product planning through the later stages of keeping the product profitably alive. The chief discussion will focus on what I call a policy of "life extension" or what Lee Adler calls "market stretching."

To the extent that Exhibits II and III outline the classical patterns of successful new products, one of the constant aims of the originating producer should be to avoid the severe discipline imposed by an early profit squeeze in the market-growth stage and to avoid the wear and waste so typical of the market-maturity stage. Hence the following proposition would seem reasonable: When a company develops a new product or service, it should try to plan at the very outset a series of actions to be employed at various subsequent stages in the product's existence, so that its sales and profit curves are constantly sustained rather than following their usual declining slope.

In other words, advance planning should be directed at extending, or stretching out, the life of the product. It is this idea of *planning in advance* of the actual launching of a new product to take specific actions later in its life cycle—actions designed to sustain its growth and profitability—which appears to have great potential as an instrument of long-term product strategy.

NYLON'S LIFE

How this might work for a product can be illustrated by looking at the history of nylon.[5] The way in which nylon's booming sales

[5] The following discussion of nylon's history draws heavily on the pioneering studies of Dr. Jordan P. Yale, summarized in his "The Strategy of Nylon's Growth," *Modern Textiles Magazine* (February 1964), pp. 32, 33, 49. Dr. Yale made his studies as part of his work at the Chemstrand Corporation.

life has been repeatedly and systematically extended and stretched can serve as a model for other products. What has happened in nylon may not have been purposely planned that way at the outset, but the results are quite as if they had been planned.

The first nylon end-uses were primarily military—parachutes, thread, rope. This was followed by nylon's entry into the circular-knit market and its consequent domination of the women's hosiery business. Here it developed the kind of steadily rising growth and profit curves that every executive dreams about. After some years these curves began to flatten out. But before they flattened very noticeably, Du Pont had already developed measures designed to revitalize sales and profits. It did several things, each of which is demonstrated graphically in Exhibit IV. This exhibit and the explanation which follows take some liberties with the actual facts of the nylon situation in order to highlight the points I wish to make. But they take no liberties with the essential requisites of product strategy.

Point A of Exhibit IV shows the hypothetical point at which the nylon curve (dominated at this point by hosiery) flattened out. If nothing further had been done, the sales curve would have continued along the flattened pace indicated by the dotted line at Point A. This is also the hypothetical point at which the first systematic effort was made to extend the product's life. Du Pont, in effect, took certain "actions" which pushed hosiery sales upward rather than continuing the path implied by the dotted line extension of the curve at Point A. At Point A "action" #1 pushed an otherwise flat curve upward.

At points B, C, and D still other new sales and profit expansion actions (#2, #3, #4, and so forth) were taken. What were these actions? Or, more usefully, what was their strategic content? What did they try to do? They involved strategies that tried to expand sales via four different routes:

1. Promoting more frequent usage of the product among current users.
2. Developing more varied usage of the product among current users.
3. Creating new users for the product by expanding the market.
4. Finding new uses for the basic material.

Frequent Usage. Du Pont studies had shown an increasing trend toward bare-leggedness among women. This was coincident with the trend toward more casual living and a declining perception among teenagers of what might be called the "social necessity" of wearing stockings. In the light of those findings, one approach to propping up the flattening sales curves might have been to reiterate the social necessity of wearing stockings at all times. That would have been a sales-building action, though obviously difficult and exceedingly costly. But it could clearly have fulfilled the strategy of promoting more frequent usage among current users as a means of extending the product's life.

EXHIBIT IV. HYPOTHETICAL LIFE CYCLE—NYLON

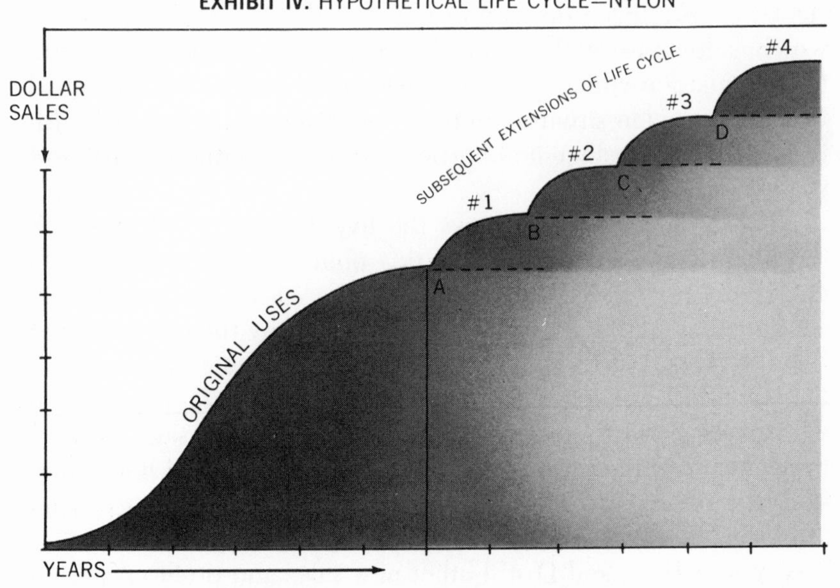

Varied Usage. For Du Pont this strategy took the form of an attempt to promote the "fashion smartness" of tinted hose and later of patterned and highly textured hosiery. The idea was to raise each woman's inventory of hosiery by obsolescing the perception of hosiery as a fashion staple that came only in a narrow range of browns and pinks. Hosiery was to be converted from a "neutral" accessory to a central ingredient of fashion, with a "suitable" tint and pattern for each outer garment in the lady's wardrobe.

This not only would raise sales by expanding women's hosiery wardrobes and stores' inventories but would open the door for annual tint and pattern obsolescence, much the same as there is an annual color obsolescence in outer garments. Beyond that, the use of color and pattern to focus attention on the leg would help arrest the decline of the leg as an element of sex appeal—a trend which some researchers had discerned and which, they claimed, damaged hosiery sales.

New Users. Creating new users for nylon hosiery might conceivably have taken the form of attempting to legitimize the necessity of wearing hosiery among early teenagers and subteenagers. Advertising, public relations, and merchandising of youthful social and style leaders would have been called for.

New Uses. For nylon this tactic has had many triumphs—from varied types of hosiery, such as stretch stockings and stretch socks, to new uses, such as rugs, tires, bearings, and so forth. Indeed, if there had been no further product innovation designed to create new uses for nylon after the original military, miscellaneous, and circular-knit uses, nylon consumption in 1962 would have reached a saturation level at approximately 50 million pounds annually.

Instead, in 1962 consumption exceeded 500 million pounds. Exhibit V demonstrates how the continuous development of new uses for the basic material constantly produced new waves of sales. The exhibit shows that in spite of the growth of the women's stocking market, the cumulative result of the military, circular-knit, and miscellaneous groupings would have been a flattened sales curve by 1958. (Nylon's entry into the broad-woven market in 1944 substantially raised sales above what they would have been. Even so, the sales of broad-woven, circular-knit, and military and miscellaneous groupings peaked in 1957.)

Had it not been for the addition of new uses for the same basic material—such as warp knits in 1945, tire cord in 1948, textured yarns in 1955, carpet yarns in 1959, and so forth—nylon would not have had the spectacularly rising consumption curve it has so clearly had. At various stages it would have exhausted its existing markets or been forced into decline by competing materials. The systematic search for new uses for the basic (and improved) material extended and stretched the product's life.

OTHER EXAMPLES

Few companies seem to employ in any systematic or planned way the four product life-stretching steps described above. Yet the successful application of this kind of stretching strategy has characterized the history of such well-known products as General Foods Corporation's Jell-O and Minnesota Mining & Manufacturing Company's Scotch tape.[6]

Jell-O was a pioneer in the easy-to-prepare gelatin dessert field. The soundness of the product concept and the excellence of its early marketing activities gave it beautifully ascending sales and profit curves almost from the start. But after some years these curves predictably began to flatten out. Scotch tape was also a pioneer product in its field. Once perfected, the product gained rapid market acceptance because of a sound product concept and an aggressive sales organization. But, again, in time the sales and profit curves began to flatten out. Before they flattened out very much, however, 3M, like General Foods, had already developed measures to sustain the early pace of sales and profits.

Both of these companies extended their products' lives by, in effect, doing all four of the things Du Pont did with nylon—creating more frequent usage among current users, more varied usage among current users, new users, and new uses for the basic "materials."

1. The General Foods approach to increasing the frequency of serving Jell-O among current users was, essentially, to increase the number of flavors. From Don Wilson's famous "six delicious flavors," Jell-O moved up to over a dozen. On the other hand, 3M helped raise sales among its current users by developing a variety of handy Scotch tape dispensers which made the product easier to use.

2. Creation of more varied usage of Jell-O among current dessert users involved its promotion as a base for salads and the facilitation of this usage by the development of a variety of vegetable-flavored Jell-Os. Simliarly, 3M developed a line of colored, patterned, waterproof, invisible and write-on Scotch tapes

[6] I am indebted to my colleague, Dr. Derek A. Newton, for these examples and other helpful suggestions.

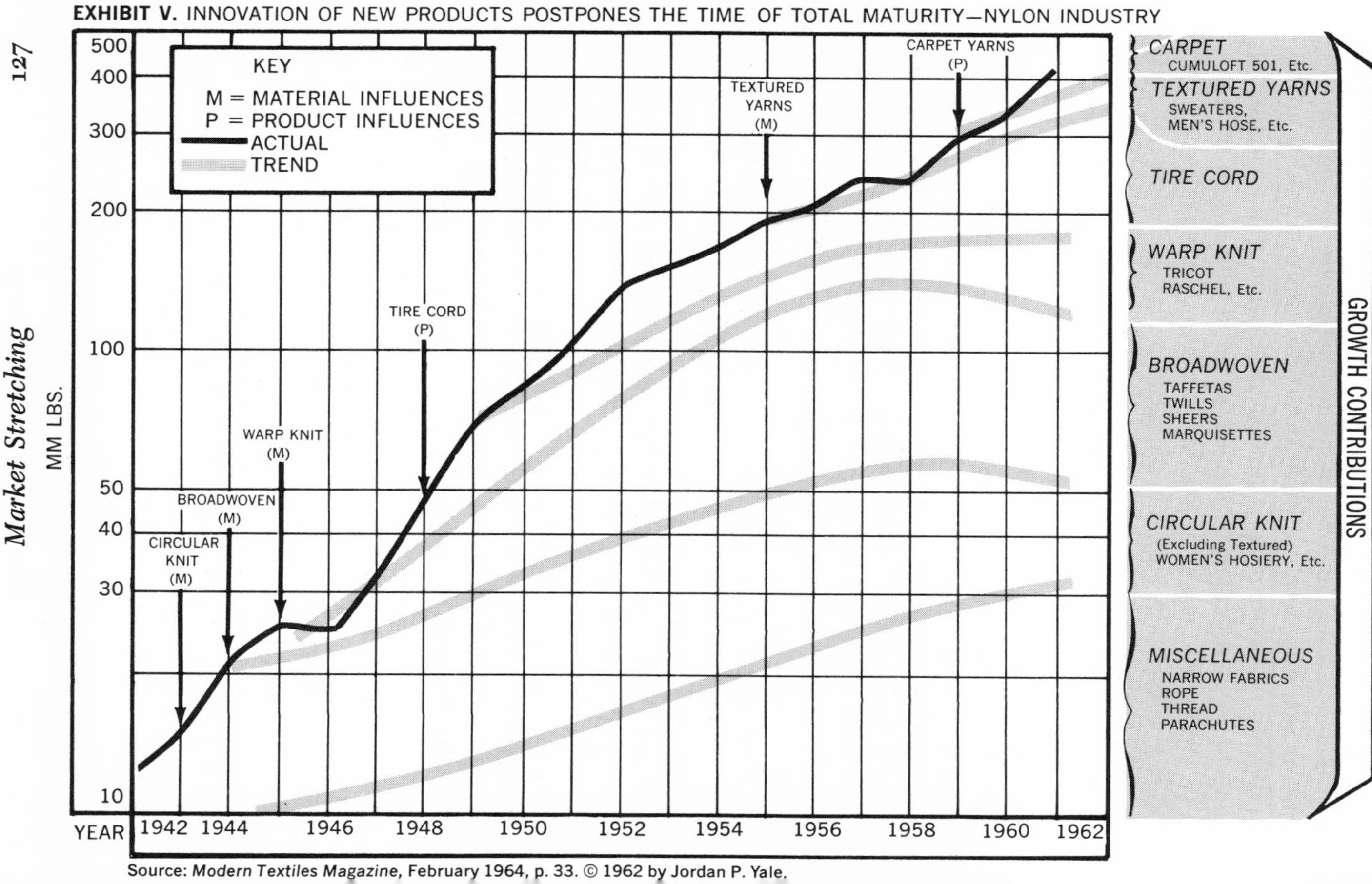

Source: *Modern Textiles Magazine*, February 1964, p. 33. © 1962 by Jordan P. Yale.

which have enjoyed considerable success as sealing and decorating items for holiday and gift wrapping.

3. Jell-O sought to create new users by pinpointing people who could not accept Jell-O as a popular dessert or salad product. Hence during the Metrecal boom Jell-O employed an advertising theme that successfully affixed to the product a fashion-oriented weight-control appeal. Similarly, 3M introduced Rocket tape, a product much like Scotch tape but lower in price, and also developed a line of commercial cellophane tapes of various widths, lengths, and strengths. These actions broadened product use in commercial and industrial markets.

4. Both Jell-O and 3M have sought out new uses for the basic material. It is known, for example, that women consumers use powdered gelatin dissolved in liquids as a means of strengthening their fingernails. Both men and women use it in the same way as a bone-building agent. Hence Jell-O introduced a "completely flavorless" Jell-O for just these purposes. And 3M has also developed new uses for the basic material, from double-coated tape (adhesive on both sides), which competes with ordinary liquid adhesives, to the reflecting tape, which festoons countless automobile bumpers, to marker strips, which compete with paint.

MORE EXAMPLES

An almost infinite variety of market-stretching examples exist in the life histories of products, manufacturing processes, and distribution facilities. There is literally no end to these examples, but rarely has any of these been the result of a consciously systematic effort. Thus the original success of air freight was an almost accidental consequence of certain shippers in effect demanding such service rather than the airline companies soliciting it. Air shipment of cut flowers, one of the early uses of air freight, resulted from the growers themselves recognizing the advantages of speed and the attendant geographic expansion of their markets.

This is an example in which market stretching worked for both parties to a single practice. It expanded the market and indeed the life of the specific flower growers. And by showing a way to raise the number of productive hours that an otherwise passenger airplane could remain in use (during the slow night hours), it, in effect, ultimately produced both lower passenger and cargo rates and, to this extent, helped expand the industry's total business.

In fact, pricing can be a particularly effective device to prolong a product's life. Interestingly, this can work both via high prices and via reduced prices in particular circumstances. One of the most farsighted recent examples of a high-priced policy to help assure a relatively strong life pattern for a product is Du Pont's Corfam—the leather substitute. The introductory policy of charging relatively high prices did more than simply assure early recovery of huge development costs. It automatically limited the product to high-style, high-price shoes. This helped legitimize the product so that when it was later made available to lower-priced products it avoided any disabling aura of synthetic cheapness. This was a quite different strategy from the original use of polyethylene in drinking cups and other kitchen uses. The prices were so low that lots of low-priced, speculative manufacturers were attracted to its use. Their products were shoddy and the consumer's experience was generally disastrous. Cups warped in the dishwater, split on the table, and in every other respect disappointed the consumer. This particular application had a booming but short life, and it was not until much later that its legitimacy was even partially and painfully restored.

But pricing is a device that can be used not only at the outset of a new product to help stretch its life effectively but also later when it approaches market maturity. One of the more common devices is to cut the price to make the product accessible to new markets. Probably the most famous example is that of Henry Ford's $500 car. He tells us clearly in his autobiography that the $500 price was not the result of his invention of the assembly line (which he did *not* invent; he copied it from Julius Rosenwald's mail-order warehouse at Sears, Roebuck), but that the assembly line was used as a means of creating a car cheap enough to give him access to a huge mass market.[7]

A similar strategy of purposely getting prices low enough to create a mass market characterized the remarkable history of transistors. At the time when Texas Instruments sold transistors at $10 to $16 each, they had only limited applications. Hearing

[7] Henry Ford, *My Life and Work* (New York: Doubleday & Co., 1923), pp. 146–147.

aids were the biggest consumer-product items. The company wanted a mass market, but its costs kept prices prohibitively high. After studying its operations, it concluded that transistors could be mass-produced to sell for as little as $2.50. The problem then was to find suitable mass-volume products for transistors. After a careful customer-oriented search, it decided that portable radios were the best bet. But since the nation's major portable producers also produced the vacuum tubes which transistors would replace, TI faced hard sledding in trying to sell the transistor portable idea to these companies.

In the end it found its only alternative was to seek out independent radio manufacturers. But since the whole proposal was so new and since most of the independents were small and unwilling or incapable of developing such small radios, TI developed the required circuit designs itself. Then it provided the other assistance that an independent manufacturer needed to bring out the first transistor radio. All told, TI invested some $2-million in this project—and built an enormously profitable mass market.

Other devices for market stretching include such things as:

1. "Going Consumer": A producer of costly soldering guns used in the manufacture of electronic circuits making a cheaper and more stylish version to be distributed to the do-it-yourself market via hardware stores.

2. "Going All-Purpose": A specialty product such as Lysol bathroom disinfectant being slightly modified (packaging and odor) and effectively promoted as an all-purpose, all-safe disinfectant and deoderizer for the entire home.

3. "Going Direct": A manufacturer of hospital soaps and waxes setting up a consumer division to sell direct to the consumer the way Avon does.

4. "Product Modification": A manufacturer of cough drops developing the same product into a spray, a liquid, a room vaporizer.

5. "Convenience Packaging": A manufacturer of nonfat dry milk packaging it into premeasured envelopes for easy quart-size preparation.

6. "Image Repositioning": Shifting the image or reputation of Mod fashions from being "beatnik" to being stylishly "in."

7. Franchising: Multiplying a single retail or service concept

(e.g., Mr. Donut, Holiday Inn) manyfold via franchising it to numerous independent investors.

EXTENSION STRATEGIES

The existence of the kinds of product life cycles illustrated in Exhibits I and II and the unit profit cycle in Exhibit III suggests that there may be considerable value for people involved in new product work to begin planning for the extension of the lives of their products even before these products are formally launched. To plan for new life-extending infusions of effort (as in Exhibit IV) at this pre-introduction stage can be extremely useful in three profoundly important ways:

1. It generates an active rather than a reactive product policy.

It systematically structures a company's long-term marketing and product-development efforts in advance, rather than each effort or activity being merely a stopgap response to the urgent pressures of repeated competitive thrusts and declining profits. The life-extension view of product policy enforces thinking and planning ahead—thinking in some systematic way about the moves likely to be made by potential competitors, about possible changes in consumer reactions to the product, and the required selling activities which best take advantage of these conditional events.

2. It lays out a long-term plan designed to infuse new life into the product at the right time, with the right degree of care, and with the right amount of effort.

Many activities designed to raise the sales and profits of existing products or materials are often undertaken without regard to their relationship to each other or to timing—the optimum point of consumer readiness for such activities or the point of optimum competitive effectiveness. Careful advance planning, long before the need for such activity arises, can help assure that the timing, the care, and the efforts are appropriate to the situation.

For example, it appears extremely doubtful that the boom in women's hair-coloring and hair-tinting products would have been as spectacular if vigorous efforts to sell these products had preceded the boom in hair sprays and chemical hair fixers. The latter helped create a powerful consumer consciousness of hair fashions because they made it relatively easy to create and wear fashionable hair styles. Once it became easy for women to have fashionable hair styles, the resulting fashion consciousness helped open the door for hair colors and tints. It could not have happened the other way around, with colors and tints first creating fashion consciousness and thus raising the sales of sprays and fixers. Because understanding the reason for this precise order of events is essential for appreciating the importance of early preintroduction life-extension planning, it is useful to go into a bit of detail.

Consider: For women, setting their hair has been a perennial problem for centuries. First, the length and treatment of their hair is one of the most obvious ways in which they distinguish themselves from men. Hence to be attractive in that distinction becomes crucial. Second, hair frames and highlights the face, much as an attractive wooden border frames and highlights a beautiful painting. Thus hair styling is an important element in accentuating the appearance of a woman's facial features. Third, since the hair is long and soft, it is hard to hold in an attractive arrangement. It gets mussed in sleep, wind, damp weather, sporting activities, and so forth.

Therefore the effective *arrangement* of a woman's hair is understandably her first consideration in hair care. An unkempt brunette would gain nothing from making herself into a blonde. Indeed, in a country where blondes are in the minority, the switch from being an unkempt brunette to being an unkempt blonde would simply draw attention to her sloppiness. But once the problem of arrangement became easily solved by sprays and fixers, colors and tints could become big business, especially among women whose hair was beginning to turn gray.

The same order of priorities applies in industrial products. For example, it seems quite inconceivable that many manufacturing plants would easily have accepted the replacement of the old single-spindle, constantly man-tended screw machine by a computerized, tape-tended, multiple-spindle machine. The mechanical tending of the multiple-spindle machine was a necessary intermediate step, if for no other reason than that it required a lesser work-flow change, and certainly a lesser conceptual leap for the companies and the machine-tending workers involved.

For Jell-O it is unlikely that vegetable flavors would have been very successful before the idea of gelatin as a salad base had been pretty well accepted. Similarly, the promotion of colored and patterned Scotch tape as a gift and decorative seal might not have been as successful if department stores had not, as the result of their drive to compete more effectively with mass merchandisers by offering more customer services, previously demonstrated to the consumer what could be done to wrap and decorate gifts.

3. Perhaps the most important benefit of engaging in advance, pre-introduction planning for sales-extending, market-stretching activities later in the product's life is that this practice forces a company to adopt a wider view of the nature of the product it is dealing with.

Indeed, it may even force the adoption of a wider view of the company's business. Take the case of Jell-O. What is its product? Over the years Jell-O has become the brand umbrella for a wide range of dessert products, including cornstarch-base puddings, pie fillings, and the new Whip'n Chill, a light dessert product similar to a Bavarian cream or French mousse. On the basis of these products, it might be said that the Jell-O Division of General Foods is in the "dessert technology" business.

In the case of tape, perhaps 3M has gone even further in this technological approach to its business. It has a particular expertise (technology) on which it has built a constantly expanding business. This expertise can be said to be that of bonding things (adhesives, in the case of Scotch tape) to other things, particularly to thin materials. Hence we see 3M developing scores of profitable items, including electronic recording tape (bonding electron-sensitive materials to tape), and Thermo-Fax duplicating equipment and supplies (bonding heat-reactive materials to paper).

CONCLUSION

For companies interested in continued growth and profits, successful new-product strategy should be viewed as a planned totality that looks ahead over some years. For its own good, new-product strategy should try to predict in some measure the likelihood, character, and timing of competitive and market events.

While prediction is always hazardous and seldom very accurate, it is undoubtedly far better than not trying to predict at all. In fact, every product strategy and every business decision inescapably involves making a prediction about the future, about the market, and about competitors. To be more systematically aware of the predictions one is making so that one acts on them in an offensive rather than a defensive or reactive fashion—this is the real virtue of preplanning for market stretching and product-life extension. The result will be a product strategy that includes some sort of *plan for a timed sequence of conditional moves.*

Even before entering the market-development stage, the originator should make a judgment regarding the probable length of the product's normal life, taking into account the possibilities of expanding its uses and users. This judgment will also help determine many things—for example, whether to price the product on a skimming or a penetration basis, or what kind of relationship the company should develop with its resellers.

These considerations are important, because at each stage in a product's life cycle each management decision must consider the competitive requirements of the next stage. Thus a decision to establish a strong branding policy during the market-growth stage might help to insulate the brand against strong price competition later; a decision to establish a policy of "protected" dealers in the market-development stage might facilitate point-of-sale promotions during the market-growth stage, and so on. In short, having a clear idea of future product-development possibilities and market-development opportunities should reduce the likelihood of becoming locked into forms of merchandising that might possibly prove undesirable.

This kind of advance thinking about new-product strategy helps management avoid other pitfalls. For instance, advertising campaigns that look successful from a short-term view may hurt in the next stage of the life cycle. Thus at the outset Metrecal advertising used a strong medical theme. Sales boomed until imitative competitors successfully emphasized fashionable slimness. Metrecal had projected itself as the diet for the overweight consumer, an image that proved far less appealing than that of being the diet for people who were fashion-smart. But Metrecal's original appeal had been so strong and so well made that it was a formidable task later on to change people's impressions about the product. Obviously, with more careful long-range planning at the outset, a product's image can be more carefully positioned and advertising can have more clearly defined objectives.

Recognizing the importance of an orderly series of steps in the introduction of sales-building actions for new products should be a central ingredient of long-term product planning. A carefully preplanned program for market expansion, even before a new product is introduced, can have powerful virtues. The establishment of a rational plan for the future can also help to guide the direction and pace of the ongoing technical research in support of the product. Although departures from such a plan will surely have to be made to accommodate unexpected events and revised judgments, the plan puts the company in a better position to *make* things happen rather than constantly having to react to things that *are* happening.

It is important that the originator does *not* delay this long-term planning until after the product's introduction. How the product should be introduced and the many uses for which it might be promoted at the outset should be a function of a careful consideration of the optimum sequence of suggested product appeals and product uses. Consideration must focus not just on optimum things to do but as importantly on their optimum *sequence*—for instance, what the order of use of various appeals should be and what the order of suggested product uses should be. If Jell-O's first suggested use had been as a diet food, its chances of later making a big and easy impact in the gelatin dessert market undoubtedly would have been greatly diminished. Similarly, if nylon hosiery had been promoted at the outset as a functional daytime-wear hosiery, its ability to replace silk as the acceptable high-fashion hosiery would have been greatly diminished.

To illustrate the virtue of pre-introduction planning for a product's later life, suppose a company has developed a nonpatentable new product—say, an ordinary kitchen salt shaker. Suppose that nobody now has any kind of shaker. One might say, before launching it, that (1) it has a potential market of "x" million household, institutional, and commercial consumers, (2) in two years market maturity will set in, and (3) in one year profit margins will fall because of the entry of competition. Hence one might lay out the following plan:

1. *End of first year: Expand market among current users.*

Ideas—New designs, such as sterling shaker for formal use, "masculine" shaker for barbecue use, antique shaker for "Early American" households, miniature shaker for each table-place setting, moistureproof design for beach picnics.

2. *End of second year: Expand market to new users.*

Ideas—Designs for children, quaffer design for beer drinkers in bars, design for sadists to rub salt into open wounds.

3. *End of third year: Find new uses.*

Ideas—Make identical product for use as a pepper shaker, as decorative garlic-salt shaker, shaker for household scouring powder, shaker to sprinkle silicon dust on parts being machined in machine shops, and so forth.

This effort to prethink methods of reactivating a flattening sales curve far in advance of its becoming flat enables product planners to assign priorities to each task and to plan future production expansion and capital and marketing requirements in a systematic fashion. It prevents one's trying to do too many things at once, results in priorities being determined rationally instead of as accidental consequences of the timing of new ideas, and disciplines both the product-development effort that is launched in support of a product's growth and the marketing effort that is required for its continued success.

■

Summary

Although most sophisticated marketing men can theoretically trace products through their four life stages of development, growth, maturity, and decline, few, if any, have put the concept to work to stretch their markets.

To exploit this concept, marketers should plan in advance of the actual launching of a new product a series of actions to be utilized at various subsequent stages of the product's existence to sustain its sales and profit performance rather than allow the usual decline to occur.

This planning offers a number of real advantages:

1. An active rather than reactive product policy: *making* things happen rather than reacting to things that *are* happening.

2. A discipline and system for infusing new life into a product at the right time, with the right sequence of steps, with the right amount of effort and degree of care. This system will provide: guidance in avoiding marketing actions now which may boomerang later; help in figuring out the direction and pace of ongoing technical research; a rational approach to establishing priorities, and determining future capital, manpower, and production requirements; and a means of prompting a firm to adopt a wider view of the nature of the product in question, i.e., to develop a comprehensive marketing vision.

6

Multibrand Entries

■

Robert W. Young, Jr.

■

Underlying the marketing strategy of multibrand entries is a basic premise: two brands tend to capture more of the available sales than one. This strategy is related to the principle of concentration: a marketer recognizes additional opportunities in a product category and pursues them with a vengeance. This strategy is also related to market segmentation in that different brands in a category, however similar they may appear to be, are, in some subtle way, carving out different chunks of the market. Furthermore, multibrand entries are a form of end-run. They enable a marketer to outflank a rival brand in a way his existing brand probably could not. And as a further illustration of the interdependence of these basic strategies, product innovation is required to provide the second and third brands.

Marketers with a broad conception of their business have learned to overcome their passionate devotion to one brand. Their vision grants them detachment; they can see that their role in life is not to nurture their brand regardless of cost, but rather to maximize profitable volume. They can also see that there will always be a few contrary consumers who will persist in buying a rival brand. So they reason that the other brand might just as well be theirs too. They know there may be some inroads into sales of the original brand, but that there will be a net gain in volume with two brands instead of one. And so they make their peace with cannibalization.

Many packaged-goods industries provide examples of the application of this strategy. In deodorants, Bristol-Myers has four brands and seven product variants: Ban (roll-on and cream), Mum (including Mum Mist and Mum Mist for Men), Trig, and Discreet. In soaps and detergents and tobacco products, examples of this strategy abound. Alberto-Culver has enunciated multibrand competition as a policy and is sending second brands into markets in which they already compete.

Perhaps the shrewdest extension of this strategy, particularly applicable when a company is first with a truly new product and can realistically anticipate competition, is to lock out rivals by bringing out multiple offerings at the time of product introduction. One food manufacturer used this approach recently in a product category segmented by flavor. Similarly, a housewares producer applied this strategy to pre-empt the key position with different-featured models in a market that segments by price. The cigarette field also furnishes examples: Philip Morris tested no fewer than three new charcoal filter brands virtually at the same time—Philip Morris Multifilter, Galaxy, and Saratoga—and Liggett & Myers introduced two—Lark and Keith—at the period when charcoal filters first became "hot."

Robert W. Young, Jr., is eminently qualified to treat this topic in detail. He has had many years of experience as a top marketing executive with consumer packaged goods manufacturers, where this strategy is most common. He can thus speak from a wealth of practical experience. Mr. Young is Vice President and Corporate Director of Marketing-Worldwide of the Colgate-Palmolive Company. He was formerly Vice President-General Manager of the Domestic Household Products Division of that company.

In Household Products, Mr. Young doubled sales and profits and developed a highly successful new products introduction and regular products revitalization program. According to a recent Eastman Dillon, Union Securities & Co. institutional research report, for example, "Mr. Robert W. Young, Jr., was appointed (1960–61) Manager of the Household Products Division and the outstanding performance of the Division in the next four years attests to the ability he brought to his job. He has recently been appointed corporate vice president in charge of the company's worldwide marketing organization."

Mr. Young organized, developed and promoted the House of Ajax: all-purpose cleaner, floor and wall cleaner, window cleaner, heavy-duty detergent categories, all of them beating both payout and investment odds for new products in these fields. Together these products built the name Ajax to its present position as the most heavily advertised and promoted weapon in the highly competitive heavy-duty cleaning business. The House of Ajax structure is now operating in most of Colgate's foreign market areas and is testing new cleaning products. Under Mr. Young's direction the division also developed Baggies, Action Bleach, Soaky, Cold Power Detergent and Palmolive Dishwashing Liquid—and revitalized Rose Lotion Vel Dishwashing Liquid and Fab with Borax.

A graduate of the Harvard Business School, Mr. Young was formerly Vice President of Kenyon & Eckhardt Advertising, where the accounts he supervised included Lever Brothers and Beecham Ltd. (Brylcreem, McClean's toothpaste), and a director and major stockholder of Golden Gift, Inc., the first company to market fruit juices in dairy cartons nationally. He sold the company profitably as the product form grew into a significant industry.

■

MULTIBRAND ENTRIES

ROBERT W. YOUNG, JR.

The stores of America are one vast cornucopia of consumer packaged goods proliferating in an ever-changing variety of packages, designs, forms, flavors, sizes, prices, and qualities to meet any need. Everyone knows that "competition" has, in some vague way, caused this; after all, competition is part of the American way of life. However, most Americans who have grown up humming advertising jingles and belonging to the brand-name cognoscenti would fail miserably in correlating many packaged-goods brand names with company names. Without some effort they would also fail to understand the concept that many of the completely independent brand names competing in the same product category to fill the same need are made by the same company. Actually, in the last twenty years, intracompany competition between brands and/or brand forms for the same specific consumer need has contributed as significantly as competition between companies to the full expansion of many of the major packaged-goods categories.

GENERAL PHILOSOPHY

Reduced to simple terms, the theory of multibrand entries can be stated thus: *Two or more brands or brand forms sold by the same company for the same consumer need can capture more sales and profits than one.* However, implicit in this thought has always been the recognition that this type of marketing would be most profitable within the climate of a mass, segmentable and expandable market; an increasing population; an increasing per capita income; and the possibility of expanding the usage of the product form to more people. On the opposite side of the coin, to stay small in a large, expanding or expanded market can be hazardous. No single product can capture all of the market nor have a vested life interest in it, because consumer demand is changeable. To protect return on capital investment it can be wiser to seek a constant or increasing share of an expanding market, and even if the market has been expanded, to meet or beat all new competition. In regard to competition, multibrand leadership or, even better, "topsmanship" in a product category tends to insure:

1. Plant, R&D, and people operating at optimum efficiency within a given area of knowledge.
2. Bottom prices and leverage with suppliers in volume purchasing of standard ingredients, packaging, and machinery.
3. Power and efficiency in sales force, advertising, and market research.
4. Financial strength to support the costs and risks of new-product development, testing, and launching; financial strength to weather unusual competition or price cutting.

The advantages of multibrand leadership are obvious if one is studying a company which basically does business in only one category of product, such as cigarettes, but the hazards multiply for companies which do business in many different product categories. An excellent track record in selling toothpaste at a profit does not necessarily insure success in selling light-duty detergent, for example. Unless the company which enters the new field completely understands why it has been successful in selling toothpaste and the differences in the new category which will require new commitment and new techniques, it may fail. A marketing vision for each category is necessary, and because a category is a business in its own right it requires its own goal definition. Companies doing business in many categories must constantly be on guard against top management's carrying assumptions from one business to another.

Failure can be costly, because multibrand marketing is not for the timid investor. As a rule, in these highly competitive categories, share of market large enough to generate a proper return on sales can never be obtained for a new product without sufficient media and promotion investment to stand out above the crowd. Profits are delayed to solidify fully the consumer franchise. Payout on a new entry can take as long as three or more years, depending on the degree of success of the entry and the normal life cycle within the category of business.

Today most knowledgeable marketers employ sophisticated methods of market research, test marketing, and feasibility/investment analysis to weigh the opportunities and risks in launching new products. The art of phasing out brands within a category which are past the point of profitable reinvestment, and the phasing in of new brands which will gain and hold a solid share of the market for a reasonable life cycle is extremely critical to the profitability of multibrand marketing. Only through a constant-category consumer research and testing program can old images and new concepts be weighed properly in the competitive investment climate.

The problems of introducing the second or third brand in a product category may involve the following considerations:

1. What unique concept can be built into the product and/or advertising of a second brand which meets or creates a consumer need not being satisfied by existing brands?

2. Will the new concept be more believable and hence more profitably used for a new product, or might it be used more effectively to reintroduce and reactivate an existing brand? Is the concept aimed at a demographic, psychographic, usage, or price segment different from those of the company's existing brands?

3. How much share of the market will be lost by the existing brand or brands when the new brand is introduced? What can be done to support the existing brand or brands during the new brand's introduction, throwing the burden on competition outside the company?

4. What will be the category return on sales and investment as a result of a new total share of the market? What efficiencies and savings can be forecast?

Unfortunately, many manufacturers have assumed that the job of bringing out new products is half over once the decision has been made to do so. Part of the overcrowding in many product categories has resulted from the introduction of partial failures or partial successes by companies which do not have the financial underpinning to phase out the new brand and try again. Most of these partial failures and successes can be directly attributed to improper evaluation of consumer receptivity and repurchase of a new product before national launching, or failure to spend adequately during launching. Partial failures are brands which take up sales-force time and the time of every company department but never generate enough volume to contribute significant profit and carry a fair share of overhead. Their cost to the company can often be incalculable. It becomes difficult for a company to sell and handle more than two, three, or four different brands within a category. Low-share brands can often get in the way of a company's drive to obtain higher and higher shares of the market. Obviously, two brands with high shares of the market are more desirable and profitable than four weaker contenders adding up to the same total share. Small- or marginal-profit brands may have to be eliminated today to make room for higher profits tomorrow. It takes managerial courage to eliminate a product weakling. It takes marketing discipline to launch only those new products which pass successfully through rigid screens of pretesting and market testing.

Many companies have made the decision to participate in multibrand marketing. Each company is faced with a different corporate position and philosophy, and each product category represents a unique marketing situation. To illustrate the complexities in multibrand marketing, broad areas affecting such marketing decisions will be discussed. For each of the areas specific examples of successful multibrand entries will be cited. The five general areas to be covered are:

1. Capitalizing on a product breakthrough to dominate an expanding category.
2. Expanding dollar volume in a static market.
3. Marketing of new forms, flavors, colors, or odors to meet or create new consumer demand.
4. Taking advantage of known market segmentation with respect to demographics and psychographics.
5. Protecting corporate franchise through defensive multibrand entries.

1. CAPITALIZING ON A PRODUCT BREAKTHROUGH TO LEAD IN AN EXPANDING CATEGORY

New chemistry in "synthetic" detergents evolved during World War II resulting in a product far superior to conventional powdered soaps and bar soaps used for clothes and dishwashing. Detergents cut grease and foamed copiously even in the hardest water. The results were very obvious to the user, both in the sink or on the line. Procter and Gamble Company recognized the advantages of the new product and, although already a large factor in the bar and powdered-soap market, they totally committed themselves to full development of detergents. They introduced Tide detergent with heavy advertising on a national basis as fast as plant could be built and used. The brand ran up to a phenomenal 30 per cent of the market by 1952. The total market expanded from $344-million annually to $478-million during this period of time. Because of Tide's success and the consequent growth of the market, P&G realized that they could increase their share even further with another entry. Cheer was introduced at the end of 1950 in blue form to emphasize "whitening" and to distinguish this product from Tide, which was sold on a tough-cleaning story. As a brand entry, Cheer added nearly a 4 per cent share to Tide, which held a 30 per cent share. The market expanded 39 per cent during this period as consumers became more detergent-prone at the expense of bar soap and cartoned soap.

Because consumers preferred the new detergents to soaps, P&G lost considerable soap volume, but so did competition. However, by recognizing the future of detergents, by total commitment, by heavy investment behind both brands, P&G assured itself ownership of a dominant position in an expanding market. This market was able to expand as rapidly as it did because the new detergents capitalized on the increased population and booming automatic washing machine ownership. By positive multibrand action, P&G ended up dominant, generating huge profits and leverage, while pre-empting competition from finding a major foothold in the market. Accurate consumer research, excellent advertising for both products, and the creation of distinct images in line with consumer needs resulted in a P&G success. If P&G had used an existing soap-powder trade mark, the import of a major scientific breakthrough might not have communicated itself as readily to consumers.

Competitors did not mobilize themselves with as much conviction or total commitment, and it took years for them to recognize new segments of the market to attack purposefully, only to be met by additional entries from P&G in defense of its major share of market.

2. EXPANDING DOLLAR VOLUME IN A STATIC MARKET

Over many years Gillette built the double-edged-blade market through heavy promotion behind both popular priced Thins and higher priced Blue Blades. Gillette owned a dominant share of the razor blade business. The company saw the market level off as the majority of men adjusted to shaving daily, and Gillette was faced with limited expansion opportunity in the face of increasing costs. Taking advantage of their position in the market, Gillette introduced a blade with a silicone-treated cutting surface. This blade was positioned as a premium-priced Super Blue blade. The superiority of the blade was readily recognizable after the first shave. Gillette's strategy paid off. The Super Blue rapidly captured a significant share of the unit market, but more importantly, increased total dollar volume of the blade business and Gillette's dollar volume.

By innovative use of multibrand entries Gillette was able to maintain dominance more profitably in the category. Although Thins and Blues lost share to Super Blues, they remained available to all segments of the male population who still preferred or wanted them. Through domination in advertising and sales, Gillette was able to optimize their multibrand strategy.

3. MARKETING OF NEW FORMS, FLAVORS, COLORS, OR ODORS TO MEET OR CREATE NEW CONSUMER DEMAND

Certain brand categories by their very nature are more highly fractionalized than others. The markets can be large, but one product form alone will not satisfy consumer needs. Examples are many and seem obvious, but without aggressive multibrand form entries, the leaders in these categories would not have achieved success or expanded usage.

A. FLAVOR VARIATION

Soups. The colossi in the prepared-soup market offer every possible variety of soup that can be sold at a profit, and probably a few which are only needed to ward off competitive inroads in retail stores (shelf space). Campbell, preeminent in this category, advertises all varieties under one trademark, emphasizing different soups in their advertising according to season, current popularity, and newness.

The market for packaged soup was expanded and developed at the expense of the soup pot through offering choices ranging across a cookbook gamut to meet the varying tastes of the consumer. One could argue that all varieties of Campbell's are one brand, but there are too many families that, for example, might have Campbell's tomato soup, Lipton's onion soup and Heinz's chicken soup on their kitchen shelves at the same time. A soup company like Campbell must cost account and phase a variety of soups in or out of the market based on the same values as a separate brand entity.

Campbell helped expand the use of canned soup through offering variety, convenience, quality, and availability at a low price. In a sense, any one of Campbell's varieties of soup is in competition with other Campbell's varieties as well as competitive varieties from other companies. Added all together, Campbell's many varieties have resulted in excellent return over the years by optimizing the phase-in-and-phase-out process.

Campbell's commitment to leadership in soup requires their readiness to meet all challengers, such as frozen soup or freeze-dried soups. Their marketing goal is to fill the soup bowl whenever it is used. Campbell's frozen and Red Kettle freeze-dried soups were launched as additional multibrand entries—both designed to re-expand the soup market and also to prevent new forms of soup from doing to Campbell what Campbell did to the soup pot.

B. FORM VARIATION

Underarm Deodorants. Deodorants are a relatively new category, which sprang up in the postwar period. In it we find another type of multibrand marketing in which various forms appear under one trademark.

The sale of products as underarm deodorants and antiperspirants was expanded both by the introduction and advertising of new brand names and by the introduction of varied forms under the same brand names to protect existing franchises. Arrid was the first deodorant to be marketed in two forms, adding roll-ons to existing creams. Procter & Gamble, observing segmentation in the deodorant market, was the first company to *launch* a deodorant, Secret, in more than one form (roll-on and cream). Subsequently Ban and other established brands were marketed in more than one form. Currently many brands such as Secret, Arrid, and Fresh are marketed in as many as three forms, including the new aerosol. Moreover, Bristol-Myers markets more than one brand name and more than one form per brand name with Mum and Ban. It is interesting to note that in this category each time a new form appeared on the market it was introduced with a new trademark, but quickly adopted for other brands as a new form entry (Stopette, Ban, Right Guard). Through multiple marketing of various deodorant forms under a single brand, a manufacturer has been able to maximize a share of the market for that brand.

Make-Up. The marketing of various forms of a product is even more aggressive in the make-up market. An example is Max Factor, which originally marketed loose powder, then water-soluble Pancake, then cream Pan Stick, then Creme Puff pressed powder, then liquid Hi Fi, and finally Sheer Genius make-up in a tube.

All these changes were dictated by fashion and changes in consumer tastes. None of these products replaced another, and all exist in today's expanded market.

C. COLOR VARIATION

Nail Polish. Revlon and other powers in the nail polish business have built the use of nail polish and made advertising pay off by offering a wide line of color choices under a house name. Twice each year color promotions highlight additions to the color line to coincide with new fashion and to create consumer demand for new colors. Colors added as a result of a promotion will remain permanently if there is a continuing demand. Similarly, colors that are moving slowly will be eliminated.

By offering and advertising such a wide choice of colors the market has been expanded by luring many women into purchasing more than one shade for use at home. Mother, who sparingly used one bottle of light pink nail polish, has been replaced by a less money-conscious, more style-conscious daughter who is capable of not finishing a bottle if she doesn't like the color, or of letting bottles dry out as she tries out a new color.

Lipstick. Lipsticks have a very similar marketing history, but complicated by their variations in form and texture as well as color.

D. ODOR VARIATION

Room Air Deodorants. The room air-deodorant category is marked by a much less definite consumer reaction than the nail polish category, but once again, expansion and profitability in this market were achieved by offering the consumer a choice of perfumes under one brand name.

The market, like soup and nail polish, is not large enough to sustain individual brand names behind individual varieties, but through adding and changing choice of odors, the business has been expanded and new customers developed. Ask any supermarket owner, and you will discover that many aerosol cans of Colgate's Florient room air deodorant are tested right in the store by shoppers to find the scent that satisfies. Brand loyalty is not high, so competitive success has to depend greatly on having a full multiodor line in stock to catch the shopper's attention and trial. If she wants pine, she will not buy your lilac in lieu of competitive pine. If she does not like perfume at all, she will only buy an odorless or disinfectant room air deodorant.

4. TAKING ADVANTAGE OF KNOWN MARKET SEGMENTATION [1]

DEMOGRAPHICS

Age, education, income, sex, size of family often lead the manufacturer into multibrand marketing in order to optimize share potential.

Age. Bristol-Myers for many years has owned Vitalis, a leading men's hair dressing. Bottled and liquid Vitalis over the last eight years has been losing its appeal to teenagers and young men (the heavy hair-dressing users), who have taken up other forms of men's hair-dressing products, especially tubed cream forms. Bristol-Myers with its "Greasy Kid's Stuff" campaign aggressively advertised to win back younger users for Vitalis to protect its franchise. The campaign was successful in protecting the franchise but did not attract a significant portion of the youth market. To appeal to the important younger men, Bristol-Myers introduced Score, a clear hair dressing in a tube, in the belief that the market is large enough to sustain two brands. A more timid marketer might have introduced Vitalis in a tube to complement Vitalis in the bottle. However, it seems doubtful that the Vitalis image could have been as successful.

By offering two forms of hair dressing to the consumer, Bristol-Myers reaches a full presentation to all age groups and has countered a trend which threatened eventually to leave Vitalis isolated as an older man's hair dressing.

Income. Although most mass-packaged goods are within the income range of most Americans, there are product categories in which price levels vary to appeal to different income groups. Quite often multibrand entries are priced at different levels to accommodate these groups. Examples would include these:

1. In cosmetics Revlon sells its Revlon line at popular prices,

---

[1] See also Chapter 4.

but prices the Ultima line higher, seeking more margin from those women who are willing to pay more in the search for beauty.

2. In the detergent field the low-sudsing detergents, such as Ad, All, and Dash, were created to appeal to the more affluent automatic washing machine owners who didn't want too high a suds level in their machines. These multibrand entries in the detergent category were sold at a higher price than the conventional high-sudsing detergents, which were used for washing both clothes and dishes. Receptivity of low sudsers by consumers who could afford a separate product to wash dishes in a sense segmented detergent users along price lines.

3. The women's hair spray category has rapidly segmented between low-priced, generally nonadvertised brands, and higher priced, advertised brands (usually the newest, which promise extra benefits) to appeal to the various income groups. Many manufacturers have multibrand entries at various price levels: Toni—Adorn and White Rain; Colgate—Respond, Halo, and Lustre-Creme.

4. In an already low-priced category, Ivory soap has maintained the strongest toilet soap franchise for years by selling an extra bar free. By long-term, excellent advertising, the Ivory image is held high, yet it is the cheapest toilet soap buy for the masses. The same company markets medium- and higher-priced bars also —Camay, Zest, and Safeguard.

Sex. Most major volume items (except for shaving cream and blades) are sold to women for themselves or the home, but:

1. Bristol-Myers is one company which markets multibrands to appeal to the sexes individually and as a family unit. Among the four Bristol-Myers deodorants, Mum is directed to women, Ban to both women and men, Trig to men, and Discreet to young men.

2. The toilet soap business also segments along sex lines. Most toilet soaps which are cosmetic in perfume, color, and name advertise to women only. The others advertise to women, men, and family. Male toilet soaps only are restricted to small volume because women make the purchase and men don't care as much about toilet soaps as they do about razor blades or whiskey. Lever Brothers, for example, markets Dove and Lux brands to appeal to women, and Lifebuoy deodorant brand to appeal to both women and men. Colgate-Palmolive Company sells Palm-

olive green and pink soap to women, Palmolive gold deodorant soap to women and men.

PSYCHOGRAPHICS

Not all people are the same in their feelings about how to live, and quite often a grasp of the major psychological segmentations among users has helped manufacturers to introduce successfully multibrand entries appealing to two or more groups which would not be reached fully by one brand.

1. Light-duty dishwashing detergents: Women seem to divide psychologically between the "I come first" group and the "house and possessions come first" group. Of course the gradations of this division are endless depending on age, income, appearance, and so on. However, in general, there seems to be a class of women who are not completely satisfied with dishwashing detergent which emphasizes mildness to hands and is cosmetic in appearance and odor. Other women look for strong, efficient cleaning products and tend to want clean dishes and pots or pans even at the expense of the appearance of their hands. Lever Brothers' Lux with Dermasil is primarily aimed at the "I come first" group, while their Swan concentrates primarily on the cleaning-efficiency group. Packaging, product, formula, and advertising tend to enhance the product image desired.

2. In the toothpaste business, a dichotomy exists between the frivolous user interested in breath, flavor, whiteness of teeth, and the health-oriented user who is concerned about cavity control. Although these psychological lines of demarcation are not clear cut and break down among various members of the family, the housewife prevails in the purchase, and the degree of her concern over cavities prejudices her decision. Multibrand entries are necessary to optimize share opportunities in this market.

3. A similar dichotomy exists in the shampoo business between one group that wishes to eliminate dandruff yet have beautiful, shiny, manageable hair, and those who have less dandruff fear (perhaps when dandruff is temporarily cured) and impute hair beauty to the more cosmetically oriented brands. Most shampoo manufacturers have or will have multibrand entries to appeal to both needs in a shampoo.

4. In the home hair-coloring business, various forms of hair coloring are sold by Clairol, Roux, and others to appeal to differently motivated women. A vast segment of the female population still does not color its hair. But once they begin, most women start tentatively with shampoo tints or semipermanent colors, and often progress to the more permanent colors because of the superior effects. At present a full line of hair colors and hair-color forms is necessary to build the market, tempting the fearful and offering choice to the more experienced users. Clairol's vision of enhancing or changing color in the hair has naturally led the company into cosmetics based on the same premise but keyed to the hair: Clairol colors from the neck up.

5. Low-calorie soft drinks represent another segmentation phenomenon requiring multibrand entries to capture differently motivated groups. With the appearance of dietary and antisweets fads on the American scene, fear of new competition made multibrand marketers of the cola manufacturers, along form as well as flavor lines. Pepsi-Cola and Diet Pepsi are for sale in the same outlets. Without Diet Pepsi, Pepsi-Cola was in danger of losing a share of the market to competition offering dietary drinks. The consumers divide between those who have no real or imagined dietary problems and those who do. No one brand entry would capture both.

6. For years the analgesic business split along simple lines: Bayer or other aspirin for simple pain; Anacin and others for more severe pain. Severe pain could be imagined or real depending on the hypochondria and pill-taking habits of the user. Some people seem to be careful; others will take only the strongest. Bristol-Myers, entering the field, brought out two brands in less than ten years: Bufferin to attack aspirin; Excedrin to attack Anacin. For the newcomer to obtain the advantages of share leadership, two brands were necessary to reach the whole market.

5. PROTECTING CORPORATE FRANCHISE THROUGH DEFENSIVE MULTIBRAND ENTRIES

To a degree, all companies which have major shares of the market with multibrand entries must become both offensive and defensive. New companies entering a category usually try to enter an innovation, and great danger to established leaders always exists from technological improvements. Unless the leaders continue their commitment to furthering technology in a category, they always are in danger of losing business. The leaders are not always first with innovations but usually are foremost when the smoke clears away, primarily because of their ability to use fully their business experience and their financial resources. Whether the leaders enter first or imitate with a new product breakthrough, every new product entry is in a sense defensive. Theoretically, all leaders wish competition would stop but are caught up in a never-ending competitive race. The quality of capitalism will probably be measured in terms of the effect of this pressure which occasionally creates technologies that outmode all previous product forms.

Razor Blades. After Gillette expanded the blade business by introducing Super Blue Blades at a premium price, they were not allowed to relax and enjoy their profit for long. Although not a new product form, long-lasting, stainless steel blades had been primarily a foreign product found only in small United States shops. Wilkinson Sword blades from England began catching hold in the eastern part of the United States in the early 1960s. Taking heart from this, Wilkinson actively began to seek greater distribution in the United States. Much like Super Blues, which were touted as premium, special, and hard to get, Wilkinson blades were soon riding a similar wave, but they were not ready to capitalize on it à la Gillette. Quickly Personna and Schick, which had been small entities in the United States market, introduced stainless steel blades in a rush to steal a share of the market before Gillette made its move. Gillette hesitated with its introduction of a premium-priced, longer-lasting stainless blade because they realized that the long-range effect of a stainless steel success could mean a significant decrease in unit and dollar volume of the market. However, Gillette saw that stainless steel would account for an important share of the market, and with its superior technology, marketing and distribution abilities, quickly introduced a Gillette stainless blade to stave off competition and hold a share of the market. Without such a move the Gillette dominance of the American blade business could have been completely shaken.

Perhaps to the benefit of the consumer, the total blade business declined as forecast.

Cigarettes. A classic in multibrand marketing, major cigarette companies have run the gamut since World War II both in building and in defending the market and their respective shares of it. From the original short regular cigarettes represented by Camel, Chesterfield, Lucky Strike, and Philip Morris, the market in turn has seen the entry of long regular cigarettes like Pall Mall; then filter cigarettes like Viceroy, Kent, Winston, and L&M; then filtered menthol cigarettes like Salem, Newport, and Bel-Air; then a rush of charcoal filter cigarettes, Lark and Tareyton, with a crossover, Montclair, incorporating a menthol charcoal filter.

A huge business is able to support advertising budgets on single brand names. In general, many of the companies lost headway and a share in the business by trying to incorporate new forms under old brand names and lines such as Philip Morris regulars, kings, and filters—or Chesterfield regulars and kings. These had little success against Winston filters and Salem menthols, for example, which were launched by Reynolds Tobacco Company as new brand entries. The business was highly fractionalized by these many entries and form variations, but no major cigarette manufacturer was able to keep afloat without meeting the major form segmentations as they came to the marketplace. The strongest defense has proved to be heavy investment behind new brand names to represent the new product form.

Cereals. Another heavily multibranded market, the cereal business is highly competitive, and the leaders own a total share of market built from various brands aimed at various demographic and psychographic groupings. For example, Kellogg's corn flakes and Rice Krispies were joined by Sugar Smacks and Sugar Puffs as presweetened cereals came on the scene with even stronger appeal to children. Kellogg then marketed Special K and Concentrate when the protein dietary fad began. The current fad is freeze-dried fruits added to cereals, which Kellogg will surely market if they show indications of becoming a significant factor in the cereal business. It is through this technical and marketing ability that Kellogg will continue to maintain leadership. Their leadership has been in direct proportion to their ability to anticipate or meet all new major trends in cereals. The investment in new products resulting from widespread cereal technology is a way of life to insure their company's strength versus General Mills, General Foods, and other cereal makers.

Home Permanent Waves. Sometimes a company which has been dominant in a multibrand category must learn new technology and market a completely new form of product for a similar use. For example, for years the Toni Company had been the leader in the home permanent wave business with multibrand entries. With the advent of hair sprays and changing hair styles, the home permanent wave became less important, especially to younger women. Unless they faced the reality of this encroachment, Toni and others in the field would have been doomed to a declining business. To counter this change in the market, Toni introduced Adorn hair spray and entered its own field from a new direction while maintaining its original home permanent business.

WHY LARGE COMPANIES ARE SUCCESSFUL IN MULTIBRAND MARKETING

Multi-brand entries may seem a panacea to the outside observer, but obviously the achievements of successful companies have stemmed from their ability in business, in knowing who they are and where they are going. All companies will have national failures from time to time, but great care is normally taken by the leaders in American packaged-goods manufacturing to test new products with consumers prior to national launching. The probability of success varies in every product category, and many new ideas are required to find a few products which consumers will respond to and which can be developed by technical know-how. This adds up to a continuing investment against the future, which must be borne resolutely. The successful new product theoretically carries on its back all the R&D, all the consumer testing, all the test marketing, all the unusual plant start-up charges, plus all the marketing and sales force time devoted to all the unsuccessful new products aborted at various stages of development.

Successful multibrand marketers offset this expense by higher product margins and lower operating expense ratios compared to the Johnny-come-lately companies. The leaders are strong where it counts, with a strong selling and distribution arm at the forefront. For example, Revlon and Clairol with broad lines and multibrand entries dominate the drugstore in their respective categories. Kellogg's, Campbell's, General Foods, Colgate-Palmolive, etc., in the same fashion are hard to match in efficient food store coverage and delivery. With efficient distribution and power at the trade level, the leaders can optimize investment in advertising and promotion. Lack of distribution and out-of-stocks are the curse of the newcomer and followers and cut into a full sales return of the invested dollar.

More than one brand generates media strength, insuring the goal of all advertisers: to reach the prime consumer at the lowest possible cost.

More than one brand normally flows from investment in R&D. Put another way, if R&D costs $1.00 for one brand, a second brand based on the same technology might bring the total investment for the two brands to only $1.05.

More than one brand using similar chemicals, packaging, and machinery can turn up efficiencies that result in greater profit or a greater investment fund. A perfect example is in the light-duty detergent category, where the majors sell three entries each with a high degree of standardization between them. Where capital investment and plant lead time is high, which is the case in many packaged-goods categories, new competition from smaller companies is obviously more dangerous when it utilizes new technology.

THE FUTURE

Today every manufacturer of packaged goods—multibrand or not—faces certain facts and trends which make the future appear quite different from what it seemed to be in 1945.

1. Most conventional product categories have been heavily expanded. Many are increasing only at the rate of population growth. New entries are, in many cases, merely fractionalizing the total market, and product life cycles are running shorter. The opportunity to invest in one, two, or three brands for the same usage need is declining because there is less likelihood of creating new consumption for new users or increased usage among current

users. The product cornucopia found in the stores and homes of Americans has become a problem in its own right.

2. Costs are rising at a faster rate in many categories of business than manufacturers' selling prices. For example, in the detergent business there has been no significant price rise in years. Although raw material costs have held, wages, salary, and employee benefits continually increase. As heavy advertisers, detergent manufacturers are dependent on advertising to promote consumer sales. However, similar to other industries which depend on advertising, they face the problem of rising advertising costs.

In addition, as competition rages hotter, marketers, with the urging of the trade, are being lured deeper and deeper into heavier sales promotion costs. At a high level and over a period of time, promotion costs between competitors tend to neutralize each other and might just as well be trade discounts or retail price reductions.

3. Since 1945 sweeping changes have occurred in trade centralization: huge chain, wholesale, co-op, and discount enterprises channeling more sales through fewer outlets. Small "Mom and Pop" stores have almost disappeared. Without distribution in major food and drug chains the average new packaged-goods product has little opportunity for success in highly competitive categories. To be heard in advertising requires investment, and once heavy investment is committed, distribution is essential to payout on investment. Over a period of time, wholesaler efforts on behalf of a product are marginal, because of the vast number of items that they carry.

To be a leader in any category, a strong, efficient sales and distribution arm becomes more and more essential. The buyers of today have IBM records and rely on an increasingly efficient use of electronic data processing. They do not look favorably on new products which have been untested and are becoming more and more adept in elimination of sizes and brands which are slow movers. The manufacturer who fails to deliver goods competitively misses trade cooperation in promotion or display and loses trade confidence. This in turn makes it harder to sell in new products, new sizes, and sufficient volume of merchandise to insure a balanced move-through of stock from warehouse to storeroom to shelf. Even with trade confidence, a major manufacturer recently had to guarantee sales on a major new product introduction to obtain full distribution of all product sizes concurrent with introductory expenditure.

Endless studies have been made to demonstrate the value of increased shelf space and display in the large chain or independent markets of today. Conversely, out of stock on the shelf results rapidly in sales below true consumer share potential.

4. Most branded merchandise has lost its consumer loyalty if the housewife cannot find it on her hectic shopping day, and most American homes will accept alternate brands, including nonadvertised private labels of major retail purveyors. This, of course, varies greatly by category of product, but all manufacturers face certain basic changes in the consumer of today as compared with the consumer of 1945. The reasons are:

(a) Television has educated, sophisticated, and changed the standards of most people. Bad or sham advertising stands out, is recognized more readily, and can actually prejudice a brand's sales.

(b) The variety of product available offers many acceptable alternatives for any product unless it is new and temporarily has a unique product advantage.

(c) Higher per capita income and higher education have widened vistas of American living to include vacation travel, boating, foreign food, eating out-of-doors, dieting, etc. The home has become less a showplace for mother's handicraft. The brand of catsup used is no longer a status symbol except in the proudest, poorest homes.

(d) The burgeoning youth market and younger housewives are TV babies and postwar products themselves. Their particular characteristics will only become intensified in the future when they replace their mothers as the heavy buyers for larger family units.

5. Government and professional groups today create greater and greater hurdles for manufacturers in the development of new products, especially those to be ingested or used on the body. In addition, the ability of manufacturers to diversify through acquisition runs full tilt into a "bigness is bad" belief, which still runs deep in the governmental agencies involved.

In general, all business recognizes and will accept measures to dignify advertising, improve standards in packaging, and protect the public from injuries or deceitful products. However, business will continue to struggle to maintain a balance with government against punitive or stifling measures which are proposed by the emotionally and/or politically motivated who show little concern for business realities and, in the end, public welfare. Extremists on both sides will undoubtedly cancel each other out, but legal and clinical expense will continue to grow for business over the years. The checks and balances concept of the Founding Fathers now definitely includes business and labor as branches of Federal government.

6. Because of governmental restrictions on acquisitions and the already large size of many United States companies, it is becoming increasingly difficult for the biggest to continually turn in sales and profit growth impressive to the financial community. Without large-scale domestic investment, diversification, or full-scale development of new foreign markets, many would be hard put to it to do better than tread water.

Encroachment through diversification is already a fact of life, and many companies have broadened their historic business to new fields. Innovations such as Johnson's wax entry into the car-wash business are a result of this need to grow. Chemical companies are anxious to capitalize on their R&D base and enter the consumer-products business as they acquire more and more knowledge of it through working closely with customers. Tobacco and liquor companies are seeking broader packaged-goods fields as their businesses come into jeopardy.

With all the forces against them, one might project that major packaged-goods manufacturers will fiercely fractionalize all major categories to a point where investment is no longer worthwhile. However, much is still on the side of the big companies. They have the people, chemistry, money, and facilities to solve their problems. They have a more diversified variety of product candidates than the smaller companies. As they head into the future, they also have new management techniques and tools to sharpen and refine their ponderous operations. Much has been written about "taking the guesswork out of business," but we are entering an era where that will be essential. The use of computers and mathematical models will force many managements to look more closely at their operations in order to put in meaningful data to get out even more meaningful instantaneous information. Just as the housewife straightens the house before the once-a-week maid comes to clean, management has to straighten its house in order to make use of electronic data processing. The future will hold great opportunity in the pinpointing of waste, the more accurate appraisal of financial alternatives, and faster decision-making.

Centralized planning and long-range planning will probably begin to make greater contributions in assisting the line decision-makers. The era ahead will see management taking more and more interest in reducing the margin of error in new-products development and marketing. The hasty rush to market of the last ten years will slow down, and interest in the higher echelons will center on sharper techniques of market research to assist in reducing waste. No company can afford too many failures, semifailures, or me-too products on the national market, or for that matter in the test market. In fully expanded categories where product differences have been slight, new product entries will probably be better planned with more obvious product differences. Head & Shoulders dandruff shampoo recently proved this in the shampoo category by obtaining a large share of the market in what was rapidly becoming an overfractionalized business. Resegmentation such as this will occur many times again in many categories as well-planned new product entries capture and restructure consumer fancy.

In other categories where single brands have held a long-term dominant share of market, such as Gillette Blue Blades or Tide Heavy Duty Detergent, it has been proved, and will be proved time and time again, that even the strongest brand will eventually decline as competition attacks the ramparts.

Major new categories of product will emanate from new chemistry, much as underarm deodorant and hair coloring did in the last fifteen years. Multibrand entries, of course, will be found in these new product categories as well as in existing markets, serving to increase total dollar volume by offering the consumer a "better mouse trap" for a higher price.

There is no point in ignoring the fact that leveling off in a great many categories of consumer packaged goods could become a problem to the thrust of American economy in the future, but certainly not in the near future. If it does, one can be certain at that time to find the peanut butter manufacturers of today busily promoting a new line of robots for the home in two forms, two prices, two colors, two sexes, and under two different brand names. It will still be true that in an expanding market two brand entries can obtain more sales and profits than one.

■

Summary

The theory of multibrand entries states: Two or more brands or brand forms sold for the same consumer need will capture more sales and profits than one.

Multibrand leadership offers compelling advantages in return on investment, bottom prices and leverage with suppliers, superior quality of marketing manpower and tools, and in financial strength.

The art of phasing out tired brands and phasing in new ones is critical to the profitability of multibrand marketing.

Multibrand marketing can operate toward five distinct objectives:

1. To capitalize on a product breakthrough to lead in an expanding category.
2. To expand dollar volume in a static market.
3. To market brands with new attributes to meet or create new consumer demand.
4. To take advantage of known market segments.
5. To protect a corporate franchise.

Economies of scale, a strong sales force, and efficient broad distribution are vital factors in optimizing multibrand marketing.

Highly fractionalized product categories, rising costs, fierce competition, sharper retailer management, channel centralization, ever-growing consumer sophistication, governmental hurdles, and incursions via diversification are among the many forces impelling a new look at multibrand strategy in the future.

7

Brand Extension

■

Theodore R. Gamble

■

Marketers' emotional attachment to products often includes the brand name. With brand-extension strategy, too, a wholesome and realistic view of the business precludes the imposition of artificial and unnecessary limitations on the use of brand names. There is nothing holy about a brand name, and if extension of it can bring about marketing good, while not discrediting or cheapening the original product or confusing the consumer, then extension can serve as a potent instrument. Thus Dristan, first a decongestant tablet, is now a nasal spray, cough formula, and medicated room vaporizer. Lustre Creme, in addition to ignoring the literal meaning of its name and coming out as a liquid and a lotion shampoo, is now also a rinse and conditioner and a spray set. Ivory, as homey and hoary a brand name as any, is as vital as ever in Ivory Flakes, Ivory Snow, Ivory Soap, and Ivory Liquid.

While brand extension has been recognized as one of the dozen basic strategies comprising our marketing weapons systems, there is virtually nothing in print on the subject, certainly no vigorous methodological studies of when you do and when you don't use an existing brand name.

The best experience on this subject is to be found among consumer packaged-goods marketers. Hence our call on the head of one of the most prominent and successful grocery products manufacturers in the country, Theodore R. Gamble, Chairman of the Board and Chief Executive Officer of Pet Incorporated. Mr. Gamble is an eminent young president, having assumed the leadership of Pet at the age of thirty-five. His entire career has been with the company. He began as an accountant in 1949 and was successively advanced to Assistant to the General Manager in 1951, Vice President and Assistant to the President in 1954, Executive Vice President in 1958, President the following year and Chairman in 1966.

Mr. Gamble was born in St. Louis, took a B.S. in mechanical engineering at Purdue University, spent three years in the Navy, then attended the Harvard Business School, from which he was graduated with an MBA in 1949. He has since won three honorary doctorates.

■

BRAND EXTENSION

THEODORE R. GAMBLE

The room was stale with cigarette smoke. The participants were voice- and brain-weary. Hour after hour the discussion had continued. The problem was what to name a new liquid diet food that Pet Milk Company planned to introduce in the 900-calorie-diet food market. The choice had been narrowed to two: Pet 900 Liquid Diet Food; Sego Liquid Diet Food.

Unfortunately, extensive consumer research had not been conclusive. On the one hand, it showed very desirable benefits to be gained from the quality and purity image built by Pet evaporated milk for over 75 years. On the other hand, Pet evaporated milk was strongly associated with its use as an ingredient item in rich foods. Further, it was in the very serious infant-feeding market, and Pet planned a "dieting can be fun" theme for its new product. An innocuous name into which "meaning" unique to diet food could be built might be the best answer. Sego also is a brand of evaporated milk, acquired by Pet Milk Company many years ago, but it is marketed in only a few western states in the intermountain area.

The final decision was Sego Liquid Diet Food. Was it a right decision? One can easily answer in the affirmative. The product has been an outstanding success. Sego and Metrecal stand today as the unquestioned leaders among canned liquid diet foods.

Yet what about those intermountain states where the same brand name applies to both evaporated milk and diet food? Has Sego evaporated milk retarded the progress of Sego Liquid Diet Food, or vice versa? There is no evidence one way or the other. The diet food is doing as well, relatively, in Salt Lake City as it is in Chicago or Los Angeles. Sego evaporated milk continues to maintain its share of the market.

This case history has been cited to underscore what may be the most significant aspect of *brand extension* as a marketing tool.

Very little has been written on the subject in any really definitive way. There are no absolute guidelines. Almost every case history of the successful application of brand extension can be countered with a case history—involving the same types of products—where comparable success was attained without brand extension.

The subject urgently needs careful study, in-depth research on a substantial scale. In an era where competitive pressures are greater than at any other time in United States business history—and promise to become even more intense in the future—a real understanding of when the impressive cost advantages of brand extension can be implemented is fast becoming a matter of top priority and concern.

Over the past quarter century the development of more and more new products, more and more product modifications, has become a way of life, particularly for consumer-product companies. As product life cycles steadily decline under the impact of accelerated competition and technological progress, this way of life has become essential to growth, share of market, and even survival. The drive for diversification has not been stimulated by a generation of empire builders; it has been forced by conditions in the marketplace.

What role can brand extension play? This discussion does not pretend to provide all the answers nor present new truths. Instead, it attempts to analyze "the state of the art" as it exists. What *do* we know about brand extension? What are the strengths and weaknesses in our knowledge?

FORMS OF BRAND EXTENSION

Basically there are two forms of extending the use of a brand name. The first is widely practiced and requires little consideration. Successive modification or improvement of a product is brand extension in the sense that it may prolong the life of a product that would otherwise become obsolete. Soap X becomes Improved X, then New Improved X, then New X with an additive, and so on. Some consumers may regard this as primarily an advertising gimmick. It isn't. Assuming the modification or improvement is valid, it is an effective marketing tool and is essential to keeping a brand competitive when technological advances create obsolescence for the existing product. The other form is the important one for this discussion. It concerns the application of a brand name to several products. Secondarily, it concerns the subject of *brand endorsement*—the use of a company name in marketing to endorse its products, regardless of brand.

There are at least four areas of opportunity:

1. *Proliferation.* In the process of product proliferation, brand extension comes into play automatically. New package sizes are added to a successful product line. Prestige, gift packaging is created for products like candy and toiletries. Sego Liquid Diet Food was introduced in two flavors; within a few years, the flavor variety had been increased to 24.

2. *Functional.* Another widely practiced extension is functional, related to product form or use. Wax shoe polish is extended to a liquid form, a spray, a stick; Ivory bar soap to liquid and flakes. In use, Sara Lee grows to embrace a broad line of desserts.

3. *Brand-Related.* This is the area of sharply divided opinion and practice. When brand extension is used, the application normally involves products with a similar base (evaporated milk, powdered milk, etc.) or a use relationship (batteries, tires, spark plugs, etc.) or a technical relationship (appliances, motors, turbines, aerospace, etc.).

4. *Unrelated.* These are found more commonly at the retail,

private-brand level than at the manufacturing level. Few manufacturers have attempted to market totally unrelated products with the same brand name. Retailers with private brands have. Currently, for example, it is reported that Sears, Roebuck and Company plans to de-emphasize its brands with a greater emphasis on Sears as *the* brand covering many different product lines.

It is quite apparent that the ease of extending a brand name successfully proceeds in the order of the four areas listed above. The first two—proliferation and functional extension—are very easy to accomplish. The latter—brand related and unrelated extensions—require the most careful consideration.

THE ADVANTAGES

A brand name applied to a variety of products adds to advertising impact for that name and can reduce a company's overall advertising costs. This can apply at the retail as well as the manufacturing level. Obviously, there are more advertising resources to draw upon with several identically branded products, each producing revenue for the common brand name.

In the battle for shelf space, too, the impact of an oft-repeated brand can significantly increase its point-of-purchase acceptability. A manufacturer with many product lines reduces his personnel selling costs. He gains economies in physical distribution by a greater use of carload shipments. He also is better able to gain and retain prime wholesale and retail outlets because he is reducing *their* costs and buying time and because he can afford to provide them with a more superior service. True, all this can be accomplished without brand extension. However, particularly with new products, wholesalers and retailers *tend* to accept a company's line with less resistance if it arrives with a highly successful brand which he knows will be recognized immediately by his customers. Further, in dealing with full-line product fields which contain many distinct and separate items—such as candy or lawn care products—it is advantageous to the retailer to deal with a single manufacturer and a single invoice for his full-line needs.

Seasonal dips can be corrected with the intelligent use of brand extension. Toro provides America with summer yard equipment and then extends its brand to the snow-removal field. Brand extension is an excellent way of capitalizing on market segmentation and fragmentation. An outstanding brand of dog food is extended to specialized puppy food. An outstanding brand of bird seed is extended to specialized parakeet seed.

A line of related, low-volume items, no one of which generates sufficient sales to support a brand name, in combination may produce adequate funds for advertising and promotional support of the brand. Little-known or very unusual products gain consumer acceptance because of a quality brand. There is no better example of this than Reese Finer Foods, a division of Pet Incorporated. Even in an America where there is an increasing gourmet interest in specialty foods, there is considerable doubt that a housewife would make her first-time purchase of snails or some other exotic and—to her—strange food product if it did not bear a very reputable brand, such as Reese, which already has satisfied her with quality condiments.

Fundamentally, however, the best arguments for extending a brand name are added marketing impact and reduced marketing costs.

THE TRAPS

Unfortunately there are a number of limitations or traps to be avoided. Poor decisions are made because a manufacturer is unaware of these and is overly concerned with cutting costs. He confuses *saving* money with *making* money.

Brand extension can dilute the best concept for an individual product. Pet-Ritz frozen foods faced very severe price competition, and Pet Incorporated could have introduced an economy line bearing either the Pet-Ritz brand or its endorsement. Instead, to preserve the high-quality concept, economy products with a different brand—Swiss Miss—were developed.

An outstanding brand of deodorant soap was extended to a complexion soap. Apparently consumer acceptance of the brand for deodorant purposes materially reduced its appeal for madame's complexion. In any event, the name of the latter product was changed.

The Pet formula nurser—the ultimate in convenience for formula feeding of infants—was first introduced as PET Formil with the emphasis on the well-known brand. There were several problems encountered in introductory marketing, and no one can say for certain that the Pet emphasis was one of them. However, the product managers decided that the concept of feeding with a relatively high-priced premixed formula might conflict with the concept of using Pet evaporated milk, an extremely economical infant food. Now, the brand name Formil is dominant; Pet has been reduced to an endorsement, and the product's acceptance has been increasing steadily.

Dilution of "the best concept" may be why an excellent brand of soups has not been extended with great success to ketchup, and an equally excellent brand of ketchup has not been extended with great success to soups.

Dilution of advertising effectiveness can be involved too. Mead Johnson faced this problem when it decided to market a diet supplement for gaining weight. The company's Metrecal brand had practically total national recognition, and the new product was quite similar in content to Metrecal Liquid Diet Food. But can you effectively advertise two products with the same brand name —one for losing weight, the other for gaining it? Mead Johnson said no. It markets the diet supplement with the brand name Nutriment.

Let us suppose you have a highly successful brand of toothpaste—a product created and advertised for its effectiveness in reducing cavities. You decide to go out for another part of the market, the vanity segment, concerned almost solely with the "whiteness" of their teeth. Would you apply brand extension? Probably not.

Another trap relates to the adequacy of product lines. Extending a brand name to even a slightly inadequate product can be quite harmful. A well-known brand of cake mixes was being introduced into a new market area, and the manufacturer was deeply concerned that the move might not be successful. Another well-known brand already was in that market. But the invasion was successful. Why? The invaders are convinced it was because their established rival then had some products in its total line that were not as good as the rest and were a negative influence on overall consumer acceptance of the line.

THE NEED FOR INDIVIDUAL OBJECTIVITY

Until United States business and industry accomplishes an impressive breakthrough to new knowledge in the field of brand extension, marketing management must continue the painstaking task of objectively making its brand decisions on an individual product basis. No rigid, established policy can cover all situations. Each product must be provided optimum positioning with respect to its packaging, price, channels of distribution, advertising, promotion, *and brand name*. There is no easy, blanket solution.

A flat policy will not work with time. Not long ago, male toiletries were introduced with the brand name of well-established female cosmetics. They were rejected. But the so-called feminization of the American male continues. Today he has accepted highly perfumed lotions, exotically branded. Tomorrow he might buy a feminine brand name, with the product tailored to his new attitudes. Thus a failure in brand extension today could be a success story tomorrow.

Essentially, the prime obligation of management is to *know the market*—where does this product fit, who will use it, how much will he use it, who is he, where is he, what specific appeals will reach him, and so on. Only with such knowledge at hand can an intelligent brand-name determination be made. Management also has the obligation to be critically aware of the competence of its brands—*and their competence today, not yesterday*. Reverence for past stature has no place in today's market. And by the same token, a current success cannot be extended in blind fashion.

Laura Scudder's is the leading brand of potato chips on the West Coast, and most of the division's snack food lines have been integrated under that brand. One product, Wampum corn chips, was not, and the case for integration seemed logical. Both Laura Scudder's and Wampum were successful brands, but the much larger sales of the former surely meant wider and greater consumer acceptance. It was known that Laura Scudder's had a broad appeal for all age groups, in contrast to what was felt to be Wampum's relatively narrow appeal to children. Why not gain the cost and marketing impact benefits of extension?

Fortunately the division thought the matter through; it did not make a blind, instinctive decision. Both brands were investigated carefully with consumers, and the results proved most interesting. Wampum and the little Indian featured on its packaging and in its advertising had tremendous recognition values. Consumers knew the little Indian for Wampum even without the name. Obviously it would be a serious mistake to lose or deemphasize such strong identification. At the same time, however, consumers clearly indicated that the endorsement of Laura Scudder's on Wampum packages increased its acceptance. The conclusion was to use "the best of two worlds." Do not dilute Wampum, but add Laura Scudder's.

And so it must go, on a product-by-product basis.

BRAND ENDORSEMENT

One should distinguish between the support of a well-known name and its use as a brand. Corporate endorsement of a brand is a subject apart from brand extension.

Pet became very deeply concerned with this subject in connection with the company's vigorous product diversification program. Brands with well-established equities were being acquired, and there was no question but that their names should be retained. But would the endorsement of Pet increase their acceptability? Would the association with "milk" prove a serious handicap?

Consumer research revealed a very positive equity in Pet's corporate name. Housewives reasoned that the company would not market a product that might in any way jeopardize its good reputation. However, the further removed a product area is perceived as being from the present image and standing of Pet, the less qualified Pet is seen to be in that product area. For example, baby foods were perceived as being close to the Pet image and were enthusiastically received as a potential Pet product. Pickles were regarded as distant and inconsistent; they were thoroughly rejected as a Pet product in consumers' minds.

A comparison of ratings of Pet-endorsed packages versus the same but nonendorsed packages showed the advantage of the former, but in varying degrees. Applesauce, baby foods, and a disposable diaper rated much higher in consumers' minds with a Pet endorsement. Candy and frozen pies were also scored higher; nuts only slightly higher. There was little difference, with or without endorsement, in consumer ratings for a brand of instant potatoes.

Thus, for a widely diversified manufacturer, the concept of constellations of related products comes into the picture. One constellation benefits strongly from the support of a good corporate name, and the endorsement should be emphasized. Others benefit less, and the endorsement should be treated accordingly.

As might be expected, the Pet research confirmed that brands with low consumer recognition to begin with seemed to benefit most from a national corporate endorsement. In this vein, although many of the leading grocery manufacturers use corporate endorsement for individual brands pretty much across the board, there is at least one of the top companies that does not. Yet it consistently endorses its new products during their introductory phase, apparently feeling that this is helpful in gaining initial acceptance.

Again, as with brand extension, the manner in which a corporate endorsement is handled—on packaging and in advertising and sales promotion—requires thoughtful consideration. It should support the brand rather than overwhelm it. It should be used with care, or not at all, when a company's brands are in competition with each other.

A study by a New York firm of marketing consultants indicates that manufacturers with highly regarded names should be using more rather than less emphasis on corporate endorsement in their advertising. In its study, women were asked to name the manufacturers of 25 leading products. Of the 25 brands, only 6 were identified with the correct manufacturer by as many as 20 per cent of the women.

The same women were asked: If they were pleased with a certain brand, would they be likely to buy another brand by the same manufacturer? Nearly two-thirds said yes. With manufacturers constantly broadening their lines, this suggests that the company name, as well as the brand name, carries weight.

BRANDING—A CORPORATE FUNCTION

We are doing business in an affluent, expanding economy. In the grocery industry many companies are experiencing failure with anywhere from seven to nine out of every ten new products they introduce, and yet they continue to prosper. Too often the branding process is haphazard, a combination of "moxie" and "flying by the seat of your pants," and undoubtedly contributes to the high rate of product failure.

As long as prosperity continues and our marketing mistakes can be absorbed without too much pain, perhaps branding will remain a matter of only moderate importance in the scheme of product decision-making.

But there are definite signs that point in another direction. Cost reduction has become a must for all of American industry. Its programs have been developed now for nearly every phase of corporate operations. The cost benefits of brand extension are certain to become more deeply involved in the cost-reduction spectrum at some point in the future, and thus demand more precise knowledge of branding.

There is yet another element to consider. President Lyndon B. Johnson and his National Commission on Food Marketing are raising storm flags over the widening price spread between farm and supermarket. National brands with their rather sizable advertising expenditures are coming under attack. Logical explanations are not necessarily sufficient in the political arena, and the lack of logical explanation can be even more vulnerable. An impressive rationale for when and why brand extension—with its potential economic savings—and when and why not, may become imperative.

A quarter century ago, a Department of Corporate Planning, concerned with intensive research in the fields of acquisitions, best directions for internal product development, and optimum uses for capital resources, was a rarity in American industry. For the most part, such planning was a part-time task, split among operating managers and corporate executives. Then came the days of severe acquisition indigestion, of too many wrong directions in R&D, of massive mistakes in the use of capital resources.

The result? These areas of corporate planning became a separate staff function, manned by executives and professionals who today have substantial expertise.

This is the vision of the future for branding. It will become a distinct staff specialty. It will be given the kind of in-depth research it requires. We will create guidelines; we will establish thoughtful policies based on specialized knowledge and precise facts. We will know the answers.

■

Summary

There are two basic means of extending the use of a brand name: by product modification or improvement, and by application of a brand name to two or more different products.

Four basic opportunities for brand extension exist: (a) when product package sizes and modes proliferate; (b) when product form is amplified, e.g., liquid, spray, stick, powdered deodorants; (c) when new products are developed related to the original product; and (d) when new products are unrelated to existing ones with the same brand name.

Major advantages of brand extension are added marketing and advertising impact and reduced marketing costs.

Among the dangers to be avoided are dilution of the standing of an existing product, evoking the wrong image for a new product and weakening the force of advertising.

There are no general rules for brand extension. Each situation must be examined on its own merits.

Regard corporate brand endorsement as a different marketing tool from brand extension. However, here, too, the "pros and cons" must be weighed carefully.

If for no other reason than marketing cost reduction, marketers must study branding more scientifically. Just as studies of the role of merger and acquisition, product development and optimal utilization of capital resources have become professionally executed corporate staff functions, so must branding take its place as a distinct staff specialty.

8

Product Innovation

■

Paul S. Gerot and Robert J. Keith

■

As in the case of market segmentation, the crucial importance of product innovation is so clear and so well understood that it requires no description here. Managing new products is managing the future of the business, no more and no less. Product change lies at the heart of many market strategies and is capable of application in a marvelous variety of ways. The essential prerequisite is a conception of a business that permits free scope to product change and, indeed, urgently demands ceaseless product change. The exact form and pattern of change will be conditioned by the marketing vision of the individual business. It will also obviously be affected by whether new concepts emerge from evolving technology, the marketplace, or a combination of both.

End-run candidates—and the concomitant avoidance of "me-tooism"—are evident in the development of essentially new products, such as cold water detergents, hair sprays, electric toothbrushes, low-calorie foods and beverages, sustained-release cold tablets.

Flank attacks are also possible by what might be called extra-benefit innovation, as contrasted with straight innovation. The typical example is in the use of an additive, for instance, lanolin, hexachlorophene, fluoride. The less typical example is the double-duty product; shampoos may also provide a color rinse, such as Helena Rubinstein's Wash 'n' Tint.

Product differentiation is the usual means of seeking a demonstrably exclusive selling edge. Taste, package size, and ways of using established products are the customary variations, as in orange-flavored analgesics for children, spray antiseptics, aerosol oven cleaners, liquid aspirin, mint-flavored laxatives, roll-on lipsticks, powdered deodorants, and travel-size packages of dentifrice.

To outmaneuver competition or to carve out new segments, the ultimate in products must come from a policy of deliberate obsolescence. But this policy is applied reluctantly, and as a result, change is forced on companies by bold innovators, or by new competitors who have no vested interest to preserve. P&G changed the detergent industry with the introduction of Tide synthetic detergent in 1946, and thus shortened the future of its own soap brands. Armstrong Cork Company entered the consumer field with a one-step floor cleaner and wax and had no compunctions about upsetting the established order. Gillette joined the stainless-steel razor-blade fray to protect its enormous franchise; because it was less than enthusiastic about it, the firm also demonstrated the high cost of being late.

Speaking from a large fund of personal experience, Messrs. Gerot and Keith challenge all of the conventional approaches to the subject. Accepting the axiom that new products are vital to the lifeblood of a firm, they wrestle with the questions of how best to structure a company so as to stimulate the function to its utmost effort. To illustrate their management explorations they use the case history of Funny Face, a children's powdered drink mix. It provides a fascinating guided tour through Pillsbury's corporate mind over a period of years in developing the new product, coincidentally demonstrating the application of many of the sound principles underlying the creation of products, as well as exploding a few shibboleths.

Paul S. Gerot is Chairman of the Board of Directors of the Pillsbury Company. Born on a farm near Riverside, Iowa, he attended Iowa Wesleyan Academy and College and Northwestern University. He joined Pillsbury in 1926 as a salesman and rose successively through the sales ranks. In 1951 he became Executive Vice President and in the following year he was elected President. During his presidency the company's annual sales climbed to nearly a half billion dollars, making it today one of the world's largest food companies.

Robert J. Keith is President and a member of the Board of Directors of Pillsbury. He began his service with the firm in 1935, holding progressively more important posts in merchandising, sales, and advertising. He became a Corporate Vice President in 1950, Executive Vice President in

1956, and President in 1965. Under his leadership the company's consumer products line grew from six flour-based items in 1950 to more than 100 by 1965. He played a key role in the development of cake mixes and is credited with leading Pillsbury's rapid expansion into refrigerated, fresh-dough products. In recent years he has piloted the firm's expansion into no-calorie sweeteners and presweetened drink mixes.

■

PRODUCT INNOVATION

PAUL S. GEROT
and
ROBERT J. KEITH

In February 1964, the critical path for introduction of our new Funny Face drink mix for kids showed we couldn't possibly meet an impending deadline for entry into the Tucson, Arizona, market.

So we threw out the critical path projections.

But we met our schedule in Tucson.

That's just one example of the need for inventiveness in marketing that can and should play an important role in the fashioning of a philosophy and structure of any new-products effort.

The Pillsbury consumer marketing effort is keenly interested in the development of new products. After analyzing our procedures and management principles we believe that we have gained considerable insight into how to improve our new-product development posture.

We have found that we need management innovation to bring about better new-product innovation. Among other things, we have learned that:

New-product search suffers under divisional (i.e., "job-oriented") responsibility because "the money" is in established "old" methods and in existing production for established, recognized markets.

A production-oriented person tends to think of new products in terms of existing technologies, habits, and market prejudices *that he recognizes.* His view of new-product opportunities, therefore, just isn't broad enough. What would be the possibility of one of our Scandinavian flour milling experts recognizing the trend to prepackaging for such ethnic foods as pizza and chow mein?

Maybe there *is* a "new-products type"—a creative, dynamic beaver who can twist the existing market or production capability and wring out something that didn't exist before. He's a man who can study the market trends and see in them something that matches the company's personality and its marketing vision—and then do something about it. If such a man exists he should be freed and put to work. (Unfortunately there is evidence that present management systems and techniques can't find him.)

The management and marketing tools we have now are not really flexible, sophisticated, or accurate enough to yield the kind of information needed about the market. The customer is still an enigma in his reaction even to established products. How much more unknown is his *possible* reaction to prospective new products!

When Pillsbury introduced Funny Face it was entering a brand-new product area and was facing a consumer audience it had never encountered before. The rules, theories, and requirements that we had learned to depend upon in our flour business—and in the marketing of our prepared cake mixes and refrigerated dough products—just didn't seem to do the job. We had to recognize requirements and react to new situations as we went along. This new line of products proved to be quite a classroom for us.

Funny Face has been a great success in the marketplace, so we feel that we did a pretty good job of marketing innovation. But we have also taken a close look at what we might have done differently.

After studying this new-product introduction we implemented a plan to streamline and unleash our new-product people, freeing them to generate ideas, rally assistance, and act with immediacy and certainty. As a result, our new-product innovators have a new profile. They're extrospective in viewpoint and are highly motivated to achieve some rather tough goals. But what is noteworthy is that they have been given the wherewithal to do the job.

We have taken a varied group of new-product people and separated them from direct divisional responsibility for present products. The Vice President who oversees this new group reports directly to the President. And the group has been assigned divisional status of its own—not only for new products but for all growth. You might say that this group is analyzing our corporate "personality."

The new separate arrangement provides these marketing innovators with more freedom. But it also accomplishes two other things. It gives the President a much closer contact with this all-important work. Because of his direct involvement, new-product activities now take on a corporate viewpoint. This permits more efficient use of time and people and eliminates a great deal of time lag and duplicated effort. Also, the President's interest and direct involvement automatically serve notice to the entire corporation of the importance we place on the new-product activity. We believe that this, too, will stimulate product innovation.

In addition to the—we hope—dynamic arrangement that we have described, we also have a corporate growth committee, a kind of "think group" that meets regularly to stimulate and utilize "free association" in our corporate organizational thinking. This may seem a luxury to some, as indeed it first seemed to us. We have found it very stimulating, however, and believe we may soon find it a pressing necessity as a management technique.

Just where is the company growing? This is one of the questions that our "think group" must answer. Remember that for most of its history, the Pillsbury Company was primarily a flour-milling firm. It wasn't until the post-World War II era that real product expansion began and the company became consumer-oriented. This was the beginning of our marketing vision of our business. A few years after that we saw that our flour-milling technology gave us a natural entry into the then-new business of prepared cake mixes. Later we expanded into the refrigerated-products area, and more recently into such ancillary products as frostings and gravies.

The remarkable results are apparent in your supermarket—the name Pillsbury is carried on products in a host of different display areas. But until Funny Face it was still all flour and baking. Now, with Funny Face, we have a wholly new, nonflour, nonbaking-food product. From here the company can move even more broadly into the food business. The effect of product innovation—

to the extent of our success in that field—is the most critical factor in this broad and inexorable enlarging of our marketing vision—and of our market.

Here is sort of a case history of our entry into the supermarket mainstream. In 1960 we bought the Tidy House Company, a regionally distributed brand of household laundry and cleaning products. Along with the rest of the line, we acquired Sweet*10, a synthetic sweetener used as a substitute for sugar. As part of our plans for Tidy House, we set about building the market for Sweet*10—not only through increasing the use of the basic product but also through introduction of new products.

Shortly after the acquisition we learned that some mothers used Sweet*10 along with a well-known multiflavored powdered drink mix for kids. The mix comes in fruit-colored envelopes whose contents are then mixed with water and a cup of sugar to make a drink. Sweet*10 was being substituted for the sugar by some women. This started us off on a train of thought that ran something like this:

FIRST THOUGHT: If a few women are using Sweet*10 for this purpose, maybe more women will buy the product if they learn about this use. Why not build our market by promoting this use?

SECOND THOUGHT: But we can provide even more consumer service by bringing out a pre-measured amount of Sweet*10, which would eliminate the need for measuring. Moreover, we could then position our product, in the store, right next to the drink mix as a complementary product. Our package concept might also be in an envelope, thereby showing some kind of "family" relationship.

THIRD THOUGHT: As long as we are going this far, why not go all the way? Why not put *all* the ingredients—including the flavoring—in our envelope and sell the complete product in competition? This would provide the utmost convenience. It would eliminate measuring, do away with the mess of spilled granules in mixing, and provide a sugar-free drink for those who wanted such a product.

And so we started development.

Next step was to conceive a marketing plan for this new product—along with the creation of a name. We evaluated many, including Fresh Ade, Tastee Ade, Instant Ade, and Quick Ade. Label designs all utilized the corporate "Pillsbury's" logo prominently, and the artwork generally included a pitcher of some kind—similar to the technique used by our competitor.

But all of this bothered us. In retrospect we recognize now that we were looking at the problem with blinders on. In short, we were stereotyping our new entry. But we didn't see this at the time—at least, not until after we pulled together our task force for additional brainstorming sessions.

We started out assuming we were selling a drink mix to mothers for consumption by kids. It was quickly established that we were not attempting to establish a new market but rather introducing a new drink that we hoped kids would select over our competitors.

Could we promise a better taste? For that matter, is a better taste important? The answer to the latter question was a resounding "no." We could build a better-tasting drink, but the kids liked the kind that was presently available.

Why then should kids want *our* product?

Because it's more fun!

There were actually more reasons than this, but it was a good point and it brought our whole marketing and creative plans into sharper focus. Our subsequent decision was to merchandise fun. We would be selling fun to kids. Therefore, let's approach our advertising and label development from that perspective.

On the label, instead of showing pitchers full of fruit drinks, let's use some crazy illustrations—ones which would be funny to kids.

What name to give it?

In the archives somewhere is a tape recording of one frenetic afternoon in a basement playroom in the home of an advertising account executive; a group of neighborhood children are talking—with occasional prompting by the ad man. We were trying to find a new name, and this was part of the hunt. The ad man had a supply of Pillsbury's new drink mix "X" in test envelopes complete with goofy drawings of humanized lemons, oranges, strawberries, etc. These were designed by the art director of our ad agency.

The kids were mixing and drinking the product when the ad

man asked one of the youngsters, "What would you call these packages?" The child answered, "The drinks with the funny faces."

We had our name! That's where it came from. Scout's Honor. It proved for us the old maxim that "the customer is always right."

Having focused on a basic theme, and having a novel name, we now moved toward other conclusions: If kids are the market, the Pillsbury identification isn't going to be very important. Consequently we will de-emphasize our corporate name in order to emphasize some more important elements.[1] Similarly, the name Sweet*10 would mean nothing to a ten-year-old. Therefore, let's also play this down.

These were not easy decisions. Tossing away the prestige of the Pillsbury name took some real soul-searching, and giving up the mention of Sweet*10 meant that we were moving away from our original purpose—to build our synthetic-sweetener business.

But we were looking at the problem from the manufacturer's viewpoint. We were guilty of thinking in terms of existing technologies, habits, and market prejudices. We did not—at the moment—have total marketing vision.

First exposure of the finished labels created some misgivings—at least in the minds of our top management people. The designs bore little resemblance to the usual Pillsbury label. The authors, particularly, had difficulty in accepting the designs and can recall having made suggestions to build up the "sugar-free" feature and get across better the "low calorie" story. Marketing people directly involved with the project, however, argued that kids don't need low-calorie foods, and that the benefit of a sugar-free product is important to the mother, not the child. They pointed out—again—that our direction was to sell fun.

These are just a few of the highlights of the inceptional problems we faced. We have revealed these facts, hopefully, to illustrate a mood which existed, namely, a willingness to try new and radically different creative approaches; a willingness to venture into strange areas of the marketplace—areas in which we were neophytes and the competition strong, places where the

[1] See Chapter 7 for a discussion of brand extension.

potential payoff was appealing but the risks proportionately threatening. This mood—this willingness—is of the essence in the management of innovation.

Remember an adage that used to be included in logic books, "It's too bad for the theory that fails to fit the facts"? The same can be said for "normal" procedures for the development of a new product. Generally there is need of an orderly process which normally requires a number of sequential actions. Usually data should be available at numerous checkpoints along the way as a basis for sound decisions. However, these standard procedures can't tell you such things as how to shorten lead time, achieve target dates, or utilize somewhat unorthodox procedures somewhere along the way.

Funny Face *had* to make the market when it did (the six-month summer sales period accounted for 72 per cent of sales for the competitor).

In a case like this, innovation is the key. A great deal of inventiveness and initiative had to be brought into play for Funny Face during the last few weeks before its test-market introduction. Here is an example of what we mean by the mood of willingness being vital to marketing innovation.

One of our more knotty problems had to do with perfecting a particular engineering process for instantizing the mix. The need was to produce a product that would instantly go into solution in cold water. Now, our company has such a process—agglomeration. It is patented, licensed to others, and really quite remarkable. Our process engineers said that agglomeration would solve the Funny Face problem of instantizing in a cold-water solution. They said that they could perfect the process for our formula in time to manufacture test-market quantities.

Their development work ran into one failure after another, and though they were learning from each defeat, the production start-up date was getting perilously close. Eventually they achieved a successful product in the pilot plant. But there was no time left to adapt the process to a regular production unit!

Ordinarily it would require months to build the unit and train the personnel. Once again imagination and dedication came to the fore. The engineers dismantled the pilot plant agglomerator in Minneapolis and moved it to their laboratory in Omaha—all in the space of five days (including two days over a weekend to truck the machinery 400 miles).

Once the machine was rebuilt, in Omaha, there were only two people who actually understood how to work it. Those two—a process engineer and a production engineer—spent the next week shaking down the equipment. During this time they worked 20 hours a day, catching occasional cat naps in their car.

Well, they made it, but during that last week before the test market, the week of February 10, they were still manufacturing the final flavor. On Friday of that week, February 14, they hadn't finished production, and it was absolutely necessary to have a quantity of product in Tucson Monday morning, February 17.

Then another innovation. Our people decided that we ought to carry the product to Tucson by personal car—to make sure that air freight schedules wouldn't kill us (an airport error could have put us behind a full day, or even two).

On Friday afternoon, February 14, one of our managers had special shock absorbers installed on his station wagon and headed off from Minneapolis. Saturday morning he was at the Omaha plant, but had to wait until noon before he could get the final run off the line. Thirty-six hours later, in the dark of night, he arrived in Tucson. We started our test market on schedule the next morning, Monday, February 17.

Ever since, the slogan "driving to Tucson" has had special significance around our place. Underlying the fun is a lot of camaraderie and a lot of respect for the total effort the trip to Tucson represented. The "journey" obviously was longer than just from Minneapolis to Tucson. It's still going on.

Now, the point is not that Pillsbury has particularly devoted or industrious managers and production people (though we have), but rather to illustrate what we meant by the mood of willingness—the key to innovation. Funny Face had involved moving production facilities, self-delivering product, avoiding corporate symbols in labeling and advertising for the first time, and even changing our original marketing concepts for the product.

Commercialization of any consumer product requires leadership which can create such dedication and solicit innovation. But lifting of restrictions to find a new way also plays a part.

Was it the lifting of restrictions that led our advertising people to forcefully bid just that extra "once more" for the distinctive nonstandard product identification—the one extra time that overcame corporate reluctance and established a whole new excitement about the product . . . for the customer as well as for us?

Wasn't it the satisfaction of defining a new technique which impelled production people to work 20 hours a day in order to make the market that particular summer, rather than next?

The past few years have seen an awesome example of innovation and alertness in the food marketing field—namely, the development of the liquid dietary market. Incidentally, Pillsbury completely missed this market—once estimated to be $200-million a year—in a classic example of lack of marketing vision.

Several years ago our laboratory developed a highly nutritional drink product. We tested this among consumers as a "breakfast in a glass." Throughout numerous consumer tests our product failed to meet our standard of acceptance, and we eventually put the product back on the shelf—preferring to pursue "more promising" ideas. About one year later the Mead Johnson people introduced practically the same product concept—as Metrecal.

Mead Johnson and Company found the product so successful that it established a separate division—the Edward Dalton Company—to market and develop Metrecal and take further advantage of the skyrocketing dietary foods potential. The fact that over 100 competitors tried to catch up with Metrecal in a sort of "me-too" effort, is testimony to the size of the market. During the height of the Metrecal rise, we're told, the Midwestern pharmaceutical firm's profits doubled—and we had shortsightedly put practically the same item back on the shelf to gather dust! The fact that we were like a lot of other companies who had the technology but not the innovative marketing sense did not make it any easier to accept the lesson.

We failed to have sufficient marketing vision because, at that time, our methods of thinking about new products were too systematized. But since then we stay much more alert to the conceptual potential of what we develop.

It was not very long ago that our research on a new product emphasized testing against some established product. Since we didn't understand the dynamics of market segmentation we used to set some pretty high standards of acceptance. Development of cake mixes is an example.

When Pillsbury was looking at a new flavor of cake, we frequently tested against a known flavor which was used as a bench mark. If the new product was not preferred over the control product by a significant degree the new idea was generally dropped. Fortunately we have since learned that a new product does not necessarily have to be preferred by a major element of the market. Often there is a small—but significant—group which will want the new product for reasons of price, convenience, and what have you. This group can represent a very sizable marketing opportunity.

It is painful to think of the opportunities that have possibly been lost through lack of understanding of this phenomenon. Metrecal is an example of utilizing the proper creative concept—a classic example of marketing innovation.

There is so much intangible human speculation in product development. (We can't help but note that how a man thinks of himself and his company has much to do with the production of his mind.) A well-defined product concept is so important—often more so than even physical characteristics. Upon it depends a company's ability to be successful in the marketplace.

But the techniques of evaluation—the tools which we use in managing product development—are still back in the flint age of marketing. This doesn't mean that the available tools aren't useful, but only in rare instances can they provide absolute, incontrovertible data for decisions. They can always be useful if we understand their weaknesses and use them intelligently.

It is for reasons such as this that we believe marketing is still more an art than a science. This is even more evident in the area of new products, simply because our knowledge there is always relatively less perfect. This leads us back to our original point—the importance of the human element in product development.

If our technical knowledge and ability are similar, where else can we have an advantage except in our people—our human resources? Such things as the ability to transfer something learned in one situation to a totally new situation, or being able to see the same facts but in a different light—this is how a company uncovers a different market segment (as in Metrecal and cake mixes) or a product innovation (as in Funny Face).

The talent to draw together conceptual relationships from physically unrelated situations is more or less important in all human activity. In corporate management it is most important—and in product innovation, it is of the essence. Consequently, if we are to gain,

. . . we must give our new-products people more freedom, fewer systems, fewer confusing traditions. (Someone once aptly said that "tradition is often nothing more than a bad habit that's been perpetuated.")

. . . we must make full use of all the tools of marketing that now exist and do what we can to increase their accuracy and flexibility.

. . . we must understand and be able to recognize change in our market and our customer.

. . . we must be able and ready to innovate.

If there is a personnel profile for the new-products man—for the innovator—we believe that it would be made up of such things as:

intimate knowledge of the tools of marketing;

willingness to take calculated risks;

ability to listen and keep an open mind;

determination to cut and go once the decision is made;

ability to stimulate others and get and keep them interested in the problem;

the intellectual acuity to expand perspective, to generate ideas, to deal with constant change and confusion, to synthesize.

Obviously it is difficult to find all of these talents in one person. But by creating a separate new-products organization and by carefully selecting our people, it is possible to assemble a well-balanced distribution of these characteristics within one group.

We have found that one of the toughest aspects of the new-product job is not what to put *into* the product development stream, but rather what to throw out. And often it is necessary to "kill" a new-product idea—from an economic, market, or conceptual standpoint. It is fairly easy to stimulate new-product ideas. The difficulty begins with the selection process—deciding which ones to go with. But sometimes another step is necessary—"ideacide." Killing off a product idea is often as important as generating them. Our company, like others, has occasionally been "hooked" on ideas that were for us, finally, unworkable.

We try to structure our new-product development toward several distinct goals. Our new products must have a market segment that allows the best profit-use of our production, marketing, and sales resources. Their concepts must be intriguing—to others as well as ourselves. Their concepts must include strong product differentiation in order to generate consumer attention and desire without unnecessarily high advertising and promotion expenditures. Finally, our products must have what some of our people have begun to call "positional exclusivity"—they must have something that makes them uniquely "ours."

We have a good example of this "exclusivity" in Funny Face. The concept of this product—aimed as it is at a particular segment of the market—is peculiarly "ours." Funny Face has a fully-developed "personality" that extends right through its advertising, packaging, and consumption phases.

Product innovation activity can never really be finalized, for there is a constant need to update and to revitalize. Certainly each successful new product developed broadens the scope of the operation, for it materially enhances the company's ability to develop still other new products. Each innovation subsequently becomes a "grandfather" for later products marketed.

At the moment we are in the midst of progress and haven't yet managed to chronicle how goals should be set and how marketing tools could be expanded—or even how to make the very best use of marketing innovation. We have learned, however, to have on hand, when and as (and if) needed, a product which suits the company from all angles, well in advance of the company's ability to use it and promote it.

This means that we must take a broad look at everything that comes our way; that we must use every means possible to survey the field (and we're constantly redefining the field we're in). We have found that it is not only flour and baking; it's food. Is it broader than that?

Perhaps!

■

Summary

Because of the vital role of new-product development in insuring the health of a company's future, it is essential to organize a company so as to permit this function to flourish. Separate status within the corporation, reporting to the President, is found superior to leaving this responsibility solely with operating divisions, typically preoccupied with today's concerns.

Beyond organization, a certain psychology must prevail to stimulate product innovation: an "experimental spirit," a willingness to try radically different approaches, and the courage to venture into new areas of the marketplace. Care must be taken that the orderly, logical, step-by-step process of product development does not suffocate what it is designed to nurture.

Successful product development utilizes several basic principles:

1. Build a "competitive edge" into the product. Answer the question: Why should someone use my new product instead of others?
2. The new entry should represent the conclusion of a harmonious dialogue between the laboratory and the marketplace.
3. A product *concept* should dictate its physical characteristics.
4. A new idea doesn't have to appeal to everyone to be a success; even small market segments can provide profitable opportunities.

The human equation is a key factor. The ideal profile for a product innovator should embrace deep marketing knowledge, willingness to take risks, openmindedness, ability to generate ideas, stimulate others, cope with constant confusion and change, synthesize, act decisively. Since this is admittedly a tough bill to fill in one person, these qualities should be embodied in the new-products task force.

9

International Expansion

■

George Weissman

■

Not only can the definition of a business be product-based, saying, "We are in the railroad industry, not the transportation industry," or conceptual in foundation, believing, "The strength of our company lies in the skillful use of media of communication rather than in our experience in this or that segment of the food trade," but the definition may also be geographic. Therefore, the vision of a business can also be liberating in this respect. Most American companies have, until recently, regarded themselves as serving the American market. The foreign market was truly foreign to their thoughts.

In contrast, companies that have the vision to see both the vast potential of the world market for basic goods and their own role in supplying it have profited enormously. Traditionally, American companies have regarded overseas markets as dumping grounds for excess or substandard production. Today the most wide-awake firms think of themselves as international rather than as United States firms that happen also to sell abroad. As William O. Beers, President of Kraft Foods Division of National Dairy Products Company, put it, "It is our goal to make Kraft an international company, rather than a company with an international division." *

Now the march of American firms overseas, especially to Europe, has broken into a run. Scarcely a week passes without another company announcing that it is buying into a European firm, setting up an affiliate, or building a plant. One of the American industries which has long recognized foreign opportunities is tobacco. Cigarette manufacturers, operating in saturated markets, did not want their growth tied to the population curve. Among the majors, Philip Morris has been a real leader in sophisticated international marketing, using every conceivable method to penetrate even the most difficult markets. Indeed, the marketing vision of Philip Morris International is constructed of two elements intertwined —*an energetic, flexible global approach to mass merchandising consumer-packaged goods.*

The author of this chapter is therefore particularly well equipped to detail the value of and sound approaches to global marketing, with many examples out of his own experience. George Weissman, as Chairman of the Board and President of Philip Morris International and Executive Vice President of Philip Morris Inc., was responsible for the direction of the company's international arm, which markets its products in over 150 countries and territories around the world. Mr. Weissman joined Philip Morris in 1952 as Assistant to the President and Director of Public Relations.

In January 1953 he was elected Vice President and was active in the company's public relations, packaging, new-products operations, and marketing. He was appointed Vice President and Director of Marketing in May 1957 and in December 1958 became a Director of the company. In November 1959 he was appointed Executive Vice President of Philip Morris Inc., and in October 1960 he assumed additional duties as Chairman of the Board and Chief Executive Officer of Philip Morris International. In September 1964 he also assumed the duties as President of Philip Morris International. Mr. Weissman became a member of the Executive Committee of Philip Morris Inc., in 1964, and was elected President in January 1967.

* *Advertising Age,* February 3, 1966, p. 3.

■

INTERNATIONAL EXPANSION

GEORGE WEISSMAN

The subject of international expansion cannot be limited to marketing concepts, strategies, and techniques. For the marketer to go international, he must have the proper organizational structure, or framework, for his activities. If he is given complete corporate responsibility for acting internationally, he must create this structure. If this basic framework is not established, the fundamental marketing procedures can well be, like Alice, lost in a wonderland of bitter experience. With the proper marketing-oriented structure, followed by the proper applications of concepts, strategies, and techniques, the world is the limit.

If Atlantis were to rise from the sea, intact and fully populated, the chances are that its first visitors would be market research teams from today's internationally-minded corporations.

For if there is any single characteristic that global companies have in common, it is their absolute *compulsion* to ferret out new markets in the farthest corners of the world. Today, as greater mobility and faster communications produce dizzying economic explosions even in the underdeveloped areas, this international scent for sales is opening up exciting new frontiers for thousands of corporations. Literally, it is changing the character and the thrust of much of our business life.

International marketing is, of course, as old as civilization. As long as men have been able to travel, they have embarked upon searches for the treasures of the world. Some found them, some did not. But the potential has always been there. And today the treasures are richer than ever before.

Billions of consumers. Unfulfilled needs. Rising levels of desire. Economies on the upswing. Entire populations moving from country to city. From earth-movers to airplanes, from kitchen sinks to submarines, from lingerie to light bulbs—the opportunities are awe-inspiring!

Yet, in terms of being able to reach out for this solid-gold ring, it is not enough to simply tick off the potential. Is the potential there for everyone? Do different companies have different potentials in different areas? How does one go about finding out? How does a company organize itself to act on what it knows?

GETTING STARTED

There are roughly 20,000 American companies known to be currently engaged in overseas sales in one form or another. Most of them are exporting. Others are licensing their products for local manufacture. A growing number have established subsidiary or joint-venture manufacturing facilities. Still others engage in all of these activities simultaneously.

Our own organization, Philip Morris International, is an example of the latter. Philip Morris' global business started as a simple export operation in the 1850s. At first it was more or less an "order-taker." Our cigarettes had been known in England, where our company began over a century ago, and gradually became known in many other parts of the world. As demand increased, we filled more and more export orders. This gave us a glimpse of the potential, which we then began to pursue more aggressively.

Perhaps it would have been less complicated (though far less exciting) if we could have continued exporting everywhere. However, tariffs, economic associations, world trade conditions, and market tastes and preferences made this impossible on a world-wide basis following World War II. To keep from losing what we had gained and to continue to grow overseas, we had to find ways to make ourselves more flexible.

As a consequence, we were virtually "forced" to expand, and adopted whichever administrative or financial arrangement made possible the greatest sales.

The result has been that Philip Morris Inc. became the largest United States tobacco company in the international cigarette business. Today its world-wide arm, Philip Morris International, reaches all areas outside of the United States. There are affiliated manufacturing and marketing companies in Australia, Argentina, Belgium, the United Kingdom, Guatemala, Nigeria, Switzerland, Venezuela, and Canada, and licensees for major brands in Austria, Benelux, Finland, France, Germany, Hong Kong, India, Italy, New Zealand, Panama, and the Philippines. And we still export directly to more than 150 countries and territories from the United States and from our overseas manufacturing centers.

Yet, as recently as 1955, when we had grown to a sales volume in excess of $350-million annually, 95 per cent of dollar sales were still within the United States market. The remainder represented exports to all other countries. Ten years later, total operating revenues of Philip Morris as a whole had doubled, but the portion derived from international marketing had better than sextupled over its 1955 dollar contribution to sales.

The transition from export order-taking to world-wide marketing may have begun slowly, but it continues to gather momentum. In the future Philip Morris will undoubtedly focus even greater attention on international markets. One of the reasons is that unit sales of cigarettes in the United States market are just over 500 billion annually, while sales elsewhere in the free world approximate 1,250 billion.

While annual per capita cigarette usage in the United States is higher (2,600 compared with 640 in the free world), per capita usage is increasing faster abroad. If the United States per capita consumption rate is attained throughout the free world, there then exists a potential overseas market more than ten times the size of the United States.

A further incentive is the world's swing to United States type of cigarettes. For example, 50 per cent of the Swiss cigarette market is now smoking United States type cigarettes, compared with less than 5 per cent when Philip Morris International first started manufacturing Marlboro in Switzerland in 1957.

In getting our feet wet internationally, we had one advantage over at least some other companies: we *knew* we were exporting. We had our own export department. We knew the countries we shipped to and who our customers were. Strange as it seems, many companies don't have this basic information about their own operations—a problem that has plagued the United States Department of Commerce in its efforts to arrive at an accurate figure of the number of United States exporters. The Department believes that products made by thousands of United States concerns find their way into overseas markets through no effort of the manufacturer. Often manufacturers sell not to their ultimate customers but to domestically-based exporters. The transaction is thus no different from one involving, say, a seller in Pittsburgh and a buyer in Chicago.

So, for many United States companies, discovering the final destination of "hidden" export sales can be an important beginning for a more ambitious expansion of international business. A consistent history of export orders from a given area is, of course, a pretty reliable indication of an even larger potential market.

RESEARCHING THE MARKETS

Identifying potential overseas markets can be tackled in many other ways. Here are some examples.

1. You can start with a totally gross look at your kind of product in relation to the entire world. In which countries is your type of product in use now? Is there a genuine need? Can a need be created? How much is being bought? How does this compare with, say, five years earlier? The United States Departments of Commerce and Agriculture can supply many of the statistics through the Bureau of International Commerce, the Business and Defense Services Administration, the Foreign Agricultural Service, and the commercial officers at United States embassies and consulates abroad.

2. Once you've zeroed in on potential markets, you will want to make your assessment from three vantage points: first, a look at each market as a whole; second, an evaluation of how your product might perform in each market; third, an inventory of legal, tax, and other factors that may affect how you enter the market or how much you will be able to sell.

These are some of the indices you will want to look for in studying the market as a whole:

population
wages
income per family
disposable income

retail sales
currency and exchange
imports versus local production
climate and topography
government
gross national product
exports
literacy
birth rate
infant and adult mortality
paved highways
airlines and airports
railroad and truck lines
ports and shipping facilities
power supply

To be useful, these data should be obtained on a comparative basis with a previous period.

A given area as a potential showcase for your particular product will then need to be examined with these points in mind:

consumption of similar goods by volume and value over a five-year period
trends in local production of similar goods
potential sales forecast over coming five-year period
competitive products, pricing, share of market, history
trade discounts, advertising allowances, etc.
retail and wholesale price structure
known distributors, agents, retailers, etc.
distribution channels used by competing products; caliber and nature of sales force, wages
import regulations: tariffs, quotas, etc.
availability of dollar exchange
packing requirements; documentation needed
availability and cost of transportation and warehousing
credit
consumer preference among competing products
number of wholesale and retail outlets available
availability of advertising and promotion assistance
government attitudes toward foreign capital investment

Finally, you will need to look subjectively at what you have learned in terms of your own company's ability to satisfy the demands of the market.

(a) How well does your product stack up against the competition?

(b) Does your product have advantages that are promotable in terms of local tastes and needs?

(c) Does your product need to be modified in terms of technical specifications, styling, packaging, etc.?

(d) Can you price to meet established competition?

(e) Do you have enough experienced executive talent available to "live with" the new market for as much time as it takes to get a foothold?

(f) Can you support an advertising and promotion program on a long-term basis?

(g) Is the potential really good enough to justify your patience and money? Can you make a projection for a break-even point? And is your top management prepared to sit it out until then?

While gross market information is generally available from secondary sources through government and other agencies, most experienced international marketers are reluctant to depend upon it exclusively. Other avenues of assistance include:

1. *Market research firms:* Reputable consulting companies are established in all industrialized countries and may be retained for a fee.

2. *Advertising and public-relations agencies:* Most American agencies established abroad engage in market and product research in behalf of their clients. A number of overseas countries have well-developed indigenous advertising and public relations industries, and market research is becoming an increasingly prevalent technique among these.

3. *A firsthand survey by an individual familiar with both the target market and your product:* This is essential. It serves to corroborate and reinforce marketing data obtained through other sources and can save your company from making costly errors in its all-important initial efforts.

The object of all this research, of course, is to help to insure that your entry into a particular market will be correct and effective.

No company wishes to repeat the experiences of an American poultry co-op which wanted to export turkeys to Europe. They put on a big promotion in Germany a few years back pegged to roasting whole turkeys. The birds cooked to a turn in the large, shiny American appliances brought along for the demonstrations. But there were some pretty red faces when the sponsors found that no amount of ballyhoo would make those big American turkeys fit into those little German ovens found in the average German home.

Organizations that regard basic market-evaluation techniques as essential domestically cannot afford to ignore this tool internationally—although too many still do.

ENTERING THE NEW MARKET

Once you've determined that a particular market holds potential for your product, still other questions must be answered: "How should we begin to penetrate the market? Can we export? Must we license? Should we manufacture? If so, should we find local partners or go it alone?"

Some of these questions will be answered by thorough market research. For example, you should be able to project whether, in a given area, your product will have strong enough appeal to be sold successfully at a price that includes high tariff or other costs.

Philip Morris has had considerable experience in this area, and our judgment is that price is simply one of many determinants of purchase—and not necessarily always the most important. We want the price to be right of course; but that doesn't necessarily mean lowest. By all means let it be lowest when it can. But in certain areas where, for reasons such as tariffs and high taxes, Philip Morris cigarettes sell for twice as much as local brands, our sales still go up nicely.

The price is an important part of the image. The sale can still be made if we give special attention to building a not-very-secret, but very special, ingredient into the product. The ingredient is quality. Let us give all due attention to efficiency and productivity and salesmanship. But let's make sure that when we tuck the whole thing in, we add the image of quality too. The customer with money is the goal, and he sets his own criteria.

Your choice of market entry may be dictated by factors other than price. Investment law is an example. Many countries have made it a matter of national policy to resist or limit the incursions of foreign capital. Some strictly forbid investment. Licensing is a traditional response. Many more specify that majority control must rest with local nationals. The joint venture is a means of complying with this restriction. And even where local law permits or encourages wholly owned foreign subsidiaries, many companies have found it wise to team up with established companies in their fields.

McKesson & Robbins, for example, enters into 50-50 partnerships with established pharmaceutical houses in Latin America to handle the distribution of its products. The resulting new company then frequently creates a wholly owned subsidiary, which is licensed by the joint-venture organization to manufacture the company's products under license.

In the tobacco industry both joint ventures and establishment of wholly owned subsidiaries are foreclosed in many areas. These are the countries in which governments have created a state monopoly to handle all tobacco affairs.

If tariffs, quotas, and currency exchanges permit, we can export to these markets. As it is not possible for us to manufacture locally within a monopoly country, we have entered into licensing agreements wherein our brands are manufactured by the monopolies, such as in France, Italy, and Austria, and the cigarettes are then sold at prices lower than if the brands were imported into that country.

In some cases there is reciprocity, such as in the manufacture in France of our Marlboro and Parliament brands, with Philip Morris Inc. manufacturing Gauloises and Gauloises Filtre Disque Bleu, two of France's most popular cigarettes, in our United States factories for distribution and sale within the United States.

Another example of flexibility is the marketing of our Marlboro cigarettes in Sweden. The Marlboros are made in the factory of our Swiss affiliate, FTR, and, as both countries are European Free Trade Association members, many of the conditions of direct export entry from a non-EFTA country are eliminated.

Most companies feel that licensing offers little potential. To many it is tantamount to exporting know-how without the full return that direct product sales offer. Yet it is a fact of international life that this is frequently the only road open. Moreover, many American companies which went the licensing route in years past are now beginning to find that the technology they exported is being returned to them. The licensees are improving the performance of the licensor.

J. H. Singer, President of Minneapolis-Honeywell Regulator Company, put it this way: "For the first time, we are becoming aware of a 'Japanese taste' and a 'German taste' in technical products, where formerly the United States design had been the international standard. It is apparent that products which have met success at home will no longer necessarily enjoy the same reception overseas."

What should your company know about its prospective overseas partners, be they licensees or joint venturers? This checklist was developed by Frank Montgomery Dunbaugh, Associate Professor of Marketing at the University of Miami.

A. Character.

1. General reputation: Consider the nationwide reputation of your prospective licensee, his local reputation, his standing with the United States representative, his standing in the trade, his reputation with suppliers or other licensors, and his relation to the local competition.

2. Standing in your particular field: Experience, manufacturer of quality products, share of market, ability to secure qualified technical personnel.

3. Connections with the United States and experience in the United States: Both are desirable, especially if licensee will be asked to adopt American methods of manufacture and promotion.

4. Licensee's outlook on business and the future in general.

5. Licensee's attitude during negotiations: Is he acting in good faith? Can you rely on his adhering to the terms of the agreement or must you expect requests for changes?

B. Capability.

1. Organization: Check corporate setup and ownership, ascertain the type of organization. When was it founded? Under

what laws? What are its functions? What is its long-term growth? Its personnel policies? Its labor history? Its record of executive development? Its compensation policies? Is there a danger of nepotism?

2. Location: Is the headquarters centrally located and easily accessible?

3. Government procedures: Is licensee familiar with intricate machinery of government which may facilitate the obtaining of import licenses? Could he count on protection from importation of competitive products once he is in production?

4. Financial participation: Your choice of the licensee may be influenced by the possibility of eventually acquiring an equity interest.

5. Management and supervising personnel:

(a) Name, title, investment in company, responsibilities, ability, age, background.

(b) Reputation—are you dealing with capable businessmen? Do you believe they are honest? Are they known for clean dealings?

(c) Who will be responsible for licensee operations? Is he qualified and able?

6. Selling organization: Physical setup, showrooms, departmental activity, number of salesmen or detailmen; how well they are trained; number of prospective salesmen for licensee department. How will territory be covered? Through branches or distributors? How many are there and where? List other lines handled by prospective licensee, names and addresses of suppliers or licensors. What are the annual sales by lines? Is there a sufficiently large warehouse? What is your opinion of the selling organization and the ability of its staff? What reputation has the company for service?

7. Technical setup: Ascertain details of technical facilities and technical organization, machinery, and equipment. Where are the manufacturing facilities? Is there enough land for expansion?

8. Forecast: What are the prospective sales in your line? What special plans are there for your line? Are these plans adequate? How high would first order be? Try to obtain forecast for first three years of operation.

C. Capital.

1. How high is the capital? Is it fully paid in? How much is unpaid? What are the specific regulations for payment of subscribed capital? What are the firm's statutes? What happens in case of death of owner or partners?

2. Who is the treasurer? Does he carry his weight? What are the firm's credit policies? What are its purchasing policies?

3. Is capital sufficient if your line is added? What additional capital can be injected and how? Will prospective licensee be able to obtain bank loans?

4. Secure local bank's opinion on present financial position. Obtain names of banks doing business with firm. What types of accommodations do banks grant the firm? Get names of local creditors doing business with firm and obtain their opinion on honesty and ability. What are their experiences?

5. Try to obtain balance sheet and profit-and-loss statements for the last three years. What does balance sheet show as to (a) amount of current assets (cash receivables, inventories); (b) current liabilities (anything due or payable within the next twelve months); (c) difference—net working capital; (d) land, buildings, deferred liabilities?

6. Do owners have resources of their own outside the business? What and how much are these resources? Are they available to business if more capital is needed?

STAFFING FOR INTERNATIONAL SALES

In Laos one does not cross one's legs. In Moslem countries an arm must not be placed around one's wife. In France business is never discussed during the luncheon entree; Danes accept the business luncheon as routine. Greeks consume endless cups of coffee during business discussions. The Japanese often fall silent for half an hour or more during negotiations. Throughout Asia one must not come too physically close to a business acquaintance. In Latin America business and social lives are generally kept quite separate.

These are just a few of the thousands upon thousands of tastes and customs and "peculiarities" that the international company executive meets in his travels from country to country. Obviously no executive can know all of them. But what he must know is that each country—often each area within a country—has its own ways of getting things done. He must have a broad sensitivity to the mores of other peoples. He must have enough respect for them and enough interest in them to want to brief himself thoroughly before he visits each particular area. And, most important of all, he must rid himself of any feelings he may have that "the American way" is the best way.

He must know, as an old friend once commented, that "what sells soap in Cleveland won't necessarily wash in Calcutta." Then he must go one step farther. He must also know that what wows 'em in Calcutta could lay an egg in Costa Rica!

Finding international executives with the experience and the sensitivity to avoid bloopers like that one is not a simple task. Yet no corporate decision is more important. It is far more critical than developing the "perfect" organizational chart for international operations.

There is, in fact, no "perfect" organization. There are only more or less flexible ones. The more flexible ones perfect themselves as they change to meet changing marketing conditions. The best of them are good because they never stay the same very long.

Our current Philip Morris International structure, which is not unusual, has four regional vice presidents, each responsible for a specific area—Canada, Europe, Pacific, and Latin America. Areas without regional vice president supervision report directly to our central headquarters. An old adage may well be considered here: "Line authority begins with the bottom line of an operating statement." In addition to the direct line functions, we provide special technical and support functions, backed by the extensive manufacturing, finance, marketing, and research facilities of Philip Morris Inc.

Once the international operation is formed, it must find a home. Actually, its precise, physical location is not too important. It must be based where there is an ease of two-way communication, including that heavily trafficked international airfield.

The site should have as its basic currency one that is in the desired classification around the world, facilities for information concerning your areas of interest, and the technical support that is required to maintain the needs of the organization and its affiliates. And it is highly desired that the host nation have policies that permit, and preferably encourage, corporations to venture outside national boundaries. Philip Morris International is located in New York, but it could function just as well from many other cities around the world.

Staffing of the international headquarters is a special problem. The international-minded individual should be hand picked for each of the required specialties, and the search for personnel should not be limited to the country of corporate origin. Technical qualifications, linguistic ability, specific backgrounds for specific areas, and personal adaptability must all be taken into consideration, as should the specific needs in the individual areas of the planned operations.

The structural organization of the multinational corporation varies from situation to situation to some degree. However, one factor should remain constant. That is, to organize internationally in such a way as to provide the greatest flexibility and local control and at the same time maintain coordination and control from the headquarters.

The organization chart for each market will differ substantially depending upon whether that country has a wholly owned affiliate, an arrangement with local partners, licensing agreements, or distributorships for direct export sales.

There is an almost infinite variety of distribution arrangements a company can make abroad. Most companies doing business multinationally have several different kinds, for the choice is often dictated by the particular way in which the market is being entered.

If you are licensing, your licensee may have his own sales and distribution organization. If you enter into a joint venture, you will perhaps "inherit" a sales force which, as a good partner, you will work to improve.

Going the export route involves other considerations. You will need agents to represent you, and these may be fully in your employ or may represent you as one of several noncompetitive companies. The selection of agents and distributors should be considered one of the most critical stages of going international. In markets of any importance it should be done by personal interview preceded by thorough field investigation. Most large companies utilize a variety of arrangements, including full-time salaried representatives, import agents, exclusive and nonexclusive wholesalers, their own sales offices, and so forth.

In the parlance of world trade organization, Philip Morris operates in a semidecentralized manner. Local units abroad enjoy a great degree of autonomy. Our manufacturing affiliates, for example, each have their own profit responsibility.

Some companies go further toward one extreme or the other. IBM, for example, sets up completely autonomous companies abroad. The Singer Company maintains fairly tight home-office supervision over its thousands of employees in Singer shops around the world. The company also utilizes the services of dealers and distributors, a few "free agents," who work solely on commission, and some merchants who buy directly from Singer at better-than-wholesale prices and resell directly to the public. National Biscuit Company has developed a network of wholly owned subsidiaries working in conjunction with its own sales organization. Caterpillar Tractor goes the route of full-time resident representatives in each country who appoint and work with exclusive authorized dealers.

So, again, you cut the cloth to fit the pocket. But however you cut it, your ultimate success will be through people as well as products.

At Philip Morris we have stringently followed the policy that local nationals, who are experts in their own field, should be employed or trained in their own countries whenever possible and that specialists from the United States should be used only to provide special technical and management advice which the company feels necessary to the maintenance of its quality performance. Our affiliate organization around the world attests to our adherence to the policy. Less than 1 per cent of all employees in our affiliated companies at overseas locations are from the United States.

Companies that have attempted to manage abroad with personnel from their domestic operations being in complete control have sometimes met with drastic failure. One major United States corporation, for example, acquired a company in Germany a few years back when that firm's products were a substantial factor in the German market. American management, without full knowledge of the market and of the cultural characteristics of the people, was installed. Today the company has lost almost 75 per cent of its former share of the market. A hard lesson, in any currency!

LEGAL AND FINANCIAL CONSIDERATIONS

Throughout the formation of an international operation there are two considerations which are thoroughly entwined with all others: legal aspects and financing. Unlike the average airline passenger, who has little or no knowledge of the theory of flight, the average foreign marketer cannot conduct his business with only a minimal understanding of the legal aspects of international trade, nor can he leave legal matters entirely to his lawyers. The complexities of trademark maintenance in counrties around the world, coupled with varying tax laws, pricing, and economic agreements between countries or among blocs of countries, make it mandatory for the competent international marketer not only to receive sound legal advice but also to familiarize himself with at least the basic fundamentals of the laws of the nations where he is operating.

In addition to the contractual arrangements that are entered into, there is often an interplay of laws among nations which is vital to the development of maximum financial return. The use of companies created in third countries, as well as industrial promotion statutes, can lead to additional complexities.

There are also new legal concepts constantly coming into play, such as the Distributor's Bill of Rights in Puerto Rico, Germany, and other countries. This concept concerns the distributor's claim to a monetary value being placed upon his total efforts for aiding in the development of a trade mark within his area. This can present problems when it is desired to change or terminate existing arrangements. Exclusive franchises in some areas are also receiving rough sledding as governments form economic agreements to develop trading areas. These national agreements may open to a rival what was given as an exclusive territory to another, with underselling and other problems being based upon a newly acquired national right. Legal misunderstandings and disputes, whether brought to court or not, may destroy a profitable relationship developed at great expense.

Restrictions of any type on a marketplace may temporarily whittle away portions; what remains is the market to be explored.

The field of finance is also closely enmeshed with all activities. It ranges from the traditional letters of credit to obtaining funds for factory construction in widely separated areas. All of the varying national regulations, and in some cases prohibitions, are involved. The balance-of-payments situation in the United States, too, can change plans, depending upon the influences that are exerted to limit or allow the use of dollars abroad. Participation in your financial activities abroad by the people of a nation where you are building can have the same benefits it does in the United States.

In essence, whether you are enlarging a factory at home to provide for an increased export volume, or you are creating a new establishment abroad, you must be capable of adapting to the financial requirements of the area involving your activity.

DEVELOPING MARKETING STRATEGY

Marketing begins with a point of view. This is no less true abroad than it is at home. If a company thinks of its international trade as "surplus dumping" it will project that image. If, on the other hand, it is genuinely concerned with pleasing its new customers, it will take steps to understand how and what to communicate to them.

Marketing strategy has its roots in several areas: how the marketer sees his own company; what market research has told him about consumer demand and consumer preference; the approaches currently being made by the competition. All of these factors will weigh heavily in the choice of image to project, how to project it, and to whom to project it.

Most international "giants" maintain a basic quality theme in their marketing which has established many United States products in the forefront of the world's marketplace. Coca-Cola and Pepsi-Cola are outstanding exponents of this philosophy of unchanging quality throughout the world. Chemstrand, which has successfully marketed its Acrilan fiber on a global basis, has maintained a quality theme while tailoring its advertising approach to suit specific markets and cultures. Armstrong Cork, Johns-Mansville, General Motors, and others all attest to the validity of this policy.

In a tobacco product quality is directly related to the taste factor and consumer acceptance of this taste. In countries where our affiliates use locally grown tobacco we have been active in improving strains of tobacco grown, field-cultivation practices, and the techniques of handling tobacco prior to manufacture. In Venezuela this has resulted in upgrading the quality of the basic material and has been helpful in aiding the switch from dark tobaccos to the "rubio," or lighter colored, varieties that are rapidly gaining in popularity throughout Latin America. Thus Philip Morris International is able to bring a fresh set of standards to an area, not only taking advantage of a switch in consumer tastes but helping to bring it about through activities in the tobacco fields and by making products available that have the more desirable taste characteristics.

There is a direct relationship, also, between the sale of a product and the rate that consumer changes in taste take place. These changes in preference make it possible for a newer brand to capture an increased share of the market without directly competing with established brands.

In Guatemala the introduction of a new charcoal filter brand, Regios, delivered a new type of cigarette to the market and obtained a large share of the newly created market for a type of filter which had not previously been available there. A dark-tobacco cigarette, Realitos, has been slower to gain, even though the majority of the cigarettes sold in Guatemala are of this type. The reason? The Realitos brand faces established, entrenched competition and does not have the advantage of a switch in taste to execute an end-run.

This change in smoking habits from darker to lighter tobaccos and from nonfiltered to filtered, is a world-wide trend. Our Muratti Ambassador cigarette in Switzerland reflected the same type of benefit as Regios when it became a charcoal-filtered brand. In this case it was an established brand name, but the new type of filter brought to it an increased share of the total market.

In Canada there is a distinct consumer preference for what is known as a straight, or Virginia type, cigarette, one that is carefully blended, but without ingredients other than tobacco. In our Canadian operation the brands that we offer conform to this taste preference, and it is extremely difficult to woo smokers to other types. We speak here with absolute authority, although with a slight blush. We knew that only an imaginary line—the world's longest undefended border—separates Canada and the United States of America. We knew that our United States radio and television messages had long been crossing the line at numerous points. We felt sure we should take the risk and market a popular American-style blended cigarette in Canada, even though preference studies indicated little market appeal.

Our logic was simple. If advertising in the United States was convincing more smokers to try the brand, would not the same reaction have taken place just a few miles north? After all, they had viewed and heard the same commercials.

The outcome of the trial was a pure testimonial for the marketing survey. The Canadian preference for the straight cigarette remained unswayed. The American-style cigarette sold right up to the border, and there it stopped. Today we're a little more careful when we counter a marketing survey with "reason."

In Australia, however, our affiliate has built its share of the market with United States type blends at the expense of the Virginia type brands. Thus it is again a matter of properly evaluating a market and adapting to it.

Similar changes in consumer desire are constantly taking place around the world. The marketer who catches them early can obtain substantial gains. In doing so, many of the fundamental strategies discussed in this book are appreciable.

Take multibrand entries, for example. Just as General Motors has overlapping price lists for its auto models to give consumers several choices at any one price level, so international cigarette marketers have developed brands on the basis that two or three or nine or ten brands in one market can attract a greater volume than one can, even though one might do very well by itself. Our brands compete, one against the other, for shares of even a segmented market. Clark gum in a number of flavors does the same, as do our razor blades. We put out a brand, and then immediately consider an additional entry that will go after the same consumers we have already reached, as well as an additional number of those we have not reached. It is the total that counts, and if that figure can be improved by chipping a few corners off our older products, we are not reluctant.

The one essential consideration is the maintenance of a profitable sales volume in any market. Whatever mechanics are utilized, they must all combine to achieve this end result.

The strategy of *concentration* of effort can be illustrated by our activities in South America. Here we began our local manufacturing operations in Venezuela, joining with a going concern there. While we do export from the United States to virtually all of Latin America, we concentrated our efforts in Venezuela until we have become the major force in that market. Subsequently we entered the Guatemalan market with a manufacturing and marketing activity there to expand our area of local manufacture.

Another instance would be the activities in Switzerland of the Philip Morris International affiliate, FTR. Promotion of Marlboro not only draws a larger percentage of the market but side benefits result from Switzerland's being such a well-traveled market; promoted brands migrate well. Thus the concentration of effort has a much greater effect through all of Europe than could normally be expected per unit cost for promotion.

"*Distribution breakthroughs*" are often a necessity on the international scene. We have boats, equipped with loudspeakers, that travel some of the rivers of South America. The loudspeakers announce their arrival, alternating music and commercials, with sales being made to consumers in areas that would otherwise be inaccessible. We also have small trucks, loaded with movie projection equipment, that circulate among small villages, providing free movies with commercial messages at the beginning, intermission, and end, and selling our wares.

Our boats and movie trucks are special techniques designed to meet special conditions, and illustrate our attitude toward adaptability. The means of distribution for a consumer product present one of the greatest challenges of international marketing. It is in this area that immense benefits can be obtained through the use of local experts. In every case our distribution depends upon local conditions. If an adequate system is available, we try to make our products available through it. If we must create a new system, we adapt to that need.

The roles of product innovation and brand extension are also apparent in many of the case histories cited. The changes that have been made in the past to established names and packages to improve marketing in the United States have also been carried over to international marketing. For example, in Venezuela, Marlboro appears in the regular rather than the long size. In some markets we sell several brands that are of the same quality, but with one brand of cigarette being smaller in diameter than the other, thus permitting competition at various price levels. And, as carton sales outside of the United States account for less than 10 per cent of sales, as compared to 50 per cent within the United States, much less emphasis can be placed on carton design. Similarly, in those markets where cigarettes are sold singly, or "by the stick," the pack is of little importance.

By these examples it can be noted that we do not subscribe to the belief that an established brand name is sacrosanct in the United States or internationally. Names, packaging, and new products in varying forms have all been adapted to meet conditions of each market. We market one item where we can, market many items where we can, but adapt them all to the individual markets.

ADAPTING UNITED STATES ADVERTISING AND PROMOTION

Two case histories will illustrate the principles involved.

1. *Tupperware:*

Tupperware, manufacturers of plastic housewares, has won wide acclaim in the United States for its "home party" policy, a sales strategy in which local women are engaged to sell the company's products. The specific technique used is to have a local woman hold a party in her home, inviting her friends and neighbors, and then display and sell the company's products.

When the company decided to try this internationally, some "experts" declared it would never work, saying that such essential differences existed among housewives in Asia and Europe as compared to those in the United States that a different method must be developed if sales were to be made.

The company went ahead with its United States method. Four years later, sales volume in over 20 countries was rapidly approaching the volume of the United States market. And house-

Realizing that its equipment could not be widely used while the dental profession in many areas abroad still clung to old-fashioned treatment methods, the company launched a series of educational events to reach this key public. It sponsored seminars, participated in trade shows, provided free equipment to schools, produced an educational film with multilingual sound tracks. It not only won a dominant sales position abroad but recently the company also received the United States government's "E-for-Export" award.

Competition frequently brings out promotional genius. Lenox does a brisk business exporting fine bone china to—of all places—Japan. The Volkswagen spurred Detroit to produce America's first compacts. An American chemical company, fearing it would be frozen out of an important trade fair in Düsseldorf by its competition, rented a Rhine River steamer and used it as a floating hotel for its fair-going customers.

General Electric, fighting a tooth-and-nail competitive war with the Japanese, redesigned and repriced its six-transistor radios for export throughout the world, including the Far East.

Overseas, as in the United States, one must sometimes find a "side door" to promotional possibilities. A New York public relations man asks:

> What to do when your enterprise cannot so clearly identify itself as a saver of foreign exchange or a developer of a new industry? Consider, for example, the producer of small packaged goods who may wish to develop new markets in Latin America. There, as everywhere else, cigarettes, powdered milk, cosmetics and other small packaged goods run into fierce competition, high tariff barriers or heavy excise taxes, or monopolistic situations.
>
> One recalls the instance in which a shampoo manufacturer got off to an excellent start in the highly competitive Mexican market. The Breck Company created great good will for itself by giving a gala reception, dinner dance and fashion show in Mexico City to which the cream of officialdom and society was invited. The fashion show featured the designs of a Mexican. Forthrightly, but in good taste, it was made known that the models in the fashion show used Breck Shampoo. What could have been merely a gimmick was publicized by the Mexican press, television and newsreels as a genuinely newsworthy event.[1]

[1] Frank Montgomery Dunbaugh, *Marketing in Latin America* (Printers' Ink Book Co., New York, 1960), p. 124.

Philip Morris itself has used this "side door" technique effectively in two recent promotions which had the added benefit of helping to solidify our company's association with leisure-time enjoyment.

In Mexico, Spain, and Argentina, large public showings were arranged for our film "Great Moments in the History of Tennis." With each showing came a personal appearance by one of the three great tennis stars who are serving as Philip Morris executives-in-training, Roy Emerson, Manuel Santana, and Rafael Osuna.

More recently our company commissioned 11 leading contemporary artists to create a pop art exhibition for us. In cooperation with our affiliates, licensees, and representatives, this show was booked in more than 20 countries abroad. In addition to associating us with the pursuit of leisure time, this particular art form helps our customers to think of our company as being as modern as tomorrow.

The line between advertising, sales promotion, and public relations is a fuzzy one at best. But this much we do know: It is not enough for us to simply sell good products; we must also be good corporate citizens. We must, in as many ways as we can, contribute to the life of each of the countries in which we operate.

Our company strives to do this in many ways. In England we honor sportsmanship by presenting a special trophy at Wimbledon. In Canada we have sponsored literary contests; in several other countries, baseball. In almost every one of our markets we are substantial supporters of reputable charitable campaigns.

We are not alone. Virtually every major company operating abroad works hard to get itself heavily involved in the affairs of its adopted countries. Some give scholarship aid for the children of employees. One offers awards for aquatic life-saving. Another supplies science-teaching kits to local school systems. Still another is sponsoring a fund drive to build a wild-animal preserve.

Activities of this kind are worth while in themselves. They are especially worth while for United States companies operating abroad because they help to take the edge off the anti-American feeling, which, lamentably, continues to persist in some areas. They help us to play a constructive role. They help us to sell our products. And, importantly, they help us to sell our country in the best soft-sell manner.

THE VISION

The international marketer's vision may be as big as the world. It is a world that is just now beginning to stir with the vitality of burgeoning economies and restless desire. It is the oyster of anyone with an honest product to sell and enough guts and enough imagination to figure out how to sell it.

Much of the restless movement of peoples everywhere is toward the city—a bonanza for the marketer of consumer products. In one recent ten-year period, one-third of the people who lived in the rural areas of Peru moved into the cities. And Peru is no exception; the trend is universal.

To the marketer, urbanization brings a similarity of habit to people who once shared nothing in common. City people tend to work in the same general patterns and to spend their leisure time in the same ways. They seek to acquire the same kinds of goods and the same kind of status. Thus the people who have moved from the country to the cities have raised their sights on the things they want from life, and in most cases they have vastly improved their standards of living and their buying power.

It has become a cliché to talk about how small the world has grown. News that the goodies made in the morning by a Brussels candy manufacturer are being enjoyed by New Yorkers the same evening is greeted by the ho-hum boredom of jet-age consumers.

Yet this is only the beginning. David Sarnoff of RCA predicts that within a very few years all the peoples of the world will be able to communicate with one another via a relay satellite, utilizing a universal language! What this would do for international marketing needs no explanation.

However, lest the heady stuff of prognostication dull our sense of the nuts-and-bolts practicalities of our business, let me repeat some guidelines.

A. C. Nielsen, Jr., has listed these 15 reasons why companies do not succeed abroad. They fail to:

1. adapt the product to the market.

2. gauge the underlying impact of custom, tradition, and racial and religious differences.

3. exploit markets in proper sequence.

4. enter potentially profitable markets because of personal repugnance toward political institutions.

5. build a strong management of nationals.

6. appreciate differences in connotation of words.

7. understand differences in advertising.

8. achieve a domestic personality.

9. understand and weigh correctly the relative importance of the various types of retailers in the distribution of the product.

10. grasp the consumer's attitude on the relationship between price and quality.

11. appraise properly the degree of acceptance of the competitive-economy principle.

12. pay attention to the various government regulations involved.

13. insulate the business from arbitrary acts of government (by building local factories, by licensing, etc.).

14. invest for the long pull.

15. provide for an adequate flow of information both to and from the parent company.

The guidelines, both the "do's" and "don't's," have been learned by experience, some bitter and some sweet. Where we have found adaptability to be our key, others have found rigidity to be the means of opening the most doors. Where we have specialized in consumer sales, others have done well marketing industrial products and services.

Competition in all areas is strengthening, however. United States advertising agencies are expanding abroad and carrying with them, for sale, the techniques that they have learned in marketing in the United States and in the nations where they are operating. The agencies, too, realize the value of the two-way flow of information that can then be further disseminated by the central headquarters for further use and adaptation. While they provide competition to those already on the international markets, they ease the route for the newer entry.

There are more United States companies entering markets

abroad and offering a wide array of products, providing more competition within any one product line and, simultaneously, providing more competition for the available supply of local currency. And the companies native to each country are modernizing their techniques of marketing to compete against inroads by the ever-increasing number of brands and products. The United States Government reports that in recent years the profit per unit of currency invested abroad is narrowing down to limits similar to those in the United States. However, there is nothing wrong with profits anywhere, and there is the additional volume to be gained through a larger marketing area.

The parent corporation must be willing to make changes that reflect on virtually every facet of corporate structure. Financing, manufacture, research, and marketing must all agree that a departure from past standardized procedures may be effected and that life will never again be the same as it was in the days of single-market selling. Teamwork within the corporation must be absolute. There must be a new delineation of areas of responsibility. And any preconceived ideas which may lead one to believe that he has an inherent right to conduct business solely according to his own social or cultural mores may well cause an abrupt awakening.

We settled upon adaptability as our international marketing concept, and have utilized our adaptability within the United States and in export activities as an experience factor, supporting it with planning, market evaluations, flexibility of organization, and all of the marketing strategies and techniques we could muster. Coupled with this vision of our business, we have established a credo of being marketing specialists to consumers. We carry it out through our activities with our established brands, our new brands, and with acquired product lines which fit our self-definition and our overall system of distribution both in the United States and internationally. We have found that localization of strategies and techniques is essential, and that every possibility should be explored. Profitability is local; therefore operations must be localized too, whether they involved manufacturing, licensing, or export sales. We maintain quality of product, for we believe in it as the most essential requirement of a product.

To market, we adapt; to adapt, we stay flexible; to remain flexible and show a profit, we market vigorously.

■

Summary

There are tremendous international marketing opportunities as urbanization increases, underdeveloped nations make headway, standards of living, consumer buying power and knowledge improve, and consumer desires grow apace. However, one should be prepared for intensifying rivalry from indigenous firms, other United States companies, and international marketers headquartered in other countries.

Thoroughgoing marketing evaluation and planning are crucial, nation by nation, prior to taking any action.

The skillful international marketer must have more than a rudimentary knowledge of legal, financial, currency, and tariff matters affecting marketing efforts in each country.

Sometimes marketing strategies and tactics evolved in the barefisted United States marketing arena can be carried over to selling abroad. However, the marketer should be prepared, much more often than not, to modify United States procedures so they work overseas. Cultural, social, economic, business, and other differences all pose challenges and demand adaptability. Meet each market's wants individually, including product, brand name, packaging, and pricing changes. Pay special attention to changes needed in advertising and sales promotion, no less than in distribution channels and methods, and in arrangements for supplies—whether via manufacturing, licensing, or export.

The parent company in the United States must display equal flexibility and permit changes in traditional policies and practices.

Nationals should be used wherever possible, limiting United States personnel to a minimum number of specialists. Organize internationally so as to provide maximum local adaptability and control, while coordinating and providing overall control from headquarters. No one organization chart will do.

In sum, though it may sound paradoxical, until we achieve One World there is in a sense really no such thing as international marketing, only local marketing around the world. In other words, the secret of success is rooted in localization and adaptability of strategies and techniques in a lot of individual markets.

10

Investment Philosophy

■

Joel Dean

■

The marketing world provides a sad, almost daily spectacle of products being sent into ferociously competitive markets by their loving but niggardly parents. To prevent nearly certain slaughter, products, especially new ones, require continued substantial support. Sophisticated marketers therefore have developed visions of themselves as marketing investors, not spenders. In the packaged-goods field, for example, current thinking includes three basic tenets:

(a) Heavy weight in advertising, sales promotion, merchandising and distribution-building, with disproportionately heavy pressure in the introductory phase of new-product launches.

(b) Substantial share of weight in whatever media and market segment(s) one competes in.

(c) Prolongation of payout periods from a "traditional" three years to four or five years, where necessary, while trying to maintain a firm hold on future profit by sharp sales forecasting and margin control. (Obviously this can't be done in fields where product life cycles are growing shorter.)

But are these practices really sound? How much should be invested for promotion? How much is "heavy"? How should marketers evaluate return on promotional investments? What criteria should be used? The raging battles regarding theory and practice in advertising "accountability" research underscore the gravity of these questions.

To deal with them, we invited Joel Dean, one of the nation's foremost managerial economists, to apply his vast experience.

Dr. Dean advances a novel conceptual approach for treating persuasion as an investment and rationing outlays on the basis of rate-of-return as measured by discounted cash-flow analysis. Dr. Dean is Professor of Business Economics at the Graduate School for Political Science and Graduate School of Business at Columbia University and President of Joel Dean Associates, an economic and management counseling firm headquartered in New York.

Dr. Dean is the author of several books, including *Managerial Economics* (Prentice-Hall, Inc., 1951) and *Capital Budgeting* (Columbia University Press, 1951) and numerous journal articles. He has had extensive experience as a corporation director and was formerly research associate of the Cowles Commission and the National Bureau of Economic Research.

■

INVESTMENT PHILOSOPHY[1]

JOEL DEAN

BACKGROUND

1. THE QUESTION

Should advertising be budgeted as an expense or as an investment?

Advertising is now bookkept and budgeted as though its benefits were used up immediately, like purchased electricity. Management thinks about advertising as if it were bookkept, as a current expense. The decision as to how much a corporation should spend on persuasion is made by the same criteria as for materials used up in the factory, i.e., its impact upon the current P&L. The advertising budget is part of the *operating* budget.

[1] This chapter was pre-published as an article, "Does Advertising Belong in the Capital Budget?," in the *Journal of Marketing* (October, 1966).

No corporation that I know of puts advertising in its capital budget. But maybe it belongs there. Several disinterested parties say so.

The stock market says it belongs there. It says that benefits derived from promotional outlays are just as capitalizable as the tangible assets that the bookkeeper does capitalize. It says this when Bristol-Myers sells at ten times its book value.[2]

Corporation presidents occasionally say it belongs there, i.e., when they invoke *investment* in advertising to justify poor current profits.[3]

New entrants into an industry say advertising belongs in the capital budget. They say it by including the promotional outlays required to build brand acceptance as an integral part of the total investment required to break into the business.

Antitrust economists say advertising belongs in the capital budget. They say it by viewing brand acceptance, which is built up by promotion, as just as substantial a barrier to entry as the investment required in buildings and machinery.[4]

It is just possible that the bookkeeper's guide to top-management thinking about advertising is wrong.[5] This chapter pursues that thought.

2. THE APPROACH

The general plan of this chapter is, first, to find whether promotion is an investment, second, to consider how to optimize it if it is an investment, and, third, to speculate on the probabilities that this novel approach, even if theoretically valid, will do any good.

My approach to the problem of how much to invest in advertis-

[2] Other companies which have very high advertising-to-sales ratios also sell at many times their book value, reflecting the value investors place on these future benefits; e.g., IBM is eight times.

[3] "Roy W. Moore, Jr., president [Canada Dry Corporation] . . . explained to stockholders at the financial meeting . . . that lower earnings in the face of an 18 per cent increase in sales was due to a heavy investment in advertising and sales promotion" (*New York Times,* July 20, 1966).

[4] Joe S. Bain in *Barriers to New Competition* (Cambridge, Mass.: Harvard University Press, 1956) found that industries where product-differentiation barriers to entry were high also had high advertising and other sales promotion costs.

[5] I do not suggest that the bookkeeping be changed. The goal of accounting is meticulous pecuniary history, comparable among epochs. This is quite different from the goal of top management in determining how much to spend on promotion. The bookkeeper's rule is a false guide to top management in this decision, as in many others.

ing is formal and objective rather than intuitive. My premise is that the overriding goal of the corporation is to maximize profits. My viewpoint is that of an economist concerned with managerial finance.

This paper is confined to the conceptual framework for deciding how much to invest in promotion. Measurement problems are not examined, nor the mechanics of application. The analysis is presented in terms of advertising but is equally applicable to all forms of persuasion. Advertising is used because it is the purest and most indisputable form of selling cost and for many firms also the largest.

My thesis, in summary preview, is this: Most advertising is, in economic essence, an investment. How much to spend on advertising is therefore a problem of investment economics. A new approach is required—economic and financial analysis of futurities. This approach focuses on future after-tax cash flows and centers on the profit-productivity of capital.

IS PROMOTION AN INVESTMENT?

To determine whether as a matter of economics, outlays for advertising and other forms of promotion constitute an investment, rather than a current expense, is our task in this section.

To carry it off we must bravely face three basic questions concerning the economics of investment in corporate persuasion:

A. Precisely what is a business investment; how is it distinguished from a current expense?

B. Just what are promotional costs; how should they be distinguished from production costs?

C. What are the peculiarities of promotional outlays; do they disqualify promotion for investment treatment?

1. CONCEPT OF INVESTMENT

What distinguishes a business investment from a current expense? An investment is an outlay made today to achieve benefits in the future. A current expense is an outlay whose benefits are immediate. The question is not how the outlay is treated in conventional accounting, how it is taxed, or whether the asset is tangible or intangible. The hallmark of an investment is futurity.

2. CONCEPT OF PROMOTIONAL COSTS

Precisely what are promotional costs? How do they differ from production costs? Promotional costs are outlays to augment the demand for the product—i.e., to shift its price-quantity demand schedule upward, so that more will be sold at a given price. Production costs, in contrast, are all outlays required to meet this demand.

This different dividing line means that some costs which are conventionally classified as marketing costs, e.g., physical distribution, are here viewed as part of production costs. It means also that some costs usually viewed as production costs, e.g., inspection, are here viewed as promotional costs, even though they are incurred in the factory.

This is the cost dichotomy needed for clear thinking about promotional investments. It is weird and at its edges it is a bit blurred and hard to measure. Nevertheless, the managerial usefulness of this distinction should not be sold short for these reasons. A clear idea of the purpose of an outlay is indispensable for a useful estimate of its effectiveness. Moreover, the criterion for optimization production costs is quite different from that for promotional costs. For production it is sheer cost minimization; for promotion it is not cost minimization but something much more intricate, as we shall see.

3. DISTINCTIVE TRAITS OF PROMOTIONAL INVESTMENTS

Do promotional investments differ from unimpeachable corporate investments in ways that make it impractical to manage them like true investments? Promotional investments *are* different from traditional corporate investments—e.g., capital tied up in machinery. The question is whether these differences call for a different intellectual apparatus for measuring productivity and rationing the firm's capital.

Promotional investments are bookkept differently. They are not capitalized and not depreciated. But this does not keep them from being investments. They tie up capital with equal inflexibility and do so with similar expectation of future benefits.

Promotional investments are taxed differently. Unlike acknowledged investments, these bastards are deductible against income fully at the time of outlay, regardless of the delay of benefits. The fact that the tax collector is oblivious to promotional investments increases their productivity. Immediate tax write-off of the entire outlay halves the investment after tax and steps up its true rate of return.

Promotional investments are generally spread out over time and can usually be adjusted in amount in relatively small steps. This trait, however, is irrelevant in determining whether or not they are true investments. It is shared with outlays recognized as investments (e.g., housing developments).

Most promotional investments have an indeterminate economic life. Brand acceptance planted in the head of a teenager by TV may influence his purchases for fifty minutes or fifty years. But uncertainty of duration of the benefits does not make the promotional outlay any less an investment. The obsolescence-life of a computer is also quite uncertain.

Promotional investments have multiple benefits which can be reaped in optional ways. The profitability of augmented demand may be taken out either in higher prices or in larger volume. But this trait is not unique to promotional investments. Factory modernization usually not only saves labor but also increases capacity and improves product quality and employee morale.

Promotional investments usually have irregular and diverse time-shapes in their benefits streams. But this is a common trait of many tangible investments. Some oil wells, for example, come in as gushers, have an unexpected midlife rejuvenation from repressuring, and live out a tranquil old age as pumpers.

Promotional investments have a benefit-stream which is hard to measure and hard to predict. But they share this characteristic with many forms of outlay conventionally classified as capital expenditures. Obsolescence of chemical-processing equipment, for example, is hard to predict, yet vitally affects its rate of return.

Promotional investments are provocative; they may induce rivals to retaliate. This trait adds to the difficulty of measuring and predicting benefits. Tangible investments, however, can also provoke rivals' reaction in ways that erode their profitability (e.g., retail-store modernization).

We conclude that promotional investments *do* have unusual

characteristics, different from those of the many other investments that now fight for funds in the capital budget. These traits, however, either are not distinctive, or if they are, do not destroy the essential investment character of the promotional outlays.

All promotional outlays are now conventionally viewed exclusively as current expenses. Some are, if the time lag of benefits is sufficiently short. Others are instead true investments, because the delay in their benefits is substantial. Most promotion is a mixture, and the richness of the investment mix varies over a wide range.

HOW TO OPTIMIZE INVESTMENT IN PROMOTION

Granted that much advertising is largely an investment in economic reality, how should a corporation determine how much it should invest in promotion? This is the central problem of this section. To solve it we need answers to the following questions:

1. Does a satisfactory solution for the problem already exist?
2. Why has such an important problem remained unsolved?
3. To what corporate goal should the solution be geared?
4. How does promotion tie into other ways of getting business?
5. What are the determinants of the productivity of capital invested in promotion?
6. What concepts of measurement are needed to calibrate productivity of capital?
7. What is the most appropriate yardstick of capital productivity for promotional investments?
8. How would rate-of-return rationing work for investments in corporate persuasion?
9. What would be the practical impacts of putting advertising in the capital budget?

1. PROBLEM UNSOLVED

Has the problem of how much a corporation should spend on advertising and other forms of persuasion been already satisfactorily solved? The problem is important: it is crucial to the competitive success of many firms and it involves vast expenditures. In the future it is likely to be even more vital. Depersonalized distribution, increased urbanization, rising consumer affluence, revolutionary advances in technology, and bigger economies of scale in some promotional media are dynamic forces which will make the decision as to how much to invest in promotion a jugular issue for many corporations in the next decade.

Surprisingly, this crucial problem is not yet solved. Despite yards of computer print-outs and millions of dollars spent on advertising research, most corporations do not really know whether their promotional outlays should be half or twice as large as they now are.

2. REASONS FOR FAILURE

Why has such an important problem remained unsolved? There are, I think, three main causes. The first cause is failure to acknowledge the importance of futurity. The full impact of most promotional outlays upon demand is delayed with associated uncertainty. Hence the conceptual framework of analysis that management needs for solving this problem is the kind that is used in modern, sophisticated management of conventional corporate capital appropriations.

A second cause is lack of a conceptual apparatus whose orientation is economic. The problem of optimizing promotional investment is basically a matter of managerial economics, i.e., balancing incremental promotional investment against predicted benefits, so as to augment sales most profitably.

The third cause of failure is the difficulty of measuring the effectiveness of promotional outlays. Their impacts on demand are diffused, delayed, and intricately interwoven with other forces. This intractable measurement problem requires a research approach which has an economic focus that is managerially meaningful. To make this kind of investment approach produce practical benefits will require an open mind, fresh concepts, substantial research spending, and great patience.

3. OVERRIDING CORPORATE GOAL

What is the corporate goal to which the solution of optimum investment in promotion should be geared? Promotional outlays, like other expenditures, should be judged in terms of their contribution to attainment of the corporation's objectives. Most companies have several goals, some of which conflict.[6] The solution for the problem of how much to invest in promotion should nevertheless be geared primarily to the goal of profitability.

The master goal of the modern corporation should, I think, be maximum profits in the long run. More explicitly, it should be to maximize the present worth at the corporation's cost of capital of the future stream of benefits to the stockholder. All other objectives, such as growth, or market share, or eternal life, should be either intermediate or subsidiary to this overriding corporate objective.

4. BUSINESS-GETTING TROIKA

How does promotion relate to other ways of getting business? A company has three ways to augment its sales: by cutting price, by spending more on promotion, or by bettering its product. The three members of the business-getting troika pull together. But, being alternatives, they are at the margin rival substitutes.

The three reinforce each other in a complex symbiotic relationship. For a product that is superior to rivals in wanted ways, promotional outlays will be more effective than for one which is inferior. A given amount and quality of promotion will produce more sales of a product which is priced in correct economic relationship to buyers' alternatives than for a product that is overpriced.

Each of the three can have delayed impacts and hence be a

[6] In many cases money-making appears to be a secondary objective. Often the primary goal seems strategic—to maintain or increase the company's share of the market, to achieve growth in sales volume or number of employees, or simply to build reputation and status. Often capital expenditures capture and embody this kind of motivation in the form of corporate monuments made "just to become the kind of company we want to be." I am thinking of welfare and prestige investments like gymnasiums, country clubs, and palatial offices.

A corporation is not single-minded. It is composed of groups and individuals whose interests conflict. The concept that management should act between employees and customers and stockholders can lead to promotional investment commitments that stray from rate-of-return rationining. When a company does let goals, such as employee-welfare or prestige, govern, it ought to know the cost. The only way to find out this cost is to determine the profitability of promotional projects and see how much profit is being passed up in order to build such corporate monuments. The cost of prestige, then, is the amount of earnings foregone by departing from a pattern of investment ruthlessly directed at profit maximization.

business investment. Their delayed and intertwining effects on sales, now and in the future, increase the problem of measuring the effects of promotional investment.

5. DETERMINANTS OF CAPITAL PRODUCTIVITY

What are the determinants of the productivity of capital invested in promotion? These need to be identified to find out whether capital tied up in advertising will yield enough profits to earn its keep. Its yield must pay for the cost of this capital in the marketplace or its opportunity costs in benefits that are passed up by not investing the money somewhere else.

The productivity of an investment in promotion is the relation of its earnings to the amount of capital tied up. This relationship requires explicit recognition of four economic determinants to be measured: (A) the amount and timing of added investment; (B) the amount and timing of the added stream of earnings; (C) the duration of the earnings stream, i.e., the economic life of the promotional investment; and (D) the risks and imponderable benefits associated with the project.

A. Added Investment

The appropriate investment base for calculating rate of return is the added outlay which will be occasioned by the adoption of a promotion project as opposed to its rejection. The investment should include the entire amount of the original added outlay regardless of how it is classified on the accounts. Any additional outlay for point-of-purchase displays or for distribution of samples to consumers should be included in the investment amount, as should future research expenses caused by the proposal.

The timing of these added investments has an important effect upon true profitability and should therefore be reflected in the rate-of-return computation.

B. Added Earnings

Concern with capital productivity of course implies that the company's goal is profits. The productivity of the capital tied up is determined by the increase in earnings or savings, i.e., net cash receipts, caused by making the investment as opposed to not making it. These earnings should be measured in terms of their after-tax cash or cash equivalents. Only costs and revenues that will be different as a result of the adoption of the proposal should be included. The concept of earnings should be broad enough to encompass intangible and often unquantifiable benefits. When these have to be omitted from the formal earnings estimates, they should be noted for subsequent appraisal of the project.

C. Durability

The duration of the stream of benefits from a promotional investment, i.e., its economic life, has a vital effect upon its rate of return. Economic life of promotion depends (1) on frequency of purchase; (2) on loyalty–life expectancy, i.e., longevity of customers; (3) on gestation period of the purchase decision as well as (4) on erosion by the promotional efforts of rivals. For advertising investments, durability is often the most difficult dimension of project value to quantify. But the problem cannot be ducked. Some estimate is better than none, and estimates can be improved by well-directed research.

D. Risks and Imponderable Benefits

Appraising the risks and uncertainties associated with a project requires such a high order of judgment that the problem should be explicitly faced and appraised by the collective wisdom of those best qualified to make the appraisal. It is only disparities in risk among projects which need to be allowed for, since the company's cost of capital reflects the overall risks. Though measurement of this sort of dispersion is difficult, some headway can sometimes be made by a necessarily arbitrary risk-ranking of candidate projects or categories of projects.

Most projects have some added benefits over and above the measurable ones. If excessive weight is given to these imponderables, there is danger that rate-of-return rationing will be sabotaged. When a low rate-of-return project is preferred to a high one on the grounds of imponderable benefits, the burden of proof clearly should rest on the imponderables.

6. CONCEPTS OF MEASUREMENT

For calibrating these four determinants of return on investment, what concepts of measurement are needed? Four are particularly useful:

A. Alternatives: The proper bench mark for measuring added

investment and the corresponding added earnings is the best alternative way to do it.

B. Futurity: Future earnings and future outlays of the project are all that matter.

C. Increments: Added earnings and added investment of the project alone are material.

D. Cash Flows: After-tax cash flows (or their equivalents) alone are significant for measuring capital productivity.

A. Alternatives

There is always an alternative to the proposed capital expenditure. The alternative may be so catastrophic that refined measurement is unnecessary to reject it. In any case, the proper bench mark for the proposal is the next profitable alternative way of doing it.

B. Futurity

The value of a proposed capital project depends on its future earnings. The past is irrelevant except as a bench mark for forecasting the future. Consequently, earnings estimates need to be based upon the best available projections. The outlays and earnings need to be estimated year by year over the economic life of the proposed promotion and their time shape needs to be taken into account explicitly.

C. Increments

A correct estimate of both earnings and investment must be based upon the simple principle that the earnings from the promotional proposal are measured by the total *added* earnings by marking the investment as opposed to *not* making it and that the same is true for the investment amount. Project costs should be unaffected by allocation of existing overheads but should reflect the changes in total overhead and other costs that are forecast to result from the project. No costs or revenues which will be the same regardless of whether the proposal is accepted or rejected should be included, and the same goes for investment.

D. Cash Flows

To be economically realistic, attention should be directed exclusively at the after-tax flows of cash or cash equivalents which will result from making the promotional investment. Book costs are confusing and immaterial. Taxes matter because advertising investments are favored over depreciable investments in after-tax rate of return.

7. YARDSTICK OF FINANCIAL WORTH

The productivity of capital in a business investment is the relationship between its earnings and the amount of capital tied up. To measure this productivity for promotional investments we must not only have a correct conceptual framework of measurements, but also choose the most appropriate yardstick of investment worth.

The concept of advertising as an investment already has some limited acceptance in new-product introduction. The measure of productivity of capital often used is pay-out period, which provides a crude yardstick. The cut-off criterion is also set rather arbitrarily to get the original outlay back in two years or three years. Such standards have no objective justification which can hold a candle to corporate cost of capital.

What is the best yardstick of economic worth for investments in persuasion? Clearly, the yardstick that is economically appropriate for investments in promotion is rate of return as measured by discounted-cash-flow analysis. The superiority of DCF for business investments in general and for investments that have the economic characteristics of promotional outlays in particular was determined over 15 years ago and is now widely recognized in the business community.[7]

A. Discounted-Cash-Flow Analysis

The discounted-cash-flow method (DCF) is a new approach to measuring the productivity of capital and measuring the cost of capital. In the last decade I have seen its use in industrial capital budgeting grow rapidly. The application is new, not the principle; discounting has long been used in the financial community, where precision and realism are indispensable.

---

[7] My views on this have been pressed so ardently over the past 15 years that I need not bore you with them here. See my *Capital Budgeting* (New York: Columbia University Press, 1951); *Managerial Economics* (New York: Prentice-Hall, 1951); "Measuring the Productivity of Capital," *Harvard Business Review* (January–February 1954).

The essential contributions of discounted-cash-flow analysis to management thinking about investment in promotion are three:

1. An explicit recognition that time has economic value; hence that near money is more valuable than distant money.

2. A recognition that cash flows are what matter; hence book costs are irrelevant for capital decisions except as they affect taxes.

3. A recognition that income taxes have such an important effect upon cash flows that they must be explicitly figured into project worth.

The discounted-cash-flow method has two computational variants. The first is a rate-of-return computation which consists essentially of finding the interest rate that discounts gross future after-tax earnings of a project down to a present value equal to

EXHIBIT I

DISCOUNTED-CASH-FLOW METHOD OF COMPUTING RATE OF RETURN FROM ONE-SHOT ADVERTISING INVESTMENT WITH FOLLOW-ON EFFECTS

Year	*Added Pre-Promotion Profits (Face Value) ($1,000)*	*Present Value Discounted @:*			
		30%	*20%*	*17%*	*18%*
0	(200)	(200)	(200)	(200)	(200)
1	96	88	87	88	88
2	64	41	47	50	49
3	43	20	26	28	27
4	29	10	15	16	15
5	19	5	8	9	8
6	13	2	4	5	5
7	9	1	2	3	3
8	6	1	1	2	2
9	4	—	1	1	1
10	3	—	—	—	—
Net Present Value		(37)	(9)	3	(1)

Rate of return is 18 per cent.

the project cost. This interest rate is the rate of return on that particular investment.

An example of a one-shot advertising investment is shown in Exhibit I. This is the case of an original investment outlay followed by benefits realized over several years. The investment profile in Exhibit II shows the initial outlay of $200,000 as a negative value on the bar diagram. The incremental prepromotion profits are depicted for each year in the positive section of the diagram.

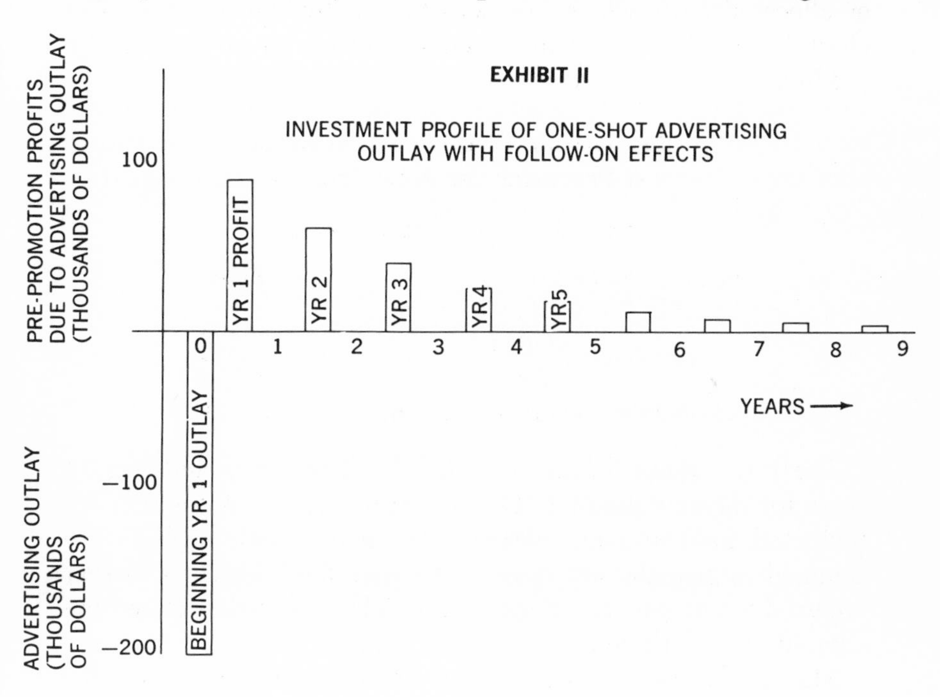

This illustrates the kind of timetable used for DCF calculation of the rate of return for such investments. The calculation format is illustrated in Exhibit I. The first column shows the prepromotion cash flows with the initial outlay shown as a negative value. In the next four columns these cash-flow amounts are translated into present value by discounting each at four trial rates of return: 30 per cent, 20 per cent, 18 per cent, and 17 per cent. The interest rate which discounts the future earnings of the advertising investment to a present value precisely equal to the investment outlay is the true rate of return on that investment (roughly 18 per cent in our illustration).

Another example is provided by the investment decision for a new product's promotion outlays spread over several years. The relevant annual incremental income for the product is projected by subtracting the variable cost from the added revenue. The variable costs include only those which are incurred by the decision to market the new product; it does not include any fixed cost or allocated costs which are not affected by the decision. The chart below shows this incremental income for a case of the product.

EXAMPLE OF INVESTMENT DECISION FOR PROMOTION OF NEW PRODUCT

INCREMENTAL INCOME PER CASE

Realized Sales Price	$17.40
Variable Costs–Manufacturing	8.35
–Other	1.05
–Total	$ 9.40
Incremental Before-Tax Income	$ 8.00

The total added income is found from the projected market share for the new product. The annual outlays for promotion are budgeted for the same period. The inflows and outflows are summed to give the net incremental cash flow, which is further adjusted to put it on an after-tax basis. The table below shows the computation of these cash flows.

The second method is a present-value computation which discounts gross future after-tax earnings of all projects at the same rate of interest. This rate of interest is the company's minimum acceptable rate of return. This should, I think, be based upon the company's cost of capital. Risk should be reflected either (a) by deflating project earnings or (b) by adjusting the cut-off rate for projects of different categories of risk. The resulting present value is then compared with the project cost. If the present value exceeds it, the project is acceptable. If it falls below, it is rejected. In addition, projects can, by this variant, be ranked by various kinds of profitability indexes which reflect the amount or ratios of excess of present value over project cost.

INCREMENTAL CASH FLOWS ($ MILLIONS)

	First Year	*Second Year*	*Third Year*
A. ADDED INCOME			
Projected Share ($'s) of Market	7.2%	7.8%	8.4%
Cases (millions)	.9	1.0	1.2
Total Incremental Before-Tax Income ($8.00/case)	$7.2	$8.0	$9.6
B. PROMOTION INVESTMENT			
Media Advertising	$7.0	$4.3	$4.3
Sale Promotion			
Dealer Display	.4		
Introductory Sampling	4.3		
Deal #1 (5% off)	.3	1.0	1.2
Deal #2 (10¢ off)	.3		
Deal #3 (½ price sale)	.1		
Other			
	$5.5	$1.0	$1.2
Total Promotion	$12.5	$5.3	$5.5
C. NET INCREMENTAL CASH FLOW			
Before-Tax Cash Flow	(5.3)	2.7	4.1
Tax (assume 50% rate)	* 2.65	(1.35)	(2.05)
After-Tax Cash Flow	(2.65)	1.35	2.05
Rate of Return = 15%			

* Assumes that company has other income to which the promotion deduction can be applied.

The DCF rate of return for this investment is approximately 15 per cent.

An example illustrating a present-value computation where there is a spread-out promotion investment is shown in Exhibit III. Here the investment outlays do not all occur at the beginning of the investment period; rather, they can be spread over several years. Column 1 shows the cumulative balance of outlay and inflow for each year. For a cost of capital assumed to be 10 per cent the present value is calculated in Column 2. With this assumed value of money the advertising investment promises plus values, since discounted incremental profits when summed are bigger than the present value of advertising outlays by $1140.00. Note that the DCF project rate of return as computed from continuous discount tables is found to be about 18 per cent.

EXHIBIT III

DISCOUNTED-CASH-FLOW METHOD
OF COMPUTING RETURN FOR SPREAD-OUT INVESTMENT

Year	*Net Cash Flow ($1,000)*	*Present Values* @:* *10%*	*18%*
1	(104)	(109.0)	(112.0)
2	(40)	(41.0)	(45.0)
3	(5)	(7.7)	(12.0)
4	30	4.0	6.2
5	50	25.0	17.7
6	65	32.0	18.0
7	175	91.4	54.0
8	115	54.3	30.0
9	75	32.1	16.3
10	50	19.3	9.1
11	25	8.8	1.3
12	15	4.8	.6
	Net Present Value	114.0	(6.0)

* Since continuous discount tables are used, each year's net cash flow must be separated into beginning-year outlay and through-year inflow before being discounted.

Both variants of the discounted-cash-flow approach require a timetable of after-tax cash flows of investment and of gross earnings which cover the entire economic life of the project. In practice the timetable can be simplified by grouping years in blocks. For projects for which investment is substantially instantaneous and gross earnings are level, simple computational charts and tables can be used to estimate the discounted-cash-flow rate of return directly from estimated economic life and after-tax payback. For projects with rising or declining earnings streams, this conversion is more complex.[8] Computer programs are cheaply available and widely used.

[8] Multiple solutions become possible if there is a recurrence of negative cash flow during the life. See James H. Lorie and Leonard J. Savage, "Three Problems in Rationing Capital," *Journal of Business* (October 1955).

B. Superiorities of DCF

DCF analysis is particularly needed for measuring the profitability of promotional investments for two reasons: first, because the outlays are usually spread out; second, because benefits, mainly incremental profits from added sales in the future, are always spread out and usually have a nonlevel time shape.

The superiorities of discounted-cash-flow analysis over rival yardsticks for measuring the productivity of capital in promotional investments are imposing:

1. It is economically realistic in confining the analysis to cash flows and forgetting about book allocations. The books, although valuable for other purposes, are irrelevant for the task of measuring investment worth.
2. It forces guided thinking about the whole life of the project and concentration on the lifetime earnings.
3. It weights the time-pattern of the investment outlay and the cash earnings so as to reflect real and important differences in the value of near and distant cash flows.
4. It reflects accurately and without ambiguity the timing of tax-savings, e.g., from expensing immediately the investment outlay.
5. It permits simple allowances for risks and uncertainties, and can be adapted readily to increasing the risk allowance over time.
6. It is strictly comparable to cost-of-capital, correctly measured, so that decisions can be made quickly and safely by comparing rate of return and the value of money to the firm.

8. RATE-OF-RETURN RATIONING

How should rationing of capital work for persuasion-investments? Rate-of-return battling among capital proposals is the essence of capital rationing. The standard of minimum acceptable profitability should (after proper allowance for special risks and for imponderables[9]) be the same for all, namely the company's market

[9] Making correct allowance for risks and unmeasurables is where top management's judgment plays its most important role in project screening. Investments which basically alter the nature of the company's risk-exposure may also change its ability to attract capital and hence its cost of capital. The general principle of rate-of-return rationing nevertheless still applies, even when measurement of the profitability and riskiness of an investment in promotion is incomplete and subject to error.

cost-of-capital or its opportunity cost-of-capital, whichever is higher.[10] Exhibit IV illustrates rate-of-return laddering of projects to ration capital, with market cost-of-capital (MCC) the cut-off rate.

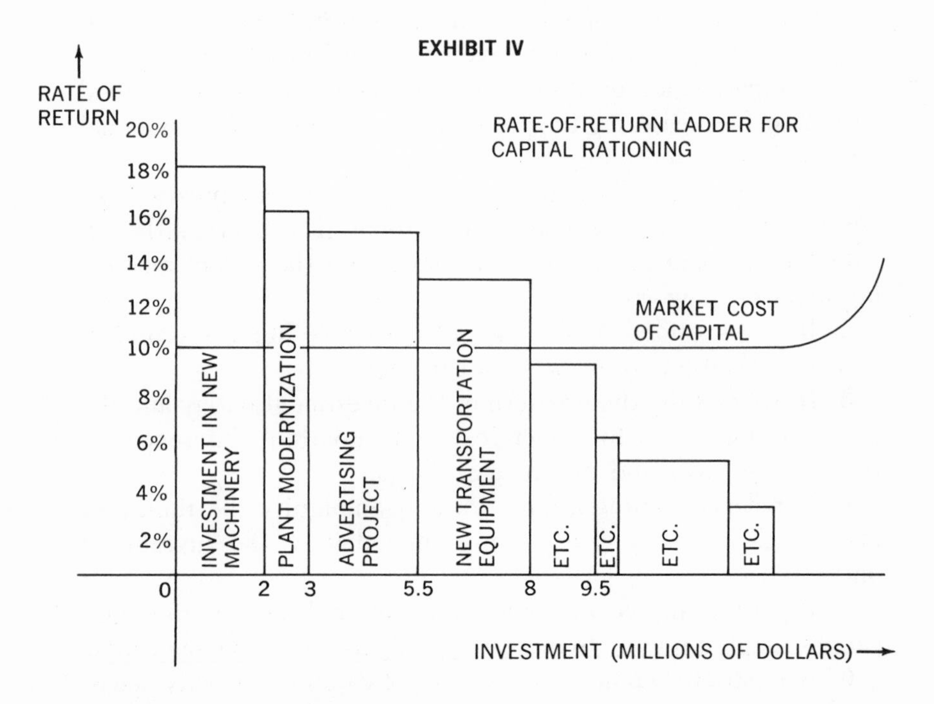

Market cost-of-capital is what the company will probably pay for equity and debt funds on the average over the future. For a large publicly held company this cost can be measured with adequate precision for rationing purposes. This is a conclusion reached after two decades of wrestling with troublesome conceptual and metrical problems of costing corporate capital. Despite the margin of error in measuring a company's market cost-of-capital I have found no better cut-off criterion.

[10] Capital controls to assure that the principles of capital rationing are actually carried out are of many sorts, including: (a) outlay controls, i.e., making sure that the expenditures are in the amount and form authorized; (b) post-mortems, i.e., auditing the project earnings at early stages to keep the estimates honest and to learn from mistakes; and (c) spending logs, i.e., comparing actual outlays with budgeted forecast outlays.

Opportunity cost-of-capital is the sacrificed profit-yield from alternative investments. Only when a company refuses to go to market for funds as a matter of policy can its opportunity costs stay long above market cost-of-capital.

Wisdom is an essential ingredient in all capital rationing decisions. But judgment is enlightened and economized when the company's cost-of-capital is explicitly quantified and when the profitability of projects is measured as fully as is economic.

9. PRACTICAL IMPACTS

Will putting advertising in the capital budget do any good? Grant that as a matter of economic principle much advertising and other forms of promotional spending are investments. Grant also that conceptually correct and pragmatically proven techniques for optimizing investment outlays are available for promotional investment. It still may be appropriate to raise the question as to whether this sophisticated and powerful mechanism when applied to promotional investments will do any good.

Most business investments are not made in ignorance of their probable impacts, whereas many of the outlays for persuasion now are. Characteristically, the amount and timing of the effects of advertising are unknown. The duration of their impact (i.e., their economic life) is unknown and the probabilities of effectiveness are also unknown. Quite possibly attempting to estimate these unknowns cannot as a practical matter improve overall results. Instead, it may move the analysis to an arena in which all the assumptions are open to challenge.

The problem of how much to invest in promotion can be solved either by intuitive and perhaps artistic processes or through a more formal and more systematic study of objective evidence. Quite possibly men of experience and good judgment can determine how much the corporation should invest in promotion by subjective judgment, whether or not advertising is formally put in the capital budget. This chapter is nevertheless limited to a consideration of ways in which sophisticated economic models and systematic quantitative study can help find the appropriate size of the appropriation for corporate persuasion. This limitation is not dictated by any necessary superiority of the objective process over the intuitive. Instead, objectivity is here preferred because discussion can never be very useful to the intuitive process, while it can indicate the most promising lines of objective inquiry.

■

Summary

Much advertising (and other corporate persuasion) is in economic reality partly an investment. The investment mix varies over a wide spectrum.

Investments in promotion are different from conventional capital expenditures, but these peculiar traits do not disqualify promotion for investment treatment.

Profitability must be the basic measurement of the productivity of capital invested in promotion. Despite the multiplicity of conflicting corporate goals, the overriding objective for decisions or investment of corporate capital should be to make money.

The main determinants of profitability of an advertising investment that need to be estimated are the amount and timing of added investment and of added earnings, the duration of advertising effects and risks.

The measurement concepts of capital productivity that must be estimated are future, time-spotted, incremental, after-tax cash flows of investment outlays and of added profits from added sales.

Discounted-cash-flow analysis (DCF) supplies the yardstick of investment worth which is most appropriate for promotional investments. By comparison, payback period, though widely used, has no merit.

Advertising belongs in the capital budget. Promotional investments should be made to compete for funds on the basis of profitability, i.e., DCF rate of return.

The criterion for rationing scarce capital among competing investment proposals should be DCF rate of return. The criterion of the minimum acceptable return should be the corporation's cost of capital—outside market cost or internal opportunity cost, whichever is higher.

Plopping advertising into the corporation's capital budget will not perform the miracle. Judgment can't be displaced by DCF analysis and computers. But judgment can be economized and improved. The most that it can do is to open the way for a research approach which is oriented to the kind of estimates that are relevant and that will permit advertising investment in promotion to fight for funds on the basis of financial merit rather than on the basis of personal persuasiveness of their sponsor.

To make this investment approach produce practical benefits will require an open mind, fresh concepts, substantial research spending, and great patience.

11

Distribution Breakthroughs

■

William R. Davidson

■

Being wedded to a given distribution system is one of the most serious obstacles imaginable to the execution of a marketing vision. It is also a frequent manifestation of marketing backwardness, because the forces of inertia, tradition, and myopia all exert their pull in the same direction. Helene Curtis' acquiring Studio Girl and Bristol-Myers' acquiring Luzier to tap the rich house-to-house sales channel are positive examples of companies building new sales highways to their markets. So, too, is Chock Full o' Nuts' signing up local licensees for door-to-door selling. Cosmetics lines that were once sold only to main-line department stores and Class A drugstores but which have now extended distribution to grocery stores are also cases in point. Indeed, one must credit supermarkets more than manufacturers for breaking out of the traditional mold of being only food outlets and creating a vast enterprise in health and beauty aids and in packaged household necessities. Moreover, one must credit retailers in general for the positive effects of scrambled distribution in all manner of goods. If a national beer brand were to franchise local brewers, taking a leaf from the book of the soft drink companies, they would be displaying the virtues of innovation in distribution channels as a basic strategy.

The author of this chapter has been described as a "channels man from way back." Dr. William R. Davidson, Professor of Marketing at Ohio State University, Columbus, Ohio, is a former president of the American Marketing Association and has been honored many times for his work in marketing, including entry in the Hall of Fame of the Boston Conference for Distribution. He is the author of numerous articles for business and professional journals and is co-author of the eighth edition of *Marketing* (The Ronald Press Co., 1967), a book which has sold more than a quarter of a million copies in previous editions. Dr. Davidson is also co-author of *Retailing Management* (The Ronald Press Co., 1966) and a contributing editor to the *Marketing Handbook* (The Ronald Press Co., 1965). He serves as a director of several business firms, and is a senior associated consultant with Management and Business Services, a Columbus consulting organization.

Professor Davidson begins with a discussion of the theoretical aspects of distribution strategy and then demonstrates with actual case histories the key role distribution considerations can play in achieving marketing advantage.

■

DISTRIBUTION BREAKTHROUGHS

WILLIAM R. DAVIDSON

Marketing management is often viewed as the task of optimizing the relationship between controllable variables in a firm's marketing mix and the noncontrollable or environmental variables. Among the noncontrollable items commonly accepted as given for a particular planning period are the nature of competition, industry demand, role of government, and the available structure of distributive outlets. In a manufacturing company the marketing effort is likely to be focused strongly upon product, price, advertising, and personal selling, these being the major marketing-mix ingredients that can be most readily adjusted to the state of the environment.

Frequently overlooked is the opportunity to make a breakthrough by applying the concept of marketing vision to distribution channels. While marketing channels are commonly regarded as a variable aspect of the marketing mix of the manufacturer, they often receive less attention than consideration of product, price, and promotion, simply because much of the channel, in the typical case, is "out there" where it is difficult to do much of anything about it, especially in the short run.

Upon reflection, almost any knowledgeable person would agree that the spatial and temporal availability of a product offering has a great deal to do with the profitable exploitation of opportunity. This is essentially the role of the distribution channel, and one too often neglected as higher priority is accorded to more highly variable matters.

Channel decisions are commonly analyzed from the standpoint of a manufacturer, with conventional discussions providing lists of pros and cons of common alternative arrangements. This conventionalism is likely to thwart a visionary approach. It will be apparent in the following discussion that real breakthroughs in distribution are likely to originate with any level of the channel, i.e., they may be the innovation of a retailer, a wholesaler, an agent or broker, as well as a manufacturer.

Since this is an area of much conceptual and semantical confusion, some clarification is in order.

CHANNEL CONCEPTS [1]

The term "channel of distribution" is part of the working vocabulary of every business executive, yet many would be hard pressed to define it. This is not surprising, because a wide variety of interpretations are available in the literature on the subject. The marketing manager should be well aware of the great diversity, for it emphasizes the great need for being very explicit about exactly what is meant in conversations, even with one's close associates.

For example, the channel has been defined by one author as "the

---

[1] Portions of the following discussion have been adapted from material previously published by the author and his associates, especially William R. Davidson, "Channels of Distribution—One Aspect of Marketing Strategy," *Business Horizons*, Special Issue (February 1961), 84 ff; William R. Davidson and Alton F. Doody, *Retailing Management* (New York: Ronald Press Co., 1966), Chapter 2; and Theodore N. Beckman and William R. Davidson, *Marketing* (New York: Ronald Press Co., 8th ed., 1967), Chapter 9.

pipeline through which a product flows on its way to the consumer. The manufacturer puts his product into the pipeline, or marketing channel, and various marketing people move it along to the consumer at the other end of the channel."[2]

Another authority states, "Marketing channels are the combination of agencies through which the seller, who is often, though not necessarily, the manufacturer, markets his product to the ultimate user."[3]

A third writer views marketing channels as consisting of "intermediary sellers who intervene between the original source of supply and the ultimate consumer." In his view, the number and character of such intermediaries "are determined primarily by the requirements of sorting and by the opportunity to effect economies by suitable sorting arrangements."[4] On another occasion, the same writer described a marketing channel as a group of firms that "constitute a loose coalition engaged in exploiting a joint opportunity in the market."[5]

Another well-known source states that "the trade channel is made up of the middlemen who move goods from producers to consumers" and that "we usually think of the channel as being made up of those merchants who own the goods and of those agent middlemen who effect sales."[6]

In another source, it states that "a trading channel exists once the terms of the franchises or agreements spanning the whole gap from producer to consumer are concluded between concerns assumed to possess the necessary marketing capabilities."[7]

Still another says that "marketing channels are institutional

---

[2] Richard M. Clewett, "Checking Your Marketing Channels," No. 120 (Washington: U. S. Small Business Administration: *Management Aids for Small Manufacturers,* January 1961).

[3] John A. Howard, *Marketing Management: Analysis and Decision* (Homewood, Ill.: Richard D. Irwin, Inc., 1957), p. 179.

[4] Wroe Alderson, *Marketing Behavior and Executive Action* (Homewood, Ill.: Richard D. Irwin, Inc., 1957), p. 211.

[5] Wroe Alderson, "The Development of Marketing Channel," in Richard M. Clewett, ed., *Marketing Channels for Manufactured Goods* (Homewood, Ill.: Richard D. Irwin, Inc., 1954), p. 30.

[6] Paul D. Converse, Harvey W. Huegy, and Robert V. Mitchell, *Elements of Marketing* (Englewood Cliffs, N.J.: Prentice-Hall, Inc., 1958), p. 119.

[7] Ralph F. Breyer, "Some Observations on Structural Formation and the Growth of Marketing Channels," in Reavis Cox et al., eds., *Theory in Marketing,* 2nd Ser. (Homewood, Ill.: Richard D. Irwin, Inc., 1964), p. 164.

configurations for directing and supporting the flows, from production to use, of things of value."[8]

This variety of viewpoints leads to lack of clarity on several points. Does the channel have to do primarily with the change of ownership of goods or with the physical movement of product? Is the nature of a given channel determined by the manufacturer, acting as a seller, or by middlemen and consumers, carrying out their role as buyers? Is the channel made up only of middlemen or intervening intermediaries, or does it include the manufacturer at one end and the consumer at the other?

THE CHANNEL FOR EXCHANGE

Given some product to be marketed, several jobs must be done. First, there is the question of arrangements for bringing about changes in ownership by performance of the functions of exchange, buying, and selling. Second, there is the logistical task of adjusting the physical supply of a product to the spatial and temporal aspects of demand. This involves the functions of transportation and storage, and related activities such as physical handling and control of inventories. Third, there is the necessity of various facilitating or auxiliary functions, such as the collection and dissemination of marketing information, management of market risks, financing of marketing activities, and standardization and grading.

Generally speaking, the functions of exchange may be considered as paramount because planning for physical supply and performance of facilitating functions do not become relevant in the typical marketing organization unless there is profitable opportunity for transfers of ownership.

It appears, therefore, most realistic to define the channel of distribution as consisting of "the course taken in the transfer of title to a commodity."[9] It is the route taken in transferring the title of a product from its first owner (usually a manufacturer) to its last owner, the business user or ultimate consumer. Such a route necessarily includes both the origin and the destination; hence it should

[8] F. E. Balderson, "Design of Marketing Channels," in Reavis Cox et al., eds., *op. cit.*, p. 176.

[9] Theodore N. Beckman and William R. Davidson, *Marketing* (New York: Ronald Press Co., 8th ed., 1967), p. 230.

be viewed as including the manufacturer and the ultimate consumer, as well as any intervening middlemen, inasmuch as all three are originators and performers of much marketing activity.

The need for considering the manufacturer as part of the channel is perhaps more obvious than the case for the consumer. In a short or direct channel all of the marketing functions that are performed by any business unit are performed by the manufacturer rather than shifted to middlemen.

Less apparent is the role of the consumer as the initiator and performer of much marketing activity. Under conditions of self-service retailing, for example, the consumer is the active doer of functions such as selecting, transporting, storing, and financing, all of which were common retailing activities prior to self-service, and which are still the ordinary middlemen functions in some channels. Not only are marketing functions often shifted to the consumer, but they also form utility or manufacturing functions in some cases, as attested to by "in factory carton" marketing of many items that require home assembly.

Middlemen in the exchange channel include both merchants, who assume title and resell on their own account, and various kinds of agents or brokers, who do not take title but are nonetheless instrumental along the route taken to effect transfers of ownership. Broadly speaking, an exchange channel can also be viewed as including marketing establishments owned by vertically integrated companies, that is, those performing marketing functions on more than one plane or level of distribution. Examples are chain-store distribution warehouses and manufacturers' branch sales offices. There is no legal transfer of title between a chain-store warehouse and the retail units it serves; however, there are ordinarily intracompany transactions that have the nature of sales or shipments, and which are comparable in nature and accounted for in a manner similar to the transactions made by alternative suppliers or distributors performing similar functions on the same level or plane of distribution.

THE CHANNEL FOR LOGISTICS

The general tendency is for the physical flow of merchandising to accompany the route of exchange. This is not, however, universally the case, and there are indications that separate structural arrangements for logistics or physical distribution are increasingly important. A few examples will illustrate a variety of arrangements for providing logistical support apart from the exchange channel of distribution.

In the field of industrial marketing and in many lines of consumer goods, manufacturers' agents are used in lieu of manufacturers' sales branches. In combining the product lines of several manufacturers, the manufacturer's agent provides economical sales coverage of a given area, and often reaches certain customers who would be difficult to contact by other means. While such agents are links in the channel used to effect transfers of title, they do not ordinarily carry stocks. The physical flow of goods is another arrangement, one that is usually direct from the factory to the customer of the agent.

In the wholesale trade (as in many other lines of wholesaling), most transactions are handled from warehouse stocks owned and stored by the merchant. A large portion of the total dollar and physical volume of sales consists, however, of so-called "direct" sales. On individual orders of large size, the wholesale merchant buys from the manufacturer and takes title at the point where merchandise is loaded on cars, but the merchandise itself flows directly from factory to customer as a drop shipment, never coming near the establishment where the sale was negotiated.

Several retail mail-order companies have worked out arrangements to establish catalogue-order departments in retail establishments operated by supermarket chains. While the facilities of another retailing organization are used as part of the route through which sales contact is made with the consuming public, the merchandise is shipped directly from the mail-order establishment.

Several food-product companies with factories located in various parts of the country and wide product lines have established gigantic regional food distribution warehouses. Such warehouses consolidate in each region a reservoir of all products in the line, permitting fast delivery of mixed cars at low freight rates to wholesalers and chain warehouses. This form of physical distribution tends to be separate from organizational responsibility for sales handled through branch offices or through food brokers, and the geographic flow of merchandise does not correspond to the location of establishments responsible for making sales contacts with customers.

In the appliance industry, some wide-line manufacturers have concentrated a physical supply of various items in the line, either by centralizing all manufacturing facilities or by providing for distribution warehouses. The wholesale distributor remains as the institution making sales contact with the retailer and assumes responsibility for developing the desired share of available market potential in the area of his operation. Many types of dealers at the retail level are able to purchase full cars containing a mixture of various items in the manufacturers' assortment, with the flow of goods direct from factory or manufacturers' warehouse. The retailer still has contact with the wholesaler as the next link in the distribution channel, but in many instances this is related to transfer of title, financing arrangements, and sales-promotion assistance, and has little to do with the physical flow of merchandise.

The last two examples, in particular, reflect a growing tendency to streamline physical distribution by setting it apart from the complex of channel links used for obtaining sales. In some companies, a new department of logistics or physical distribution combines a number of previously scattered activities, including finished goods inventory control, transportation and traffic warehousing, order processing, container design, and sometimes even manufacturing scheduling.[10]

While the flow of exchange activity and the flow of physical distribution still tend to coincide in many cases, it is increasingly recognized that this coincidence may be only one of a large number of theoretical possibilities. The concept of separability of exchange and supply activities, in instances of traditional coincidence, may comprise the vision for new breakthroughs.

The exchange channel is primarily concerned with those activities that increase demand and bring about changes of ownership, such as selling, advertising, display, product information, trade and consumer credit, etc.

The flow of logistical services includes those activities having

---

[10] John F. Magee, "The Logistics of Distribution," *Harvard Business Review*, XXXVIII (July–August 1960), 89 ff.; Edward W. Smykay, Donald J. Bowersox, and Frank H. Mossman, *Physical Distribution Management* (New York: The Macmillan Co., 1961).

to do with the location, movement, and size of the physical supply of a product, and the adjustment of it to demand.

Contrasted with promotional effort, which involves many personal, psychological, and subjective considerations, logistics can be organized in a more systematic or scientific manner. Some reasons for this are: [11]

1. Personal contact is great, but not inherent, in carrying out logistics activities.
2. Logistics goals often can be more clearly defined than those for promotional efforts.
3. Alternative methods to achieve goals are becoming better known.
4. Logistics-systems alternatives lend themselves to quantification and mathematical analysis.
5. Mathematical tools to attack the more complicated logistics-systems problems are becoming available.

Logistical considerations, while sometimes innovative, can also be destructively apathetic. Consider the example of large meatpacking companies that remained married to branch houses located along the railroad tracks long after refrigerated trucks, chain supermarkets, centralized buying, prepackaged items, and new meat products had entirely changed the meat-distribution business.

STRUCTURE OF DISTRIBUTION

It is important to distinguish the concept of distribution channel from that of distribution structure. A *single* channel of distribution is brought into being when a particular set of exchange relationships is established linking a manufacturer with an ultimate consumer. For example, a single channel would be established when an insecticide manufacturer begins selling to a given hardware wholesaler, thereby establishing consumer contact through the retail stores served by the wholesaler. From the wholesaler's point of view, a single channel is formed by the establishment of trading relationships with any given store. Thus, any one manufacturer may actually be utilizing a large number of specific or single chan-

[11] J. L. Heskett, Robert M. Ivie, and Nicholas A. Glaskowsky, Sr., *Business Logistics* (New York: Ronald Press Co., 1964), p. 9.

nels, even in one marketing area. This is true in the sense that there are many traceable or separable flows of exchange or ownership.

As indicated above, if the physical flow of product does not accompany the route taken in the transfer of title, there may be many additional specific logistical channels.

The structure of distribution for a product type is composed of all of the networks in use at a given time to connect all of the manufacturers of that product type with all of the ultimate consumers or industrial users of that product class. It includes all of the exchange flows and all of the logistical flows when these are separate.

In marketing management, it is often said that the structure of distribution is a given environmental factor. The individual firm may make choices among the various routes or channels that are in the structure. The structure itself, however, is taken as a noncontrollable variable.

While this may be a good assumption to make for various short-term practical purposes, it may make one blind to great opportunities that a more visionary approach would unfold. A real breakthrough in some cases is the successful discovery of a route not previously used by any firm in a given industry. Then the new channel arrangement would be new to the entire structure of distribution as well as to the first user of it. Such an innovation, as will be shown by later examples, may originate from visionary approaches taken at any level or plane of distribution, by manufacturers, wholesalers, or retailers.

CHANNEL CONTROL AND CHANNEL "COMMANDERS"

Much recent attention has been given to channel control, by which is meant the ability of one member of a marketing channel for a given product or brand to stipulate marketing policies to other channel members.[12] Channel power may be achieved by the use of sheer economic power, political or legal means, superior knowledge, more effective promotional programs, or in other ways. The

---

[12] Louis W. Stern, "Channel Control and Inter-Organization Management," in Peter D. Bennett, *Marketing and Economic Development* (Chicago: American Marketing Association, 1965), 655 ff.

channel member who is able to use such means to achieve control over the bargaining process with other channel members obviously has a major advantage with respect to all aspects of relationships.

In many discussions of the subject, the manufacturer is cast in the role of "commander" of the channel situation. When introducing a new product or when making a major change in distribution policies, he examines a wide range of possible alternatives with respect to kinds and numbers of wholesale and retail outlets, weighs a number of factors that have a bearing upon sales volume, costs, and profitability, and selects the arrangements that best serve his purpose.

The types of decisions to be made by a manufacturer in choosing a channel may be divided into two classes: *vertical* considerations, which relate to the number of different levels or stages in the route used to effect transfers of title; and *horizontal* considerations, which pertain to the density or selectivity of distribution and the classes and number of outlets on a given plane (for example, wholesale or retail level).

Vertical choices may be illustrated by alternatives of the following kind that might be available to a manufacturer of home furnishings. He could choose (1) to sell direct to the consumer without use of any middlemen, perhaps by means of catalogs; (2) to sell to retail furniture stores by means of a manufacturer-employed sales organization; (3) to sell to furniture stores through wholesale merchants; (4) to sell to wholesale merchants by means of manufacturers' agents who also sell other related lines; (5) to use manufacturers' agents who call directly upon retailer; or (6) to use some combination of the above channels in order to reach different geographic markets or various classes of stores, perhaps differentiated on the basis of sales volume.

Horizontal choices may be illustrated by listing the channels open to a manufacturer of home furnishings who has his own sales organization calling directly upon the retail furniture trade. He must decide whether to (1) continue confining his distribution to retail furniture stores; (2) sell also to furniture departments in regular department stores; (3) offer his merchandise also to variety-department stores operated by certain variety chains that are expanding their merchandise offerings of this general type of merchandise; or (4) sell to various forms of discount houses.

Conventional discussions of channel problems have tended to devote more emphasis to questions of the vertical kind by stressing the factors that determine whether or when it is feasible for the manufacturer to move forward in the channel, assuming within his own organization the functions normally performed by various types of middlemen. He thereby carries his own marketing effort as close as possible to the final user. Among the various factors generally believed to contribute to the feasibility of short channels are a high unit value of product, a wide line of items marketed together, geographically concentrated markets, and financial strength and marketing know-how in the manufacturing company's organization.

In recent years several factors have tended to make decisions of the horizontal type appear as matters of greater decision-making significance. For one thing, various types of retail outlets have greatly diversified their merchandise offerings, thereby invading what was once considered the private province of establishments in other categories. As a consequence, there is a wider range of alternatives at the retail level, and each class has unique operating problems, buying procedures, and operating philosophies. Second, choices at the horizontal level are more likely to cause frictions and tensions in channel relationship. For example, antagonism among regular household-appliance stores and a possible withdrawal of sales support by them may occur when a manufacturer decides to solicit business aggressively from various types of discount houses. Similar frictions exist at the wholesale level when distributors in one line of trade find that new outlets in another trade classification are selling identical products formerly distributed in a more confined way. Third, decisions to use particular types of outlets at the retail level—a horizontal choice—may often dictate the kind of channel to be used in a vertical sense, since the retailer customarily uses certain sources of supply and a traditional outlook on buying arrangements.

As an illustration of a strategical horizontal channel choice, it has been reported that Armstrong Cork entered the household wax and polish business via the less competitive hardware and department store outlets, in order to gain something of a consumer franchise before engaging in shelf-space rivalry with S. C. Johnson and other well-established companies in supermarkets.

The Middleman. In numerous situations, the manufacturer can realistically be regarded as the channel commander, at least in the short run. It is rather common for the manufacturer to call the plays when he is large and powerful, when he has developed high public status by his demand-creation activities, when he finds it feasible to use a limited number of distribution outlets, and when distribution outlets operate under the terms of a franchise and would be seriously handicapped by the withdrawal of it. This tends to be the case with automobiles, some lines of household appliances, and major brands of automotive petroleum products sold through gasoline service stations.

In many other instances the manufacturer is channel commander not in any basic way but only in a derivative sense, owing to the strong position of middlemen in the channel. This circumstance stems from the twofold role of middlemen as distributors of manufacturers' goods and as suppliers of the purchasing requirements of their customers. When the middleman carries a variety of items drawn from many original sources, he tends to be more strongly oriented to the latter role than to the former.

Briefly, it may be noted that the manufacturers' freedom to select among conceptually available alternatives is practically limited by conditions and attitudes prevailing among middlemen. Many circumstances limit the potentialities for distribution in certain types of channel situations, whether the choice be of a vertical or horizontal nature. Examples of these circumstances follow:

The manufacturer finds that the most desirable types of outlets have already been pre-empted by strongly entrenched competitive organizations.

The middleman, already using his space and capital resources to the maximum, is reluctant to add additional items to his line, since such proliferation poses serious logistics problems, particularly in terms of available display space, warehousing space, catalog or stock control listings, capital required for inventory investment, and so forth.

The pricing or discount structure on the item is not sufficiently attractive to induce middlemen to devote promotional effort adequate to ensure movement to the consumer.

The manufacturer mishandles consumer packaging or shipping

containers so that neither is acceptable under the conditions of selling or merchandise handling typical in a particular line of trade.

The manufacturer has created tensions or frictions in trade channels, either by using distribution techniques that place him in direct competition with some possible outlets or by distributing through various outlets in different lines of trade with varying margin and sales-supporting requirements. He thereby generates antagonism, which makes his products unacceptable or, at best, only marginally acceptable to certain types of potential outlets.

When the manufacturer encounters conditions of such a nature, he often learns that the middleman, in his role as a buyer and selector of sources of supply, really determines the nature of the channel of distribution.

The Consumer. Even when middlemen, whether they are wholesale distributors or retailers, are more strongly entrenched than manufacturers as channel commanders, their role too is more derivative than basic, owing to their need to adjust to constant changes. In a private-enterprise economy characterized by high levels of buying income per family, the consumer has a wide range of choices when it comes to satisfying those wants that can be met in the marketplace. The consumer can, for example, decide whether to use more of his purchasing power to eat better, to travel more, to buy more clothes, or to purchase new appliances for his home. If the choice is for appliances, he can satisfy his needs at a department store, an appliance store, a mail-order company, a furniture store, a discount house, an automobile-accessories store or, in some areas, a supermarket or consumers' cooperative organization. His choice will ordinarily be the outlet that has best harmonized its marketing mix with the buying interests of the group of consumers of which the individual purchaser is a member.

In the long run, therefore, the buying decisions of consumers determine the adjustments that occur in the relative importance of different kinds of channels of distribution. As adjustments occur at the retail level, they naturally have their impact in a vertical sense, by modifying the relative positions of various kinds of channel links between the manufacturer and the retailer.

HISTORIC BREAKTHROUGHS

The manner in which marketing vision has led to major distribution breakthroughs may be illustrated with several classic examples. From the many historic cases that might well be chosen, three have been selected because of their varying nature and because of the manner in which their long-standing effects are still apparent. Attention is given to A&P's cash-and-carry stores, to General Motors' dealer structure, and to several breakthroughs associated with Sears. It is observable in each instance how an innovative mind conceived the opportunity to achieve a differential advantage by viewing the process of distribution in a new way.

A&P's Cash-and-Carry Stores. The Great Atlantic & Pacific Tea Company, founded in 1859, developed originally as a service retailer, characteristic of its times. It had trading stamps, delivery service, charge accounts, and premiums for promotions. In 1912, John Hartford, a founder's son with marketing vision, observed an unusual New Jersey store that did a large volume of business on the basis of limited service and low prices. Sensing a possible distribution breakthrough, he got approval for an experiment at A&P. This involved a small unit that could be operated in many cases by one man. Services were cut to the bone by eliminating stamps, streamlining the inventory, and operating on a cash-and-carry basis. Traditional grocery-store gross margins at the time were about 25 per cent. With its new stores, A&P had a differential of about 10 to 15 per cent of sales, thus giving it a cost-protected price advantage over service competitors. So successful was this breakthrough that the company opened 7,500 stores of the new type within three years--about seven per day. John Hartford was quoted as saying, "We went so fast, hoboes hopping off trains got hired as managers." [13]

The Dealer Structure of General Motors. Prior to 1920, automobile distribution was largely from manufacturer to "distributor-wholesalers" who resold to dealers within their respective territories. Gradually manufacturers took over the wholesale function. During the 1920s, the prevailing manufacturer attitude was that

[13] "Pinching 500,000,000,000 Pennies," *Fortune* (March 1963), p. 172.

the manufacturer was responsible for the product, the price, and the advertising, and the rest of marketing was up to the dealer. Under conditions of large untapped primary demand, this worked well for some. Henry Ford, by stressing continually enlarged production of standard models at lowered prices, brought Ford to a position of strong sales leadership.

At the same time, executives of General Motors realizing the growing complexities of marketing under conditions of increasing ownership saturation and trade-ins, began to give more attention to retail distribution. Alfred P. Sloan, Jr., as chief executive officer, fitted up a private railroad car as an office and traveled all over the United States, visiting five to ten dealers a day in their own towns. It was apparent to him that the economic position of dealers in the mid-1920s was deteriorating and that dealer franchises were less in demand. There were increasing problems of achieving market penetration, liquidating inventories at the end of model runs (then the financial responsibility solely of the dealer), of maintaining communication between manufacturers and dealers, and of preserving dealer financial solvency.[14]

Sloan and his General Motors associates decided that something drastic had to be done not only for the sake of dealers but also for the soundness of the enterprise as a whole. The decision was to involve the corporation, to an extent wholly unprecedented in the industry, in the retail distribution of its products, while still retaining independent franchised dealers. The resulting program involved, among other things, the following: (1) scientific local-area studies of market potential, to locate and establish dealers with respect to market opportunity; (2) shared manufacturer and dealer responsibility for year-end liquidation of old models; (3) the development of proper accounting systems on a departmental basis (new cars, used cars, service, parts) to permit internal and comparative analyses of financial position and operating results; (4) improved management and marketing approaches; and (5) the development of financing methods whereby able persons with inadequate capital could be assisted in the establishment of new dealerships.

Sloan has attributed much of the success and stability of Gen-

---

[14] Adapted from Alfred P. Sloan, Jr., *My Years With General Motors* (Garden City, N.Y.: Doubleday & Co., 1964), Chapter 16, "Distribution and the Dealers."

eral Motors in the years that followed to these early changes in relationships in the distributive organization.

Distributive Breakthroughs at Sears. Few indeed are the business organizations that could vie with Sears, Roebuck & Company with regard to outstanding visionary developments in distribution.

The two companies most prominently associated with the development of the mail-order business—Montgomery Ward & Company, Inc., and Sears, Roebuck & Company—date, respectively, from 1872 and 1893. In the early days the initial success of the enterprises founded by Montgomery Ward and Richard Sears is attributed to the failure of country merchants to adjust to changing conditions. In the post-Civil War period, country general stores and small-town merchants were characterized by high costs of operation, limited variety, frequent out-of-stock conditions, and high prices. Their failure to respond to rising income levels among farm families and industrial workers paved the way for mail-order pioneers. Sears won the confidence of customers by truthful descriptions of goods illustrated in catalogs and in a firm "money back" guarantee. Merchandise was bought in large quantities and priced to appeal to a rural target market.

The early success of the Sears pattern of mail-order distribution is an outstanding case of response to changing environmental conditions. The company took maximum advantage of the early availability of rail transportation to provide delivery to remote places. Rural free delivery service provided an opportunity for accelerated distribution of general and special catalogs, as well as bringing to rural America more information of all kinds which tended to make people more dissatisfied with offerings of inadequate small-town stores. Another impetus in 1913 was the inauguration of parcel post service, bringing small-package delivery right to the farmer's door.

Location became a major differential advantage of Sears as the mail-order business began to mature in the early 1920s, and more people had automobiles and access to city stores. Sears began to open retail stores in the 1920s, and 324 establishments were opened in the 1925–29 period.[15] General Robert E. Wood, then the principal Sears executive, was the only major department store executive with the vision to anticipate the future influence of the auto-

[15] "Sears Makes It Look Easy," *Fortune* (May 1964), 120 ff.

mobile and suburban living. While other merchants concentrated upon downtown locations that were oriented to public transit facilities, Sears expanded rapidly in newer outlying areas. At the time the company was often criticized or ridiculed by competitors for building stores upon "farmland." Once established, however, these stores often had a spatial monopoly that went largely unchallenged until the post-World War II era, and they had only to perform to Sears standards to grow substantially.

The nearly complete vertical integration of the channel of distribution found in the contemporary Sears organization is often a subject of envy on the part of manufacturers who must devote considerable marketing effort to the obtaining of good will from thousands or tens of thousands of independent middlemen in their various channels.[16] A more recent chief executive officer, T. V. Houser, has contrasted the Sears method of distribution with the typical channel situation of the large manufacturer. According to Houser's account, the products of such a manufacturer are ordinarly distributed by a very large number of small retailers. There are likely to be independent or manufacturer-controlled wholesale functions in the channel. The manufacturer attempts to exert the marketing leadership in the channel, by preselling the product through advertising, and then to secure distribution on the basis of established demand.

The Sears type of system is just the reverse pattern of distribution. In Houser's account, the large retail distributor furnishes an outlet for great numbers of small manufacturers. Product determination becomes the responsibility of the retail distributor and marketing or channel leadership comes also from him through product advertising, display, direct sales effort, and customer-credit arrangements. The concept of channel commander is illustrated by Houser's statement: "So long as the customer is free to buy from competing sellers and producers, the function of the business closest to the customer must carry weight in influencing the decisions that determine the character and cost of the product." [17]

---

[16] T. V. Houser, "The True Role of the Marketing Executive," *Journal of Marketing* (April 1959), 363 ff.

[17] *Ibid.*, p. 364.

CONTEMPORARY ILLUSTRATIONS

Distribution breakthroughs need not bring into being new types or methods in the sense that they were previously unknown. The breakthrough may involve a new approach to working with a given type of situation, of utilizing a type of capability with reference to other products, or of applying concepts that have been perfected in some other field. Some contemporary cases are illustrated in the following paragraphs.

Coca-Cola as a Distribution Network. Depth of marketing vision has been explained as the successful seeking of the understanding of the essential being of a company, its distinctiveness of differential advantage with respect to ability to exploit profitable opportunities.

This was well illustrated in Chapter 1, where the inner being of The Coca-Cola Company was described as a remarkable distribution network. Distribution through more than 1,600,000 outlets of every kind, type, and description, has, in the words of a former president, put the product "within an arm's length of desire." With 1,000 franchised bottlers supplying this myriad of retail outlets, the ability to gain rapid distribution of a new item in the product line is readily assured.

Programmed Merchandising at Scott's. The O. M. Scott & Sons Company of Marysville, Ohio, is the leading manufacturer and marketer of lawn products. The importance of distribution in the company's marketing mix is illustrated by the following statement: "There are three basic components for marketing success by a business such as Scott's: (1) Products must be those that build leadership because they satisfy the customer; (2) Advertising and promotion must be of the type that translates this leadership into buying interest; (3) Products must be available at the time and place required to convert favorable attitudes into sales."[18]

During a period of rapid post-World War II expansion, a policy of highly selective distribution was followed, with all but a very small proportion of sales made through hardware stores and garden and nursery stores that adhered closely to a standard Scott program. Each store was called upon directly by a company sales-

[18] O. M. Scott & Sons Co., Annual Report, 1965, p. 9.

man, known as an account executive, and physical distribution was handled from company-controlled distribution centers direct to stores.

In the mid-1960s, consumer market research in a number of major market areas indicated that a large proportion of medium- to upper-income home-owning families did not use even one bag of lawn fertilizer in a year. This fact, along with other considerations, led the company to the decision to expand its distribution greatly, increasing the exposure of the product line to the nonusing segment of the general public.

While Scott's had significant distribution among department stores, the sales achieved in most such outlets were usually quite disappointing. In the summer of 1964, a careful study was made of selected typical department store cases.

The Scott lawn seed and chemical line was ordinarily merchandised as part of the housewares department. Top management of most such stores was oriented to fashion apparel or home furnishings, or both, often with minimal interest in lawn products. Thus there was little internal pressure upon the department manager to maximize his opportunity. In housewares the department manager or buyer sometimes had as many as 200 merchandise suppliers and several hundred merchandise items. The merchandising requirements of the Scott line, as developed with primary attention to hardware and garden stores, did not usually fit the operating method of department stores, thereby often generating friction between store and supplier.

Merchandising is commonly thought of as having the right merchandise at the right time at the right place in the right quantities and at the right price. A consultant to Scott's emphasized the concept of merchandising in terms of the opportunities to be wrong in the distribution channel, no matter how good the product or its promotion.

For example, a large department store was expected to have about 40 Scott items in stock. It had, in a typical case, a downtown and four branch stores, with five total locations. There were five distinct merchandising seasons with different quantity requirements to meet consumer needs. And there were at least ten key marketing activities to be handled at the retail level (dealer advertising, sales training, display, etc.). This is $40 \times 5 \times 5 \times 10$

or 10,000 opportunities to be wrong, assuming the variables are multiplicative, which was approximately the case.

Owing to the lack of top-management store interest and the buyer's orientation to different product classes, the "wrongs" were sometimes more numerous than the "rights."

The solution was for Scott's to become much more highly involved in department store merchandising activities. Special programs were worked out in detail for each major department store account that could be interested in substantially expanding its volume of lawn-products sales. Plans for monthly sales by product were developed by Scott account executives. These were projected to dollar totals and incorporated into the store's departmental plan well ahead of each six-month merchandising season, thereby automatically generating sufficient "open-to-buy" to cover planned sales. Promotional activities for each month (each week for the peak seasons) were detailed in advance, with responsibility clearly defined for each store location. All operating requirements were oriented to the conditions at the individual store. Some of these programs involved 50 or more pages of plans developed for an individual account. They were so comprehensive that the department manager rarely had to make a personal judgment that was not covered.

A fortuitous circumstance was that a trade magazine, *Department Store Economist,* featured prominently in its October 1964 issue the concept of *programmed merchandising*—something very much like the Scott department store program. This made it possible to popularize the new approach to department stores as programmed merchandising.

Many department stores were on this program of Scott-planned retail distribution activities within their companies in the fall of 1964. Sales increases were very large among this group. This provided the company with many success case histories for further expansion of the program among similar outlets in 1965 and 1966, and the extension of similar distribution approaches to other new classes of trade for the company, including mass outlets and supermarkets.

Total Supplier Distribution at Cotter. The retail hardware trade has long been dominated by the small independent merchant. According to Census of Business figures for 1958, single-unit independents accounted for more than 85 per cent of total hardware store sales and chains of more than ten units accounted for only 7 per cent. During the period 1948–58, the total number of hardware stores remained nearly stable at about 34,000, and the sales of such stores dropped from 1.9 per cent to 1.5 per cent of total retail trade.

Increasingly, the typical independent was finding it difficult to compete effectively with the pricing and often superior merchandising of branches of department stores in suburban centers, discount outlets, upgrading of units of variety store chains, general merchandise diversification in some supermarket companies and drug chains, and catalog retailing.

In the late 1940s and 1950s, distribution in the hardware trade was originally quite complex, with many contacts between retailers and the various agencies that supplied them. Much of the effort at the wholesale level was devoted to competitive activities, as one wholesaler vied with another, attempting to get a larger share of the dealer's business. This also meant that vast quantities of the retailer's time were taken up in contacts with order-taking salesmen of many suppliers.

For example, in a study supervised by the author in 1952, based on a sample of 10 Columbus, Ohio, independent hardware stores, it was found that the average (per store) number of suppliers included 7 general-line wholesalers, 10 specialty wholesalers, and 13 direct-selling manufacturers, for a total of about 30 regular or consistent suppliers.[19]

Perceiving the inefficiencies and competitive limitations of such a distribution pattern, a small group of hardware retailers had earlier banded together in Chicago. Under the guidance of John Cotter, a recognized leader in the hardware trade, they established a retailer-owned cooperative to serve as a complete supplier to members. It was named Cotter & Company. This program adapted various merchandising approaches and operating methods that had been developed earlier by chain stores and by voluntary chains in other lines.

As is the case with other retailer cooperatives, each member

---

[19] Harold Spielbert, *Purchasing Practices of Independent Retail Hardware Stores Located in Columbus, Ohio*, unpublished Master's thesis, deposited in library of Ohio State University, 1952.

buys stock and receives patronage dividends from the wholesaler, in proportion to his volume of purchases during the year.

By getting a large proportion of the total business of each member dealer, and by handling this with a simplified mail-order method from catalogs, the order-taking salesman of the traditional wholesaler was eliminated. Savings in credit and bad debt expenses were also realized by concentrating on better-financed dealers. These, plus other efficiencies associated with larger average order size, are claimed by Cotter to amount to direct savings in the range of 6 per cent to 8 per cent of sales at the wholesale level, as compared with traditional methods of hardware wholesaling.

Cotter executives feel that certain intangibles are even more important to the health of merchant members. Thus there are programs of store identification ("Value Service" or "True Value"), mass advertising by direct mail and in national media, bin-ticket stock-control systems, store-modernization counsel, pricing guidance for volume sales of key items, buying of promotional items in massive quantities for merchandise cost savings, and resource relationships with direct-shipping manufacturers.

For a small service fee, Cotter handles contacts with those manufacturers that normally sell direct to retailers, arranging for their participation in Cotter promotions, and handling the billing and collection for the manufacturer, who receives settlement in one sum for all outlets, without worry about bad-debt losses.

By utilizing some ideas and working with proven principles of closer integration of efforts between channel levels, Cotter has achieved fabulous growth in the fairly stable hardware trade. From 25 members in 1948, it grew to 1,885 in 1965. Wholesale volume increased from $385,000 in 1948 to a projected $106,000,000 for 1966.

With similar growth on the part of several other well-known hardware groups, distribution conditions have greatly changed. This has made it necessary for many manufacturers to realign their marketing effort accordingly.

Such changes have not, of course, been confined to retailer cooperatives. Many progressive, independent hardware wholesalers have also developed aggressive mechandising programs, thereby extending their influence forward in the distribution channel, and bringing about a more highly integrated relationship between wholesaling and retailing, often with some shifting of functions from the retail level to wholesale organizations.

EVALUATION OF CHANNEL-OF-DISTRIBUTION RELATIONSHIPS

The general discussion in the early parts as well as the more specific historic and contemporary examples just presented provide ample evidence that a channel of distribution is something more than a marketing choice that is made by a manufacturing company. It shows, moreover, why many manufacturers have had to modify their thinking about factors that influence channel choices. In any company that follows a program of modern, consumer-oriented marketing management, considerations relating to consumer requirements are elevated to paramount status, and factors relating to company situation are subordinated, at least in the sense that the latter must be adjusted to the former. This means that the manufacturer must look beyond his own circumstances and beyond the situation of intermediaries in the channel, so that he is attuned to the wants and interests of the consumer in the market segment he is trying to reach.

CHARTING THE CHANNEL

Too often channel relationships do not receive due attention, since they involve matters that are "outside" the company and hence are more easily taken for granted than other activities, such as marketing research, advertising, or personal selling. These "internal" functions come up for more frequent review or appraisal since responsibility for them tends to be fixed on the organizational chart or in job descriptions, and the cost of them is conspicuously identified on accounting statements.

In manufacturing companies, opportunities for more frequent and more realistic appraisal of channel problems and relationships might be provided by new approaches to charting the organization of marketing activities. An organization chart might well show not only the various departments within the marketing division of the company, but also all of the vertical links in the channel used to effect transfers of title to eventual users, and, moreover, the different types of outlets on each horizontal plane or state of distribution.

Another recommendation is to prepare operating statements that reveal sales performance and cost situations through the channels used. At the top of such a statement would be sales, stated in terms of prices paid by the ultimate user, and showing as expenses the costs of marketing through the various channels in use.

In any event, manufacturers will have made progress in solving channel-of-distribution problems when they recognize two considerations. First, channel activities must be thought of as only one aspect of the total marketing mix and one that must be coordinated with other ingredients, as these contribute to the objective of reaching a defined market; second, in the long run, the nature of channels is determined from "the bottom up" rather than from "the top down."

Finally, it may be concluded that the ability to achieve a differential advantage in distribution through marketing vision is related to ability to perceive the ways either in which wants are satisfied or in which satisfaction is being thwarted. By focusing attention upon values created through distribution, or upon values desired but remaining unfulfilled, some firms will look beyond the more readily controllable factors of product, price, and promotion, and achieve real breakthroughs by innovation in the flow of ownership transfer and product movement through distribution channels.

■

Summary

Marketing management tends to concentrate on things over which it can exercise sway—product, price, selling, marketing research, advertising—to the neglect of the vital role that distribution arrangements can play in implementing marketing visions.

Defining the channel of distribution as the "course taken in the transfer of title to a commodity," requires inclusion of the manufacturer and the ultimate consumer in the channel.

Streamlining physical distribution by separating it from the route of exchanges of title provides a foundation for enunciating new marketing visions.

Major examples of visionary approaches occur in evolving new distribution channels for particular products.

Distribution breakthroughs also come from a new approach to an existing channel and from applying concepts or capabilities perfected in other fields.

12

Merger and Acquisition

■

Paul van der Stricht

■

The growing tide of mergers and acquisitions testifies to industry's awareness of the potential benefits of corporate marriages. Yet many curious matings raise questions about the vision of the corporations initiating them. This is not to argue against a most unlikely merger of a business whose vision is management talent for buying depressed situations and upgrading them or a business whose core is financial wizardry. But these are special circumstances. For most companies, mergers are a serious drain on manpower, time, and resources. Blind worship at the shrine of the Great God Diversification may hinder or arrest opportunities to blend the benefits of diversification with logical extensions of a business. Sound mergers take sound vision.

Chiclets are quite different from Bromo-Seltzer, Richard Hudnut Shampoo, Anahist, and DuBarry cosmetics, yet the purchase of American Chicle by Warner-Lambert marries dissimilar products with similar characteristics of packaging, rapid purchase-repurchase cycles, channels of merchandising, and advertising response. By the same principles, the subsequent merger of American Chicle with Smith Brothers cough drops is a further logical development of the Warner-Lambert vision.

The merger of Coca-Cola with Minute Maid and Duncan Coffee simultaneously with soft drink line extensions in different flavor categories with Sprite and Fanta and the low-calorie category with Tab represents the application of a twofold vision of the business. One aspect of the vision has already been noted—an extraordinary distribution skill that Coca-Cola management can contribute to the acquired companies, though outside the bottler network, of course. The second is the definition of the firm as being not in the carbonated cola beverage field, nor even in the soft drink field, but rather in the refreshment business, or indeed, in the beverage business. To these instances of horizontal mergers can be added vertical ones, such as cosmetics companies acquiring chemical interests or, more frequently, chemical and ethical drug producers entering cosmetic and proprietary drug fields.

To discuss fully the role of merger and acquisition as a marketing strategy, we have obtained the contribution of Paul van der Stricht, Vice Chairman of Warner-Lambert Pharmaceutical Company, for here is a firm which has made eminently sound use of this strategy.

Mr. van der Stricht, who has spearheaded Warner-Lambert's merger program, is thus able to cover the philosophy and mechanics of mergers with great practical wisdom. He outlines with sharp clarity the marketing values to be sought, the do's and the don't's, with concise case histories to illustrate his major points.

Mr. van der Stricht joined Warner-Lambert as Director of European Operations in 1953. He subsequently was named Vice President for European Operations and in 1957 became President of Warner-Lambert International. In 1961 Mr. van der Stricht was promoted to Executive Vice President of the corporation. In addition, he retains responsibility for all international operations. He is also an officer or director of a number of foreign companies affiliated with the Warner-Lambert group.

Mr. van der Stricht was graduated from the University of Ghent with the degree of Doctor of Law and the University of Brussels with an M.A. in admiralty law. He was associated with the New York law firm of Davis, Polk, Wardwell, Sunderland, & Kiendl from 1934 to 1942, when he joined the United States Army. He was awarded the Legion of Merit, French Legion of Honor, and French Croix de Guerre with Palm. In 1945 Mr. van der Stricht was attached to the United States Embassy in Paris. In 1946 he obtained an honorable discharge from the Army with the rank of Colonel. From 1946 to 1953, prior to joining Warner-Lambert, Mr. van der Stricht was associated with the chemical and antibiotic industry.

■

MERGER AND ACQUISITION

PAUL VAN DER STRICHT

One of the most potent, immediate and effective tools available to management in attaining corporate objectives is the merger.

The fact that more than 10,000 mergers have taken place since World War II indicates that management is well aware of the existence of this tool. For instance, of the 500 largest United States industrial corporations, as compiled by *Fortune*, 486 have made at least one acquisition in the last ten years. The Federal Trade Commission reports that 1,893 mergers took place in 1965 alone. Since 1950, the nation's 200 largest manufacturing firms are reported to have acquired more than 2,000 companies through merger. The further fact that about one-third of all these mergers, according to the American Management Association estimates, has proved unsuccessful suggests that it is a tool to be used with some care, restraint, and advance planning.

Much has been written on mergers—possibly too much. Numerous checklists and other mechanical procedures to evaluate the potential of a merger are readily available. One such questionnaire consists of 230 points, not including subheadings. Another, compiled by and for personnel directors, covers 66 subjects and includes the question, "Has every employee of the about to be acquired company filled out a job description?"

Given this backlog, it would be extremely difficult in the course of this single chapter to improve upon the existing body of "how to" information concerning mergers, and I do not intend to try. Rather, my comments will essentially be a reflection of personal views and personal experience of how a merger can strategically serve to achieve specific marketing objectives. Also, I will speak throughout this chapter from the buyer's viewpoint. (An entire book could well be devoted to how to sell a company.)

Before starting, one factor bears mention, because it cannot be solved by the checklist system and because it probably has caused more mergers to go sour than any single other one. I refer to the human component in the merger equation.

Just as the perfect recipe for the perfect marriage has never been developed because in every marriage individual people are involved, so too in the world of corporate marriages no formula, however capably developed and applied, will yield the secret of a perfect merger. No two mergers have ever been or ever will be exactly the same. They can be similar in intention or characteristics, but since people are inevitably involved, they will present distinct and different problems.

Carrying the marriage metaphor one step further, the history of a merger divides readily into three recognizable periods: (1) the search for a partner; (2) the courtship; (3) settling into married life.

THE SEARCH FOR A PARTNER

Because it is a massive and tortuously complex subject in itself, I will omit from this discussion any reference to or consideration of the antitrust aspects of mergers and acquisitions. This omission is in no way intended to minimize the importance of the question—quite the opposite. Never have the courts and the government bureaus dealing with antitrust matters been more prolific—and in some measure more confusing—in handing down key decisions or rulings affecting mergers. Candidates to merger will do well to study exhaustively the legal implications of their actions.

I would also like to assume that the reader rejects "bigness for bigness' sake" as a valid reason to merge. As one investment banker with extensive experience in acquisitions recently observed, "In some of these cases, the main objective of pushing the merger through seems to be to permit the executives to fly bigger company planes." There is a clear distinction between healthy corporate growth by merger as a result of planning and policy, and mere fattening of volume.

Before following the path of growth through merger, it is essential that management pass through a process of thinking along the following lines:

(a) the development of a plan for the enterprise—a clear and comprehensive definition of exactly what is the business of the company, and what it wishes to become.

(b) the determination of whether implementation of that vision can best be served by acquisition and merger, or by development from within.

(c) should the corporate decision be to develop at least in part by merger, a determination of the type and approximate size of the company to be acquired.

It is only when these three steps have been carefully dealt with that a search into the availability of companies fitting the plan should be undertaken. To begin the search at an earlier date is to court disaster. Mergers, like marriages, may be contracted in haste. But both are then often repented in leisure or lived with in uneasy resignation or tolerance.

THE COURTSHIP

Once a candidate to merger has been identified, a preliminary study of strengths and weaknesses should be undertaken, never losing clear sight of the strengths and weaknesses of the acquiring company. To be fruitful, an acquisition must be the means for both partners to fulfill basic needs; it must enable both to achieve together objectives which neither could reach alone. It must, in arithmetic terms, satisfy the equation: two plus two equals five.

In human terms, this equation may be read to mean in most cases that you did not "buy out" a concern solely for the naked reason of dollar profit or immediate benefit, but with the hope of obtaining lasting and willing cooperation. For it is this cooperation which in the long run is the safest, most effective way to turn an acquisition into an investment and a dynamic enterprise, rather than into just a purchase.

After analysis has been completed, and if the conclusions point to the soundness of the merger, the next step (the importance of which is very often overlooked) is to select with great care the company representative who will carry on the courtship. It goes without saying that tact and diplomacy are among the essential qualifications of the suitor's representative. He must be thoroughly versed in the complex techniques of mergers. In addition, he should have a full understanding of both the motivations and objectives of seller and buyer. He must also possess sound psychological insight, and be able to assess quickly the personnel and particularly the management of the company to be acquired. Before getting married, it's wise to meet the family.

Soon after the chosen negotiator has determined that there is genuine interest on both sides, he must attempt to identify those elements in a merger which will appeal most to the other party. In the light of this information he will frame the terms of the offer which are most likely to sound attractive. As a matter of course, the framework of these terms will have been carefully prepared and agreed upon by his own management, based on studies carried out during the search period. In practice, these studies will probably involve an evaluation at different levels. As a rule of thumb, evaluations based solely on balance-sheet figures or profit-and-loss performance may lead to frustration and disillusionment.

It is during this stage of negotiations that the human element tends most often to be shunted aside in favor of more tangible short-term considerations. The acquiring member, in his haste to achieve his immediate goal, often is tempted to measure his acquisition in terms of what he must pay rather than in terms of what he is getting.

This should be the time for flexibility, the time to assess and evaluate the human factor. It is, for instance, crucial at this stage not to make promises or representations which will be forgotten as soon as the formalities of the merger are completed. The formalities merely signify a change of ownership, and the beginning of the most difficult phase of the merger—integration. That phase will take time, and it is bound to fail if it must be built on the foundation of broken promises.

SETTLING INTO MARRIED LIFE

Just as in its personal analogy, this third phase in corporate marriage is more difficult to chart than the first two. Possibly the best advice available consists of two words: "Go slow."

There will inevitably be problems of parallel staff functions, of the obvious advantage of moving certain products or even entire product lines from one company to another, of consolidating manufacturing and research facilities, of radically changing long-established trade practices.

It is undeniable that among the many attractive features of most mergers is precisely this kind of overhead-cutting and efficiency-promoting reorganization. It is part of the input of the 2-plus-2-equals-5 formula.

But in the interest of lasting, long-term success, it is the responsibility of the managements of both partners to effect these economies with a minimum of damage to the human factors involved. As a general rule, it may be said in summation that any skillful group of technicians can effect mergers that are legally and financially sound, but only outstanding managers can make them succeed psychologically. Perhaps, in the long run, that is why they are outstanding.

With this generalized *caveat* of all mergers, we can turn to some of the specific strategic motivations that have impelled a number of recent marketing-minded mergers.

Essentially, and again barring the "let's get bigger together" kind of merger, a company will seek a merger to achieve a specific purpose. Thus it may want:

1. To acquire a means of distribution.
2. To penetrate a geographic market.
3. To acquire or pool managerial know-how.
4. To enter a new field.
5. To achieve vertical integration of existing products.
6. To acquire a manufacturing base or raw-material sources.
7. To extend existing marketing lines.
8. To serve newly developing marketing needs.
9. To buy time.
10. To improve the effectiveness of its existing marketing effort.
11. To avoid cyclical and seasonal instability.
12. To acquire consumer franchises.

1. *To Acquire a Means of Distribution.* Many recent examples in this class have been reported, among which is the acquisition by Georgia-Pacific of Vanity Fair mills. G-P, of course, has long been basic in timber and timber products. It also had the facilities, through a subsidiary company, to manufacture household tissues. However, the management of G-P is said to have felt that it lacked

both the salesmen and the established contacts with wholesale and retail distributors to make a go of this very specialized kind of retail product. It therefore instituted a search for a small but active company that had outstanding talents in this rather specialized marketing field. In Vanity Fair it found an organization that had proved its effectiveness in the distribution and sale of private-label products in the field. Both the reasoning and the integration process have apparently been successful, since G-P has been able within less than three years to become a profitable, growing challenger in its chosen field.

Other examples can be cited: Evans Products Company, one of the important factors in the United States plywood industry, is reported to have felt that it was being hamstrung by independent jobbers who were reluctant to carry the company's line. To solve this difficulty, Evans bought control of two plywood-specialty manufacturers owning between them 35 warehouses throughout the United States.

These acquisitions incidentally had a basic effect on the whole nature of the company. Formerly it had concentrated on serving the needs of large single users. Now, with its distributions problems solved, it is increasingly expanding into the building-materials field.

It is interesting to note that here is a case of a merger that not only helped to solve an immediate marketing problem, but also placed the company in a position from which it could re-evaluate and reformulate its total planning as described above. It should be noted that the development and acceptance of a plan is not a once-and-for-all historic milestone. A successful plan should have built into it provisions for continuous review and adaptation to future opportunities.

Another recent merger largely motivated by reasons of distribution was that between Arwood Industries and the Cast-O-Matic Company. The former is in the investment casting field; the latter in the die-casting field. Both needed to support relatively expensive technical field sales forces which frequently called on the same kinds of customers—aircraft and aerospace manufacturers, etc. By merging, the two companies have been able to jointly provide better sales service, at lower costs.

2. *To Penetrate a Geographic Market.* In today's business world,

there is an increasing trend toward thinking in world-wide terms, rather than in local terms. This realization has led many companies to consider—and consummate—mergers which would have appeared less justified only a few years ago. The recent merger between Warner-Lambert Pharmaceutical Company and the American Chicle Company is a case in point. Warner-Lambert enjoyed a wide international marketing network, while American Chicle had not yet penetrated several key parts of the world, notably Europe and Asia. As a result of collaborative efforts after the merger, the new American Chicle Division has been able to increase materially its overseas sales in a very short time.

It should be pointed out that while the geographical "fit" was one of the most impelling factors that militated in favor of the merger, there were many others as well. Both companies were mass marketers of nondurable packaged goods sold in large measure through similar channels of trade.

3. *To Acquire or Pool Managerial Know-How.* As the state of technology becomes increasingly complex and specialized, many companies have found it to their mutual advantage to marry their skills and resources in differing, but related, fields and disciplines. To use another example with which I am personally acquainted, the acquisition by Warner-Lambert of Research Specialties, Inc., of Richmond, California, is a good illustration of this strategy. Research Specialties has extensive know-how and capability in the instrumentation field. Warner-Lambert, through its Warner-Chilcott Laboratories Division, has long served the medical profession and understands its needs. By pooling skills, the two companies hope to become a factor in the rapidly growing field of medical electronics—the application of advanced engineering techniques to solving difficult problems in the health field.

4. *To Enter a New Field.* The search for diversification is perhaps one of the commonest spurs to seek out mergers, particularly among companies that have long been associated with a single product or a single narrow field. There is something vaguely comforting, fashionable, and modern about striving for diversification. Eggs, we learn early, should be distributed among many baskets. Furthermore, segments of the financial community—and particularly securities analysts—have in recent years looked benignly upon managements bent on expanding the sphere of their activity,

while at the same time showing mild impatience with companies that stay within their established lines of business.

It is usually a poor decision to purchase an enterprise simply because it is available and because it will provide more baskets. At the same time, it is equally poor and dangerous to accept too narrow a vision of an enterprise's true nature. Thus had someone asked the great, pioneering railroad builders of the nineteenth century what their business was, they would almost certainly have replied that they were in the business of moving goods and passengers from one place to another along their rights-of-way. This they did with great success and considerable profit—for a time. Had they instead thought a little further and replied that their business was *transportation,* rather than just laying tracks and sending iron horses coursing over them, it is a safe supposition that railroads would be in an entirely different position in our current economy.

By imaginatively and exhaustively pursuing an answer to the question of what a business is, or wishes to become, there should emerge a clearer guide to what constitutes rational diversification.

The application of this formula could well have suggested to two leading soft-drink companies that they were really not just in the business of bottling and distributing carbonated beverages, but in the business of providing refreshment. Seen in this light, the recent acquisitions made by these companies take on additional significance.

In a totally different field, IBM waited until recently to make the first acquisition in its history—that of Science Research Associates. In one sense, it put IBM into the relatively new field of education and publishing. In another sense, if IBM's vision of itself can be defined as a major factor in the business of collecting, assimilating, storing, and utilizing information, then the acquisition becomes a logical extension of the parent company's activities.

When examined in this critical light, many recent mergers—CBS and Random House, ABC and ITT, Ford and Philco—take on new significance. Naturally, there are also many mergers where the partners have nothing in common except the desire to marry. Many of these succeed, possibly because they also fulfill one of the 11 others purposes. But many also fail.

5. *To Achieve Vertical Integration of Existing Products.* Here

too there are any number of examples of companies, notably in the chemical, metallurgical and extractive fields that have set for themselves policies of improving their profit margins by further refining or processing their products. Characteristically, they have often used mergers to expedite the process by acquiring certain skills and facilities which they did not themselves possess.

Thus American Cyanamid Company recently purchased Wasco Products, a fabricator and distributor of methyl methacrylate panels and components, as part of its planned entry into that segment of the building-products field. Thus, too, Standard Oil of Ohio purchased the Pro-phy-lac-tic Brush Company, which despite its name had become to a considerable extent a fabricator of plastic parts for which Sohio already had the raw materials.

Total vertical integration—from manufacturer to the ultimate consumer—could well be the goal of the future for nearly all industry. Quite obviously, the merger route will often be the shortest and most attractive one.

An economist for a giant manufacturer ticked off just a few of the advantages of vertical integration: the buying and selling costs (the expense of salesmen, advertising, sales promotion, sales management, buyers and purchasing departments) between different levels in the integrated firm are eliminated; risk and credit costs are reduced; bad-debt losses and administrative credit investigation costs are eliminated; transportation and storage costs are reduced because of better scheduling of deliveries and better coordination between distribution levels.

It may well be that the traditional position of processors and manufacturers: "We don't want to compete with our customers," will soon be just a voice from the past.

6. *To Acquire a Manufacturing Base.* Even as industrial giants are busy reaching upward in their integration plans, a reverse movement is taking place among many major retailers, largely to remain competitive. Possibly encouraged by the long-term success of Sears, Roebuck, other retailing giants such as Rexall, Walgreen, A&P, Woolworth, and Kresge have added manufacturing facilities to their distribution networks.

Walgreen, for instance, now owns seven ice cream plants, manufactures over 300 drugs and cosmetic products, and even has its own coffee-roasting plant. As for Rexall, in 1964 roughly 70 per cent of its net income came from manufacturing operations, including the highly successful Tupperware line of plastic housewares.

7. *To Extend Existing Marketing Lines and Franchises.* This is perhaps one of the most complex—and by compensation one of the most rewarding—of marketing strategies. It seeks in effect to transfer brand equities earned in one area to new products in another related area. Thus, the B.V.D. Company, which for years was known strictly as a manufacturer of underwear, has begun acquiring producers of private-label wearing apparel such as shirts, ties, and slacks, and marketing the products under the B.V.D. name.

In the food field it is fairly common for established companies, such as Del Monte and Green Giant, to acquire local or regional processors and subsequently put their products under the national name. In fact, the all-time United States records for acquisitions may well be held by a food company—Beatrice Foods. Since 1951 it has made 204 acquisitions.

The temptations and rewards of this strategy are both considerable. It costs literally millions of dollars to establish a national-brand franchise; it costs an equivalent and sometimes even greater amount to acquire one. The enterprise which owns one or more such franchises therefore has an exceedingly valuable asset—valuable and fragile.

Can a commodity such as a hair coloring find shelter and a favorable climate of growth under the umbrella of a well-known brand name in the cosmetic business? Can a national reputation for excellence and reliability in providing household appliances in one area be transferred to another area? If the answer is yes, it is easy to see how an enterprise can by-pass the cost of developing or purchasing a national franchise simply by acquiring the necessary technological and productive capabilities—with the anticipation that the resulting new product will come into the world not as a stranger, but as the newest member of a well-known and respected family.

8. *To Serve Newly Developed Marketing Needs.* A somewhat more specialized but clearly identifiable strategy may be illustrated by the continuing acquisition program of TRW, Inc., formed by

the 1958 merger of auto and aircraft parts maker Thompson Products, Inc., of Cleveland, and California's Ramo-Wooldridge Corp., a company engaged in aerospace work. Analyzing opportunities available in the electronics field, TRW identified the "component" segment of that field as being particularly attractive because (a) it was an expanding field; (b) a well-established "component" business had stability not usually found in companies that make complete military hardware systems; (c) the component segment of the electronics industry was made up of many smaller-sized companies and thus easier to enter.

Further, they found that generally component companies were only marginally effective in marketing their products, that they generally had only limited resources, and that the increasing predominance of the military market with its insistence on reliability created problems for these small companies that they were poorly equipped to meet.

Thus, on the basis of the two-plus-two-equals-five formula, the stage was set for mutually beneficial merger explorations. TRW would provide distribution effectiveness, marketing management, and field engineering support. The component makers would provide product position and manufacturing capabilities.

9. *To Buy Time.* One of the most attractive features of a merger as a management tool is that it becomes effective now, as of the date of closing. It can thus cut several years off the time required to bring a planned program to fruition.

When Litton Industries was organized in December 1953 as an electronics company, its top management prepared a carefully thought-out five-year program. Among other projects it included a plan to enter the office-equipment business.

It would have been possible to create a national sales and service organization to market commercial products resulting from Litton's own research and development programs, but the best estimate was that it would take at least eight years to do the job properly. Because they felt the time was too long, management considered acquisition of a concern already established in the market instead. Late in 1957 negotiations were completed with the Monroe Calculating Machine Company, which owned 350 sales and service branches within the United States. In the seven years since the acquisition—time during which Litton would have been establishing its own organization—sales of Monroe business machines have nearly doubled.

10. *To Improve the Effectiveness of Its Existing Organization.* On the simplest level, mergers of this kind include such combinations as manufacturers of business-office supplies who acquire companies that produce rubber cement, mimeograph equipment, and the like. The obvious advantage is that the same salesman calling on the same accounts would have more items to sell.

But on a more sophisticated level, the thoughtful application of this kind of thinking to an entire, complex enterprise can produce fascinating results. One of the best examples may well be the Singer Company. Though it had been one of the most progressive and enlightened companies in the world, the Singer Company decided in the late 1950s that the sewing-machine field could not effectively utilize all of the capital which was available for expansion. In early 1959 Singer President Donald P. Kircher issued a lengthy memorandum to fifty of his top executive associates. The purpose of the memorandum was to encourage investigation of possible paths of diversification which the company could usefully undertake. At the core of this document was an analysis of the company's existing resources. They included: (a) an ability to operate anywhere in the world; (b) engineering and production skills in the manufacture of precision electromechanical products; (c) a strong world-wide marketing network; (d) a healthy world-wide capital position; (e) experienced and well-established world-wide capability in the financing of customer receivables.

The question which was most asked was: Given these descriptive qualifications, what is the best business that we can enter immediately?

Extensive studies were undertaken, including a systematic review of all industries contained in the Department of Commerce 2-digit Standard Industrial Classifications. Out of this developed the basis for deciding that the business-machines and data-processing-equipment field was a promising one for Singer to enter. A further study of available candidates in the field narrowed down to Friden, Inc. Formal negotiations were begun and within less time than a year the merger was consummated. It has since proved to be eminently successful and has paved the way for at least half a dozen subsequent acquisitions.

The point is that had it not been for the preliminary thinking-through process, it might never have occurred to the world's largest manufacturer and distributor of sewing machines that its best future potential lay in the business-machine field.

11. *To Avoid Cyclical and Seasonal Instability.* Many industries by their very nature are sharply cyclical in character. While this is easy to define as a problem, it is not always as easy to solve. A classic example is the many coal merchants who are also equipped to sell ice. On a higher level of marketing sophistication, the attempt to overcome cyclical demand has impelled manufacturers of electrical refrigerators to look for merger candidates among producers of space heaters, humidifiers, and dehumidifiers.

More recently, Smith Kline & French is reported to have acquired Sea & Ski, a well-established line of sun-tan products, to make it, from a seasonal standpoint, the logical companion to the company's existing proprietary products in the cold-remedy field.

12. *To Acquire Consumer Franchises.* In this instance, a company which already has both the means of distribution and the established reputation as a marketer will seek to add established product lines to its marketing mix in the expectation of increasing volume and therefore profitability. Again, there are many examples of the application of this marketing strategy. Warner-Lambert's acquisition of the West Indies Bay Company, manufacturers of a most distinctively packaged line of franchised men's toiletries, was motivated by just such consideration.

These are twelve specific purposes which mergers can be used to achieve. Nor is the list by any means exhaustive.

The point, I think, is that if you are contemplating a merger or acquisition, you must determine what you want to accomplish and then search for what you want, not wait to have a business offered to you. The history of many mergers shows that some of the most successful acquisitions have been companies which did not need to sell for any particular reason and which, in fact, had not even considered a business marriage. Never forget that at worst the prospective bride you approach can only say "no."

Assuming that the answer is more encouraging, it is well to heed two precautions:

(a) Get the facts, or to put it another way, don't take action on first impressions alone.

(b) Be absolutely certain that at all times lines of communication between the two groups are kept free and open.

Should the courtship eventually prove successful, it is a good idea to put your own house in order before the deal is completed. Too often managers have the optimistic expectation that somehow an anticipated merger in spite of all of its concomitant problems of adjusting budgets, organizations, and plans, will magically solve existing problems.

One final *caveat.* Once the merger has formally taken place, one should remember that no groups of people can work together without a mutual understanding of objectives or of the controls necessary to achieve these objectives. Management should not hesitate to define closely these objectives and controls. People have a surprisingly great capacity to accept and deal with reality. It is only uncertainty which troubles and confuses them.

There is for the professional manager a certain fascination about a successful merger or acquisition. It can bridge both time and space; it can help solve seemingly impossible problems; it can help achieve objectives otherwise seemingly unattainable.

But—and this is fundamental—the objectives have to exist first, to be firmly established and preferably reduced to a written statement.

To buy a company for the right reasons, at the right time, and price, is not particularly difficult. Unfortunately, the consequences of such "impulse buying" are often disillusionment and frustration.

To buy a company for the right reasons, at the right time, and with the proper painstaking follow-through is something else. It is the exercise of management skills and science at its best and most effective level.

Summary

It is vital for a company to decide on its corporate vision, and whether merger and acquisition are the right tools to implement that vision before any action is taken.

A merger must be synergistic. It must give each marriage partner benefits they could not achieve singly. As Mr. van der Stricht says, two plus two must equal five.

The human equation is perhaps most basic. For this reason there should be a long enough engagement for the couple to get to know each other—and their relatives.

There are at least twelve basic marketing-oriented reasons for seeking a merger. A clear realization of the reason or reasons applying to a particular situation must be enumerated before the courtship goes too far.

Mergers can help achieve brilliant end-runs. They can bridge time and space, solve apparently insoluble problems, help attain seemingly unreachable objectives. But the objectives must exist first.

13

Iconoclasm

■

Peter G. Peterson

■

One of the hallmarks of the practical application of a creative vision of a business is a willingness to depart from customary ways, to seek unorthodox solutions to orthodox problems. This iconoclasm runs as a common thread through the success stories of the period after World War II. Icon-breaking is necessary even in applying the most sophisticated marketing strategies.

Indeed, every strategy and every example cited in this book represent a casting away of the familiar and the stultified. That our list of strategies to execute marketing vision starts with end-runs and concludes with a challenge to marketing dogma is no accident. For the two are intimately related. Both attack the conventional, the traditional, the routine. Both demand creativity in marketing, the formulation of sparkling new visions to reap the rewards the future holds in store.

One of the foremost young business leaders in the post-World War II generation is Peter G. Peterson, President of Bell & Howell Company. Because of his concern with creativity in marketing and with loosening the bonds that paralyze creativity, his role as the final contributor is especially appropriate.

Mr. Peterson is the second contributor to this book to have reached the top by the age of thirty-five. He was elected President of Bell & Howell in 1961, having joined the firm in 1958 as an Executive Vice President and member of the Board of Directors. In 1963 he was named Chief Executive Officer.

Before the move to Bell & Howell, Mr. Peterson spent ten years in a variety of marketing jobs. After graduation from Northwestern University in 1947, he went to work for Market Facts, Inc., a Chicago-based marketing research company. The pattern for his rapid succession was set early, for he was appointed Associate Director of the firm in 1949 and Executive Vice President in 1952. The following year he became Director of Marketing Services at the Chicago office of McCann-Erickson, Inc. The next year, at the age of twenty-seven, he was appointed Vice President. General managership of the Chicago office came in 1956 and an agency directorship in 1957.

Along the way Mr. Peterson took an MBA degree from the University of Chicago, co-edited a book, *Readings in Market Organization and Price Policies* (University of Chicago Press, 1952) and received many honors and awards, including a 1962 citation by *Life* as one of the "100 Most Important Americans Under the Age of 40."

■

ICONOCLASM

PETER G. PETERSON

"Dogmatic" is a word nobody likes to apply to himself. Indeed, if we were to conjugate it, most of us would say: "I am *positive*, you are *opinionated*, he is *dogmatic*."

As a foundation for my thesis, I want to discuss first some dogmas in marketing. Let us begin with a few goals that are both commonplace and startling. It has been predicted that the United States can have an $835-billion economy by 1970, a mere three years away.

By 1975, according to an extrapolation by *Business Week*, our economy can rise to over one trillion dollars—and by 1980 to nearly one trillion, three hundred billion dollars—a figure, until recently at least, so large and unprecedented that it can hardly be grasped by the mind, except as some vague abstraction, like the distance between stars.

To achieve this fantastic rise in the economy, there will need to be at least a *one-third* to *one-half* increase in consumer expenditures. This is the prime marketing challenge that should concern us—the increase in *total* consumption. To achieve it will require a rebirth, I believe, of truly creative marketing.

My thesis is a simple one. It is this: Most of us spend most of our time, money, and energy, not as creative marketers who build new markets and total consumption, but rather at what might be called "share of market" gadgeteering. We have become highly proficient at doing the same things a little bit better.

Perhaps this thesis is unwarranted. I hope it is. I would like each of us to test its validity by answering a question. In the past six months, how much of our time and thought went into really creative marketing effort—effort that often creates *new kinds* of products or sells new kinds of customers our existing products? And how much of what we euphemistically refer to as creativity is actually a kind of chrome-polished creativity—where we put a bit of shine on the same old products and selling techniques?

I am sometimes amused to read best sellers that portray the marketing man as a monster, who constantly creates huge markets where none existed, who manipulates masses of consumers to buy things they don't want or need—like some gigantic Svengali with the public under hypnosis.

It is a fact, a melancholy one perhaps, that we know better. We know in our heads and our hearts that much of what we call marketing is rather timid attempts to increase our share of markets that already exist.

In fact, if we are monsters, we are timid monsters. If we are dragons, many of us are reluctant dragons. If we are tigers, many of us are paper tigers. If we are bulls, I believe we may be closer to Walt Disney's creation, the bull with the delicate ego—Ferdinand.

This is not to say, of course, that we are incapable of truly creative marketing. In a number of areas, we have proved otherwise. In the area of new-product categories that have built total consumption, take, for example, the new "convenience" foods; in the last few years, they have had ten times the growth of foods in general. Consider the hi-fi market of the last decade; this has been a created market for people who had traditionally been quite unsure of their taste and ability to discriminate between "good" and "bad" sound. And consider the compact cars, and the new interest in sports cars, both of which have filled needs that had probably remained dormant in the public for some years. And, of course, television.

In the field of marketing, the record clubs by direct mail are a creative marketing concept that revitalized the entire record market—much to the surprise, I might add, of the traditionalists and dogmatists.

Thus, to meet the tremendous challenge of 1975—which is really just around the corner, as the business calendar goes—marketing executives need to invigorate themselves with the conviction that one of their main tasks is to create new markets, not just to feed on existing ones.

If it is true—and I think it is—that we are not spending enough of our time, talents, and energy on marketing that truly builds new markets, what are the reasons for our negligence?

One of the most important reasons was expressed recently by that distinguished anthropologist, Margaret Mead, in a perceptive article called "Must Capitalism Crawl?" In this article in the *Harvard Business Review,* Professor Mead made the incisive comment that "Businessmen suffer from the accumulation of overwhelming quantities of data, prematurely treated as 'information.' " She went on to explain what she meant by this, and I quote her at some length because she says it so well and so concisely: "In his business activities, each administrator knows too much about all his competitors—what their market is, what changes they are making, how they are diversifying, retrenching, and expanding. When knowledge of a field was very limited, the imaginative man made an informed guess and forged ahead, and his success or failure—in actual profit—gave him a measure of his achievement. But today, when every field is researched, we have the spectacle of each company copying its competitors and, in so doing, limiting the profits of them all."

Professor Mead concludes by saying that "this kind of living in a closed, competitive world, trying to follow a trend (which might be called *trending*), is one of the situations that makes our business administrators, who should be our boldest and most adventurous thinkers, feel trapped. Continuous competition within a closed system results in greater and greater standardization of behavior, product, and imagination."

It is ironic that while we, as businessmen, pay lip service to individual initiative, risk-taking and boldness, we are driven by our own passion for security—and, in our case, it is the passion to *know for sure* what can only be estimated at best. Like all passions, this is fundamentally irrational.

Thus one of the first dogmas of marketing that we must subject to a critical scrutiny is our over-reliance on facts and figures, statistics and surveys—our passion for statistical security.

Now, there is nothing wrong and much that is good about surveys and statistics—if they are used as *tools,* and not venerated as deities—if they stimulate our thinking, and do not merely replace it or stultify it—if they lead to a *creative grasp of new situations* rather than petrify our old prejudices and make us passive in the face of change.

Our exaggerated hopes and dependence on the computer illustrates this passion. In the first place, by its very nature, computer information is wholly and only quantifiable; that is, it is concerned only with what can be measured, weighed, calibrated, tabulated, and processed in the physical or statistical sense. This should be enough to warn us of its limitations in that area of social behavior known as "business." For business is, by its very nature, filled with intangibles and imponderables.

It is difficult to overestimate the force of the psychological undercurrents—and cross-currents—in business behavior; and these, up to now, have not been objectively measured. The danger of the computer is not the science-fiction fear that machines will begin to think like men, but the more realistic apprehension that *men will begin to think like machines.*

Let me offer an analogy that may strike most forcibly among those who are addicts of that pleasurable pastime known as bridge.

There is a familiar character in every bridge club known as the "unlucky expert." He has been written about humorously in many bridge books. He knows everything objective there is to know about the game—how to make double squeeze plays and end-plays, all the complicated percentages, all the most delicate and "scientific" bidding conventions and slam tries. But, over the table, he almost always loses. Why?

Because he so often lacks what the bridge experts call "the feel of the table." It is exactly what I am talking about. It is an intuitive understanding of what is going on *among the players and not merely among the cards.* All the bridge champions *play the cards* with the same degree of proficiency, but the winners *play the players* better than the losers do.

Unless a man has "the feel of the table"—the conference table as well as the bridge table—he will lose out in the end because he will be substituting sterile knowledge for a vital and intuitive grasp of changing situations.

The really successful executive, it seems to me, has above all the ability to imagine and do the unexpected.

Thus, too much insistence on the dogma that facts "prove" the worth of a creative idea tends to freeze the creative impulse. The tendency is to accept the obvious conclusions and to do what everybody else would do in similar circumstances. This may be a good system for "face saving" when we want to avoid the risk of being wrong and taking the blame for it; but it is not for this trait that a man has been elevated to senior executive status of a corporation. It is precisely for the reverse ability—the ability to do what others will not.

This current paradox in which business finds itself reminds me of a fine cartoon in *The New Yorker* some years ago: The Chairman of the Board is addressing his directors with the statement: "What we need, gentlemen, is a completely brand-new idea that has been thoroughly tested."

A second reason we are not often truly creative is that we cling to *marketing folklore* that no longer is true, if it ever was. Along with our exaggerated faith in science, we retain (ashamedly, perhaps, but tenaciously) old superstitions that have little basis in reality.

For example, we yearn to discover "the" marketing generalization, "the" selling trend, "the" market. It is more comfortable and easier to think in such simple terms. But we know they are not realistic terms—for people are different and therefore markets are different. And even if they weren't, people's responses change and therefore markets change.

Perhaps these twin dogmas of "scientism" and "folklorism" ought to be replaced by a new dogma the *principle of opposites,* which would be a refutation of previous dogmas. Almost all significant marketing innovations were *opposites,* were direct contradictions of what until then had been accepted as irrefutable principles.

I mentioned earlier the record clubs as an interesting marketing innovation. The dogmatists, the folklorists had long accepted the "irrefutable" principle that people *had* to play the record before buying it. That this wasn't necessarily so soon became evident when, under the impetus of direct-mail clubs, the total market grew dramatically.

Another striking example is in the cosmetics field. It was a truism for many years that, to buy cosmetics, the woman had to be presold by advertising. Since 1950 Avon has been selling door-to-door with something more than modest success. Sales have increased 17 per cent per year, profits have increased 26 per cent per year; the company has achieved a "modest" 34 per cent return on investment.

The history of American business successes is filled with men with vision, with a commitment, and blessed with ignorance of or disbelief in the prevailing folklore—which, as you know, dogmatically tells us what can and, more emphatically, what cannot work.

To repeat, our great challenge is to create really new kinds of products and new ways of selling them for the markets of the future . . . and too much of our current energy is expended upon giving the customer minor, perhaps even trivial choices.

How are we going to meet the creative challenge this implies?

At this point the economist would tell us that the real question is how much and what kind of resources we are willing to allocate to the task.

Let's start with where we are today.

In the world of marketing today, we spend millions of dollars in marketing-research programs defining with increasing accuracy what has happened or is *now* happening. We spend additional millions of dollars that may improve the readership of our advertisements a bit, the impact of our commercials a bit, the selection of media a bit, and so forth.

I hope I would be among the first to recognize the great value of these incremental improvements in marketing *efficiency*. But the essence of a successful business is one that deals effectively with the present *and* the future.

While I know of a few magnificent exceptions to this rule, I believe it is true that in most companies, and in the organizations that serve them, only a very small amount of their human and financial resources in the area of marketing is devoted to the task of planning and creating the markets of the *future*, and the significant marketing innovations of the *future*.

Let me compare this to what we would normally think of as the *physical* world of business—the world of manufacturing and technology.

Here, too, a good deal of money is spent on the essential work of improving productivity, of improving operational *efficiency*, of doing the same things cheaper, better, faster.

We have cost-reduction engineers, quality-control engineers, time- and motion-study engineers. With rising costs and increasing competition, particularly from abroad, these productivity improvements are essential to profitable survival.

But of course we at the same time find major financial commitments to tomorrow—to research and development programs that deal with the unknown, the speculative, the innovative. And we assign not money alone. We have seen fit in American industry to assign an even rarer resource—some of our brighter and most inventive people—to the task of developing the future; that is, in the physical world of business.

If marketing is going to play its full role in the partnership of building a dynamic tomorrow, it too must devote more of its resources to the important task of creating the significant new choices of tomorrow.

I use the word "partnership" advisedly. While there is much we have learned about how to invent in the physical world, I believe we are in a state of relative infancy about how to translate this inventive genius into human satisfaction, into products and services that significantly affect the way we live our lives.

We can all point with justifiable pride to some of the really new products and, in fact, the new businesses that have come out of the advanced technology of our country. The computer and television are two such businesses that have significantly changed the lives of our people. But in relation to the billions of dollars our economy has invested in research and development, about $100-billion in the past ten years, these are all too few examples of new products of real significance to *people.*

And the unique contribution of marketing must ultimately be in terms of *people.* Whereas the laboratory inventor is a physical scientist, the marketer deals with the social sciences, and until these disciplines are merged, we are likely to continue to have a wide gap between the inventions of our laboratories and products that have meaning in the lives of human beings.

The marketing person, if he is to make his full contribution to the partnership, must see himself as no less an inventor. His discoveries are "cultural inventions," that deal with people's needs and ideas, but no less important.

Thus I would propose that we must first make a commitment to ourselves that marketing can be a full partner in creating significant new businesses. And with this commitment must come the investment of the full time of some of our best people—people who would make up the *advanced-development* unit of the marketing function. It needn't be more than a relatively small handful, but it should be a handful of our very best people, committed and devoted to the future of the business.

With the commitment of some of our very best market-oriented people to the *future* of our businesses—and *not* to this month's sales quota or next month's promotion—I believe we would see the experience of our R&D laboratories repeated in the field of marketing; that is, a greatly accelerated rate of invention.

For example, these people could become the "distant early warning" group. The group that feels and senses what may be coming. The group that deals with the people of tomorrow . . . the culture of tomorrow . . . the human needs of the future.

We see today the emergence of large mass markets in sports cars—or at least the sports-car feeling—and of diet drinks and foods. As we think back, I am sure there were "distant early warning" symptoms of the human needs and desires that have been tapped. After all, the fringe markets of yesterday are often the mass markets of today.

Nor would this advanced-development marketing group deal with new-product concepts alone. There is much that needs to be done in innovative *marketing* of existing products.

Surely none of us is willing to admit that the economy that innovated credit installment buying, direct-mail selling, and the supermarket has discovered the ultimate truths in how to sell and distribute products.

Such a group, incidentally, would by its temperament be much interested in experimentation with, or study of, the *unusual,* of the untried selling approaches. It would also concern itself with the awkward, embarrassing exceptions to "the" trends that we all like to ignore—and the companies that don't believe the current marketing folklore and the current dogmas.

These advanced-development people would probably be most innovative if they dealt with a few outside people as well. The history of America's successful innovations has taught us to be careful of the inside specialists, who know perhaps too much about what can't be done. In short, this particular group should put a kind of special value on ignorance.

Speaking of outsiders, it is significant that many of the world's greatest inventions and discoveries were made by men completely *outside the field.*

The three greatest discoveries of surgery, without which modern surgery would be impossible, are anesthesia, asepsis, and X-rays—and none was discovered by a surgeon! Of the four most important railroad devices at the turn of the century, not one was invented by a railroad man! It was not a physicist, but a physiologist, who discovered current electricity!

And in this setting up of an advanced-development marketing group, let us not forget the much maligned professor. As the book *Sources of Invention* points out, even in this century of the large R&D industrial complexes, the majority of the significant inventions of the twentieth century were made by lone, and perhaps lonely, professors.

I see no reason why the same concept would not apply to the field of social sciences—to discovering and projecting the human needs of the people of tomorrow, and the cultures of tomorrow.

By this I am hardly suggesting that we delegate the future of our businesses to academicians or to any outside group. But I am saying that the businessman tends to be isolated within his occupation, and in his own way lives in an ivory tower more remote from realities than many an academic person. Part of the shift we need from the "specialist" to the "generalist" is getting the businessman to "cross-pollinate," as it were, with the cultural community, the academic community, and the nonsuburban community.

Here time is our enemy. More and more of our working time is spent in monumental trivialities which bear only the dimmest relationship to the work we are really paid to do. By the time we extricate ourselves from these irrelevancies, and get down to the business at hand, we are commonly too tired to cross-pollinate with anyone at all. It's as much as we can do to be civil to our own wives and children at the end of that kind of—typical—day. This occupational fatigue, perhaps, may explain in part why we yearn for "the" simple generalization that covers "the" market.

Let me sum up in this way:

The man of business is proud of being "practical." But he must also, in some sense, be a visionary—with a vision of what our businesses *could be,* not what they are or have been. He is proud of being "pragmatic." But he must also be *experimental.* He is proud of being an "expert" in his area. But he must also become a "generalist," and learn how his area relates to other areas in our complex and increasingly interrelated world.

But it is a world that is much more than this. An entirely new world is opening to us—a world undreamed of even by Jules Verne or H. G. Wells. If marketing cannot come to grips with this world of the not-so-distant future—if we fail to exploit its potentialities, not merely for profit, but for the flowering of the human personality—then we will be left far behind by a society that has "researched" *us* and found us wanting.

I hope, I trust, I believe, this will not be the case.

■

Summary

In order to capitalize on the tremendous growth in our economy lying ahead of us, a rebirth of truly creative marketing is needed instead of minor tinkering with existing products and sales techniques. The main task before marketers is to build new markets, not just to feed on existing ones.

Several factors discourage creativity in marketing:

(a) Continuous competition within a closed system, which results in greater and greater standardization of behavior, product and imagination.

(b) A passion for statistical security.

(c) Clinging to marketing folklore that is no longer true, if it ever was.

Marketers must become full partners with physical scientists in creating significant new businesses by inventing products that have significant meaning in the lives of people. To achieve this, companies must invest the time of some of their brightest and most inventive people, organized into an advanced development group, to plan the future of the business. Some features of this group would include:

(a) An interest in experimentation.

(b) Curiosity about the unusual, the mavericks.

(c) A special value placed on "ignorance."

(d) A link with outsiders, notably academicians, to provide a fresh perspective.

About the Editor

Utilizing sophisticated marketing research techniques, Lee Adler has helped leading companies develop effective marketing strategies.

He currently holds a key marketing position with The Interpublic Group of Companies, Inc., the world's largest marketing communications organization. He has been deeply involved in a wide cross-section of American business, both in consumer and industrial areas. Before he joined Interpublic, almost ten years ago, Mr. Adler was a marketing consultant with Amos Parrish & Company.

Mr. Adler is the author of three provocative articles in the *Harvard Business Review*. He has also written for the *Journal of Marketing*, the *Journal of Marketing Research* and other professional publications. In addition, he is the co-editor of *Attitude Research at Sea* (American Marketing Association, 1966) and contributed to *Modern Marketing Strategy* (Harvard University Press, 1964). He is a Director of the American Marketing Association.

Mr. Adler pursued doctoral studies at the Sorbonne, has an M.B.A. from New York University, and a B.A. from Syracuse University.

Away from the office, Mr. Adler moves from the world of statistics and indices to painting. A professional in the fine arts, Mr. Adler has had his oils exhibited in a number of shows, praised by critics and purchased by collectors.

He lives with his wife and son in a renovated pre-Civil War brownstone in Brooklyn Heights, and summers on Fire Island.